I0606125

GRIFFINOLOGY

GRIFFINOLOGY

THE GRIFFIN'S PLACE IN MYTH,
HISTORY AND ART

A. L. McCLANAN

REAKTION BOOKS

Dedicated to the boundless curiosity of my students, whose enthusiasm helped hatch this endeavour and granted it flight

Published by Reaktion Books Ltd
Unit 32, Waterside
44–48 Wharf Road
London N1 7UX, UK
www.reaktionbooks.co.uk

First published 2024

Published with assistance from Furthermore: a program of the J. M. Kaplan Fund.

Printed and bound in India by Replika Press Pvt. Ltd

A catalogue record for this book is available from the British Library

ISBN 978 1 78914 846 6

Contents

Introduction

Over 5,000 years ago, the first images of a griffin appeared in art and this conundrum of a creature has been reimagined in Western visual and literary history ever since. Usually conflating features of an eagle and a lion, it offers a kind of supercharged predator whose territory encompasses both land and air. One of the main stories in this book is the diffusion and flexibility of the griffin's representation, across the gamut from the 'magic wands' used by ancient Egyptians to safeguard childbirth to the neon sign for a Las Vegas bar (see illus. 48, 27). Their presence over vast periods of time and in such varied places makes us wonder: how and why did the griffin become so popular across different cultures and forms of media? Examples have been discovered in settings spanning much of the global north. Thus, many of the works in this book present puzzles about the people who crafted them, and the recurrence of this question is meaningful; the image of the griffin is that extensive.

No art-historical monograph has looked at griffin imagery beyond the confines of a specific period.[1] The folklorist Adrienne Mayor's book *The First Fossil Hunters* is, as its name suggests, mostly about early (classical-era) interest in fossils, but proposes a theory about griffins that, though widely adopted, is here reconsidered. Throughout this book, I consider this and other specialized studies about griffins. While I may occasionally question their conclusions, I hold a profound appreciation for the groundwork they have laid. It is this very foundation that has enabled the scope of this book spanning the griffin's long journey through history. The two earlier general books about griffins in English, while well-crafted, were both slender volumes published in the early 1980s, and a bit more focused on pictures than history or analysis.[2]

Academic sub-fields, such as monster studies, also bring insight to our topic, and the interesting heritage of the word 'monster' is informative. In the fourteenth-century text attributed to John Mandeville, *Livre des merveilles*, a monster is defined as 'a thing deformed against kind, both of man or of beast' – and as a composite, griffins might fit the bill. While griffins are often portrayed with an unquenchable thirst for riches and conflict, and in this excess are monstrous in a certain sense, there are enough depictions outside of that vein to make it misleading to refer to griffins as 'monsters' in this book. Instead, I've opted to use the words 'hybrid', 'composite' and 'creature' for their more neutral tenor. We will also tease out the nuances implied by spelling variants 'gryphon' and 'griffin'. In modern English, 'gryphon', with its archaic flourish, comes up mostly in fantasy novels and kindred contexts, whereas 'griffin' is preferred in academic writing, although sometimes the spelling more common in modern French, *griffon*, appears. 'Griffin' as a name is also examined at several points.

Overview of Chapters

To reflect the diverse representations of griffins, the book's chapters intentionally adopt distinct approaches – some emphasizing themes and others delving into specific historical moments – to showcase this superabundance. Explored in Chapter One is how the griffin emerges in the interconnected cultures of ancient West Asia and Egypt, alongside the question of what gets labelled a griffin in this book, by no means a self-evident matter for a fictional beast depicted across millennia of art-making and writing. Among the various forms of this hybrid, the version with lion hindquarters and a blend of eagle front features emerges as the dominant depiction. This form later becomes part of the shared visual language in the eastern Mediterranean. A topic throughout the book is the substantial disconnect that often exists between the representation of the griffin in texts and images. Griffins are primarily a visual motif, yet their distinctive art history has sometimes been ignored or misunderstood, so Chapter Two refutes a popular recent theory that mistakenly asserts that the ancient Greeks invented the idea of the griffin through contact with dinosaur fossils – a hypothesis that disregards thousands of years of preceding griffin imagery and clear evidence of cultural transmission of the visual motif from Greece's trading partners in West Asia and North Africa. Archaic-period Greeks rediscovered the image of the griffin through high-status imported goods and then wove their own story of conflict with Arimaspi around it.

Chapter Three shows how griffin imagery combines with that of a range of deities across the ancient world, including a second- to first-century BCE Buddhist stupa in India. While the griffins accompanying Apollo often lead the scholarly narrative, the prominence of griffins with Nemesis (personifying retributive justice), who enjoyed widespread appeal, culminates with the creature actually becoming a stand-in for that goddess on objects from exquisite statues to humble bread moulds. Griffins conjoin with other goddesses, ranging from the fearsome Minoan woman in an Aegean fresco to (maybe) that on an imposing Iron Age silver vessel from Scandinavia. This adaptability must surely be a large part of the motif's persistence. Their connection with the god Dionysos links with the griffin's ongoing presence in both the decor of social drinking spaces as well as the objects used therein, as Chapter Four will show. Expressing both transformation as well as opulence, we can find griffin imagery on drinking vessels across a wide swathe of cultural spheres, from ancient Greece to Baroque France.

Chapter Five considers how the griffin's legendary ferocity positioned it as a ready symbol of military potency, and *Griffinology* ranges freely through time periods along this and each chapter's thematic lines. The creature's portrayals vary widely from a commanding Roman sculpture of Mars Ultor (the Avenger) to recent visual branding by the United States Air Force (see illus. 33, 39). Griffins, whose intermingling of two apex predators readily broadcasts their warlike identity, functioned in this widely understood language that extends far beyond its roots in ancient West Asian and North African visual culture.

Roughly contemporary with ancient Greece, the griffin imagery of Central Asia is considered in Chapter Six. Shedding the usual reliance on classical authors such as Herodotus, it is more informative there to ask how shamanic religious experiences can inform the motif's meaning. These steppe societies possessed both distinctive and shared traditions of eagle–lion hybrids. Griffin imagery was an important part of expression from Achaemenid Persian goldwork to the tattoos adorning the Pazyryk people of the Altai Mountains, and these early representations of griffins continue to be repurposed in body arts and political insignia today (see illus. 46, 47).

Chapter Seven considers how griffins' reputation for vigilance leads to their representation as guardians (a reciprocal loop). Ancient griffins could be shown safeguarding and nurturing their young, and many, many doorways and other transitional spaces across time have been guarded by griffins. Their symbolic protection powers extend to vessels used in ritual cleansing, such as medieval aquamanilia. Video games and commercial architecture traffic in this common conceptual language, as with the griffins that guard the pedestrian entry of the Mandalay Bay Casino Resort in Las Vegas, and video game *The Last Guardian*'s namesake creature (see illus. 102, 109).

Chapter Eight details how the motif's inclusion in elite spaces built by the Byzantines and Sasanian Persians taps into venerable links between radiance and power, but also pulls in new, medieval meanings. Many versions of the creature exist, including a fire-breathing griffin that once celebrated an emperor's fascination with the heavens. Likewise, Chapter Nine delves into some of the many griffins rendered as luminous creatures and inhabitants of the heavens, whether in their role powering Alexander the Great's flight through the sky in legend, emanating light on lamps or accompanying a saintly host on the facade of an Armenian church.

In Chapter Ten, we see how Islamic and Byzantine silks with griffin patterns came to enshroud precious relics of saints in western Europe. Perhaps ancient associations of the griffin with transcendence and death persisted (or were reinvented) in the Christian medieval world? This linkage might help us understand the many instances encountered in Chapter Eleven of griffins figuring in funerary arts and paradisical imagery. William Blake's re-envisioning of Dante's *grifone* and Gustave Moreau's 'splendid dreams' of a griffin each resonate with earlier concepts of transcendent griffins.

From the above, one could assume that griffins provide uplifting examples in the moralizing texts of the medieval and early world, but Chapter Twelve shows nothing is ever so simple with this hybrid creature. Medieval bestiary manuscripts might originate in ancient writers' clichés about animal behaviour but lead us to the nascent study of natural history in the early modern world, when uncomfortable questions about the griffin's existence start to be raised. If anything, for most writers from St Jerome through Milton, the griffin symbolizes avarice and duplicity, but there are instances, such as the imagery of the *Bird's Head Haggadah*, that valorize it as part of a response to the devastating loss of life in the antisemitic Rhineland Massacres of 1096. That ambivalence dissipates in the heraldry examined in Chapter Thirteen, where the griffin becomes a standard-bearer for aspirational attributes like tenacity and bravery, which in turn leads to griffins being used as corporate logos or as school mascots in sports.

Chapter Fourteen shows how the imagery of fantasy-based stories, from chivalric tales to travel writing, uses the creature as a kind of narrative gateway. This yields some surprising outcomes including the curiously griffin-related origins of the place name California, lately reimagined by the painter Walton Ford (see illus. 100). In Chapter Fifteen, the interplay of image and word is central to my interpretation of the Gryphon from *Alice's Adventures in Wonderland*. In contrast, the griffin in the *Harry Potter* series stands largely as an invisible ideal, though the hippogriff's inclusion hints at broader, interesting patterns of transmission, too. The importance of the protagonist's identity as a golden griffin (Gryffindor) arcs across all seven original books, and the connotations of Harry's school house derive from the griffin's earlier martial meanings, representing qualities such as valour. Gryffindor identity serves as an important anchoring concept in online domains including fan fiction. In this way, the final chapter shows how the griffin motif continues to serve as a site of identification and fantasy.

Familiarly Unfamiliar

While the chapter organization by theme offers potential wayfinding for the exploration of the many modes of rendering this one creature, specific griffins often themselves hybridize multiple meanings. For instance, the remarkable Pisa Griffin – acquired as war booty and installed atop a cathedral – voiced overlapping ecclesiastical, economic and military messages for its audiences over many centuries (see illus. 38). Likewise, the griffin features as both image and artefact in medieval churches, appearing in decorative programmes as well as in the form of *realia* in church treasuries inventoried as griffin claws and eggs. Palaces, temples and video game storyworlds can all showcase griffin imagery, but the meanings of the same creature can seem as manifold as its settings. Given this multiplicity, one wonders if their role at times can be as a kind of exclamation mark, an amplifying frame for whatever the griffin is represented alongside.

This vast array of images, whether on wine vessels, belt buckles, tattoos or weaponry, often falls beneath the attention of art history. Because of a scholarly habit of privileging texts over images, even within art history, important aspects of how and why griffins appear in art and particular routes of transmission across cultures have before been neglected.[3] While premodern textual mentions of griffins again and again dwell on predation and greed, often centring on the Arimaspi conflict as recounted in Herodotus, imagery carries far more wide-ranging connotations. In visual culture the most stable element in the griffin motif is the addition of wings to a land-bound predator (although even that unambitiously generic description has exceptions). Wings can suggest transcendence or transformation, making the banal and earthbound extraordinary.[4] The griffin motif yokes the airborne and terrestrial, and this cognitive dissonance leaves it equally strange and recognizable. Even when they were widely depicted within a society's visual culture, such as in ancient Greece, they can be written about as perennially foreign, for instance by classical authors who refer to their images as 'Persian griffins' and situate their existence at the edge of the known world.

Griffins' being imagined at the boundary of the graspable might account for how many examples explored in the book seem crafted to elicit a sense of wonder and even awe in their viewers. Whether the proto-robot abilities of the Pisa Griffin, the allure of a 'griffin claw' in a *Wunderkammer* (Cabinet of Wonders) or the experience of archaic Greek viewers encountering a startling new kind of realism in art, this aspect – of griffins manifesting the marvellous – resurfaces across chapters. The creature can encapsulate moments of encounter, which fuses with their bellicosity in figures styled as world conquerors, such as the god Dionysos and Alexander the Great's many reinventions. In this way, griffins routinely have a sidekick role in the Macedonian general's later reimaginings made from France through Mongolia until the early modern era, even when texts describe the scene with other winged beasts, including the roc, eagle or phoenix (see illus. 61–4).

The book in your hands thus introduces the cultural history of this mythic beast's representation, ranging far afield chronologically and geographically – across North America, Europe, Central Asia and North Africa – to find important connections and contrasts. Many intriguing renderings regretfully had to be omitted, for within this limited space I tried to balance relatively famous works with those less renowned. While some parts of the discussion are diachronic, showing the transformations of the griffin motif from ancient times to the modern day, this isn't meant to imply a teleology. Rather, the motif moves through different lines of transmission that aren't always the expected ones – in particular, we will see the West sometimes copying the art of the East and not necessarily 'improving' on it. Rather than a single march in lockstep to arrive at a monolithic 'Griffin of Today', the pathways of the motif will be seen chaotically splitting apart, circling back and commenting on each other, in the process transforming in unexpected and dazzling ways.

Chapter One

What Is a Griffin?

Early Depictions from Ancient West Asia

At sunrise, when Anzud cries out,
The earth in the Lulubi Mountains shakes at his cry.
He has shark's teeth and eagle claws;
In terror of him buffaloes scatter into the foothills;
Stags flee into their mountains.

***The Return of Lugalbanda*, a third-millennium BCE Sumerian text**

The variety we will encounter in griffin images raises the question: what precisely does the term 'griffin' even mean? The label has been applied to many different creatures mixing attributes of predatory birds and felines. The raptor characteristics are typically those of an eagle or, less commonly, a hawk, or even another bird of prey, with lion's features typically providing the feline details. The boundaries defining the griffin motif are elastic and culturally specific; sometimes, in medieval and later heraldry, the term is used so broadly it covers almost any imaginary creature, while at other times it is delimited much more rigorously. Later chapters consider when the notion of a 'griffin' seems to converge with other creatures such as the dragon – a creature bearing an even more loosely defined perimeter of meaning.

Biologists argue about where to draw boundary lines between species of real animals (and even what a species exactly is), so it is hardly surprising that the identity of an imagined composite beast continues to be redefined. Thus the griffin is best understood as a concept based on overlapping similarities rather than a static definition (whether visual or textual). An idea from the twentieth-century philosopher Ludwig Wittgenstein, 'family resemblance', can help us surmount some of the more perplexing and fascinating challenges of defining the griffin as a 'thing'. First set forth in his *Blue Book* and then revisited in *Philosophical Investigations*, Wittgenstein's concept is cogently summarized by a later commenter: 'Family resemblances are nests of properties, similarities, and relations that the things falling under a general term have and have to each other. They are elaborate and not summarizable networks of features that are exhibited across the range of items to which the term applies.'[1] It is telling that the philosopher reportedly often quoted *King Lear* – 'I'll teach you differences' (Act 1, Scene 4) – for he rejects an essentialist approach to meaning. I adopt this pragmatic approach here – that is, if a representation has conventionally been referred to as a griffin, it falls into this book's purview – rather than a more idealized, proscriptive approach proceeding from an unvarying definition of what a griffin is supposed to be or look like across time and space.

Following this framework, the griffin motif first appeared in art of the Bronze Age among the first groups of people to live together in the earliest cities.[2] Correspondingly griffins were well established in ancient Egyptian art by the late fourth millennium BCE, likely inspired by imagery on goods coming from the Iranian plateau as well as Mesopotamia.[3] There are also arguments to be made for griffins (depending on how you define the term) originating more precisely in northern Syrian sites such as Karkemish or in Elamite centres like Susa, but the main point to bring from those discussions is the astonishing richness of composite animal imagery already in the late fourth millennium, featuring many leonine–avian hybrids.[4] Although a number of interesting examples survive, and are analysed in upcoming chapters, griffins are relatively less common in Egyptian art compared to their frequency within surviving Aegean and ancient West Asian (also known as ancient Near Eastern or ancient Middle Eastern) art. Lion–eagle hybrids in Mesopotamian images and their Egyptian counterparts are part of a rich visual vocabulary of animal composites that flourished in those early civilizations.[5] These earliest depictions lay the groundwork for some of the themes we'll see in the millennia to follow. The lamassu (a winged human–bull composite) and sirrush (another bird–lion hybrid, with serpentine details) are just two of many other composite beasts from this era – but the griffin has proven to be the longest lasting of the hybrids.

Three distinct lion–eagle composites in ancient West Asia have traditionally been labelled griffins by scholars. The earliest is the Anzû bird, a lion-headed eagle. The second type, a lion's body with an eagle's head, appears on cylinder seals and other media – this creature comes closest to what in later eras' art usually gets called griffins. Third, historically the latest to appear, is the 'griffin demon', a standing human man with the wings and head of an eagle, with no leonine elements. The definitions of hybrid beasts have rather porous boundaries, so the question comes down to how broadly we want to recognize the 'family resemblance'; the Anzû bird, for example, indeed intermixes lion and eagle, but with its leonine head and raptor's body, it reverses the formula of the later, more familiar griffin. All three types have parallels and connections worth exploring, and the variability illustrates just how much what gets identified as a griffin depends on contextual cues.

Anzû Birds, the Thunderbird and the Winged Lion

The southern Mesopotamian people of Akkad and Sumer in the third millennium BCE developed much of the visual vocabulary for animals used by later ancient West Asian cultures – 'heraldic' beasts symmetrically positioned, pairs of fighting animals

1, 2 Cylinder seal depicting serpopards with Anzû birds, with modern impression above and ancient seal below, from Uruk in modern Iraq, c. 3500–3100 BCE, *green jasper.*

and the pervasive utilization of composite creatures to bridge the divide between the earthly and divine.[6] Cylinder seals from Akkad and Sumer feature Anzû birds – for example, a green jasper seal found at Uruk carved more than 5,000 years ago, between 3500 and 3100 BCE (illus. 1, 2).[7] These seals were rolled across wet clay to mark an object and proclaim ownership; in our first example the lion-headed Anzû bird flies above beings with leopard or lion bodies with fantastically long, serpentine necks (serpopards).

In sources such as the Sumerian tale of Lugalbanda, from the late third millennium BCE, the Anzû bird is said to inhabit wild mountain regions. It menaces the farthest highlands, and – like later griffins such as those in the medieval *Kudrun* saga, whose ability to fly while carrying prey far larger than themselves testifies to their strength – surges through the air with a live buffalo in its talons and a dead one slung across its back.[8] When not called griffins, images of lion-headed eagles are typically 'Anzû birds' in scholarly writing, and debate persists as to whether these pictorial examples can be, with certainty, identified as the Anzû bird written about in texts.[9] Anzû bird representations peak in the Early Dynastic period (*c.* 2900–2350 BCE), have an interval of disuse, then re-emerge in first-millennium BCE neo-Assyrian art.[10] If scholars have correctly connected images with texts, some Anzû birds were possibly intended to fend off evil while also evoking, more generally, weather and, particularly, storms.[11] The lion-headed eagle remains a mainstay especially in contexts associated with war and kingship.[12]

Our next lion–eagle hybrid comes closest to the later visual formula for a griffin, combining a leonine body with aquiline wings and a beak. An Akkadian cylinder seal from circa 2340 to 2150 BCE (illus. 3, 4) shows a winged lion pulling the chariot of the storm god and his consort, the rain goddess.[13] The storm god holds the reins of the yoked griffin, which lowers its head to spew fire or lightning. This griffin occupies an intermediary role, striding between the divinities and their libation-pouring worshipper. This winged lion is part of the wider proliferation of hybrid beasts in Akkadian art, and despite being visually distinct from earlier lion–eagle hybrids, its meanings may be tangled with those of the Anzû bird and storm personifications since Mesopotamian art often interweaves meanings and associations from earlier periods.[14] Bronze Age griffins from the region that is now Syria and Lebanon could be quite eclectic, such as examples including Hathor crowns and other features derived from Egypt.[15]

The Griffin Demon and Bird-Apkallu

A third type of figure written about as a griffin is the 'griffin demon' and is particularly popular in Assyrian art. In scholarship about ancient West Asian art, 'demon' refers to a bipedal, human physique with an animal head; the most common type is the griffin demon, which combines a winged human body with an eagle's head, without any leonine elements. Griffin demons are often accompanied by a lion-bodied griffin, as in this Middle Assyrian chalcedony seal from circa 1200 to

3, 4 Cylinder seal depicting fire-breathing griffin drawing chariot of storm god and rain goddess, with modern impression above and ancient seal below, Akkadian, c. *2340–2150* BCE, *shell.*

5, 6 Cylinder seal depicting griffin in the grasp of a griffin demon, with modern impression above and ancient seal below, Middle Assyrian, c. *1200–1000* BCE, *milky chalcedony.*

1000 BCE (illus. 5, 6), interpreted as an epic battle between the forces of life and death. On the left, the lion griffin rears up in lethal fury, in the role of an angel of death. Its opponent, the humanoid griffin demon on the right, defends the forces of life. Wielding an alarmingly sharp dagger while grasping the embattled lion griffin by the foreleg, the demon seems to have gained the upper hand. The kneeling bull below provides a symbolic and visual anchor and could represent the divine bull in Mesopotamian texts, a child of the sun god Shamash.[16]

While the griffin demon first appears in Middle Assyrian art (as in the thirteenth-century BCE wall paintings from Kar-Tukulti-Ninurta), its popularity peaked in ninth- to eighth-century BCE neo-Assyrian art.[17] The ruler Ashurnasirpal II populated the walls of his northwest palace at Nimrud with griffin demons, as in his room warded with low reliefs of these protective spirits, 'sacred trees' and the king himself (illus. 7). The griffin demons hold a bucket in one hand and lift a cone-shaped object in the other, signifying both purification and fertilization of the sacred trees abundantly carved in the same room (the cone's shape resembles a male date plant's spathe, but the inscription calls the cone 'purifier'). Some palm trees require pollination by a human cultivator to bear fruit, so one possibility is that the griffin demons and king are shown cultivating sacred trees. The griffin demons' buckets may be for a protective, purifying ritual, supported by the presence of two ritual knife handles peeking out above the strap across each demon's chest. Considering the palace setting and the king's presence, though, this panel may also depict the leader in the persona of an enlightened sage.[18] Archaeologists have discovered sets of seven 'sage' statuettes, *apkallu*, buried in brick boxes under the foundations of structures at many Mesopotamian sites. These groups of seven figurines, ceremonially buried at house entrances and under interior rooms, both purify and protect buildings and their inhabitants. An eagle-headed figure that can likely be identified with the griffin demon is consistently included in these sets of *apkallu*, but is not specifically mentioned in texts, marking another crucial divergence between the worlds of images and that of texts.[19] Chapter Seven looks into other griffin imagery with a protective, purifying role.

Griffins communicate as part of a visual vocabulary shared across disparate eastern Mediterranean societies. A fourteenth-century BCE haematite cylinder seal (illus. 8, 9) taps into this visual language, foregrounding griffins in its spectacle of predation. A griffin attacks a stag, side by side with a belted hero between two lions, another hero between dogs and a double-headed eagle above – all squeezed onto the surface of an object slightly over 2 centimetres (0.8 in.) tall. The sharp-beaked griffin rears up, looming over the stag, whose head arcs backwards in a gesture of pitiful collapse, a posture signalling a wounded animal in Aegean art. This seal could, however, have been carved anywhere in the eastern Mediterranean – the first of many examples in this book of griffin imagery with an ambiguous place of creation. It is one of many 'intercultural-style' seals conveying conquest through brute force, with the griffin's relentless attack on its prey encapsulating that message.[20]

7 Ashurnasirpal II *wall relief of king flanked by 'griffin demons', from Nimrud in modern Iraq, neo-Assyrian* c. *865–860* BCE*, gypsum.*

An Ivory Griffin from Nimrud

The griffin motif continues as part of a shared visual syntax into the Iron Age, but now with a spectrum of potential meanings, and so a peaceful griffin graces this exquisite ivory from about 800 BCE found at Fort Shalmaneser, Nimrud (illus. 10), excavated in 1963 by Max Mallowan (the archaeologist husband of Agatha Christie). The griffin cranes its neck to nibble a palm tree, its front paw elevated on an outcrop to facilitate the beast's elegant reach towards the foliage. Part of a group of nine ivories found near each other with similar style, all with tenons suggesting a role as furniture adornment, in each one the composite beast approaches a tree.[21] Ivory was a prized material usually imported from Africa by this time, as the elephants of the Syrian river delta were driven to extinction from over-hunting. At Fort Shalmaneser, neo-Assyrians collected ivories carved in a visual style different from that used in the decoration of their palaces. Several attributes of the griffin on this ivory – its long, curled mane and slender proportions – are hallmarks of Levantine origin or influence. Iron Age Levantine sculptors were adept at adapting their output to suit the tastes of specific export markets, and the ivories came to Fort Shalmaneser likely as war booty or tribute payments.[22] Where the Ashurnasirpal II relief shown earlier in this chapter hinted at the ritual significance of palm trees, griffins and palms have solar associations in ancient Syrian seals,

8, 9 Cylinder seal depicting griffin attacking a stag, 'Master of Animals', and double-headed eagle, with modern impression above and ancient seal below, eastern Mediterranean, c. 1400–1300 BCE, hematite.

10 Furniture plaque depicting a griffin nibbling a palm, found at Fort Shalmaneser, Nimrud, c. 800 BCE, ivory.

which is likely the case here – this would echo depictions on an eighteenth-century BCE mural from the Syrian palace of the king Zimri-Lim (or one of his predecessors), where griffins flank solar symbols.[23]

The 'Persian' Horned Griffin

This sixth- to fourth-century BCE gold plaque (illus. 11) splendidly typifies an Achaemenid Persian horned griffin – the body is mostly leonine, making the eruption of hybrid attributes all the more alarming and powerful, with flamboyant curving horns, large bull-like ears and a feathered neck emerging above the wings.[24] The heavy rings on the reverse of the plaque suggest it may have decorated a belt, rather spectacular personal adornment. In later chapters we'll see that griffins were favoured belt decorations of the Avars and other nomadic people across early medieval Eurasia, and belts were a masculine accessory throughout antiquity (and in some settings continue to be 'gendered' – consider the connotations of championship belts in boxing). The ongoing popularity of the griffin motif on belts, as well as in male-identified spaces as in the ancient Greek *andron*, suggests it was, at times, construed as masculine; yet other instances, namely Aegean Bronze Age connections with a female divinity, and later with the goddess Nemesis, complicate that picture in interesting ways (see illus. 17, 22, 26). While the plaque's version is often called a 'Persian' horned griffin, the curved-horn griffin appears widely across time and places beyond the Persian Empire, in settings as disparate as a late fourth-century BCE Macedonian tomb at Agios Athanasios and a seventh-century CE Byzantine imperial palace in Istanbul (see illus. 55).[25] A loose pattern one sees in upcoming examples is that so-called 'lion griffins' have either short or curving horns, as opposed to the longer, pointed ears of what are sometimes distinguished as 'eagle griffins'.

This chapter introduces distinctive elements of the earliest representations of griffins, from many thousands of years ago. Their wide variety makes clear hybrids uniting lions with birds of prey were well-established elements of visual culture well before their entrée into ancient Greek art and literature. Scholars, particularly Wengrow, have linked the rise in the depiction of composite creatures such as the griffin with the 'first age of mechanical reproduction', seen in the new media, cylinder seals; these technologies spoke to the needs of a newly urban population that had 'the bureaucratic imperative to confront the world . . . as an imaginary realm made up of divisible subjects, each comprising a multitude of fissionable, commensurable, and recombinable parts'.[26] This interpretation, situating the rise of composites among the exigencies of a freshly emergent role for humans – the urban bureaucrat – offers an important corrective, suggesting these animal hybrids are emblematic of a profound cultural transformation. The rise of these lion–eagle composites makes sense in the context of the early cities. The Anzû bird, griffin demon, lamassu and sirrush didn't make the leap from the civilizations of ancient West Asia to their neighbours and successors, but the eagle-headed lion

11 Plaque with horned lion-griffins, Achaemenid Persia, c. *6th–4th century* BCE, *gold.*

and winged lion were here to stay. The diffusion of the griffin motif in this region is crucial to understanding its representation during the classical period. It is this context, as we will see, that has sometimes been ignored.

Chapter Two

Golden Griffins of Ancient Greece:

From Image to Word

Beware of the sharp-beaked hounds of Zeus that do not bark, the gryphons, and the one-eyed Arimaspian folk, mounted on horses, who dwell about the flood of Pluto's stream that flows with gold. Do not approach them.

***Prometheus Bound*, fifth-century BCE tragedy, attributed to Aeschylus**

We have seen griffins prominently included in ancient art extending back to the fourth millennium BCE, but the objects that most illuminate how Herodotus and other classical-era Greeks thought about griffins were those that were on imported goods emulated by their Iron Age artists beginning in the eighth century BCE. Contrary to a popular theory that will be questioned here, griffins strode into ancient Greek culture on the luxury goods that circulated around the eastern Mediterranean through trade, war and high-level gifts. 'Orientalizing' bronze cauldron protomes, silver vessels and vase painting tell a story here of how this composite beast became part of Greek culture, and later chapters delve into further depictions including on Greek temples, coins and armour.

The ubiquity of griffin heads as protomes (a head or bust used as adornment) on ceremonial cauldrons at this moment of transition in Greek art is suggested by the remarkable number that still exists – over six hundred griffin protomes have been catalogued from that era, almost 3,000 years ago. Griffin cauldrons could serve as a votive offering – part of how people might proclaim milestones like winning an athletics competition, by thanking the gods. Thus, at Olympia, the uptick in their use coincides with the expansion in 776 BCE of the famed Panhellenic Games at that site. While their use as such offerings has often been emphasized, not many cauldrons actually have votive inscriptions, so they likely had a wider range of meanings for their audience. At Greek sanctuaries, and especially at that of the goddess Hera on Samos, excavated remains show griffin cauldrons were integral to the kind of Cabinet of Wonders of astonishing, rare objects that these sites offered visitors.[1] Especially in contrast to works from the preceding phase of Greek art, the much more abstract 'Geometric' period, it is

12 Cauldron from Tomb 79, Salamis, Cyprus, c. 700 BCE, *bronze.*

probable such works were intended to dazzle their viewers and evoke a sense of awe, an interest testified in that period's descriptions of artworks that suggest their potential to inspire wonder. In a pattern of evidence that we will see in upcoming chapters, though, griffin cauldrons are mentioned much less often in ancient writing than the tripod cauldrons also produced in the seventh century, although griffin cauldrons were used over a much wider area.[2]

The first Greek griffin cauldrons were probably made in the Aegean, with a strong influence from north Syrian works among their many catalysts. Cyprus is on the eastern edge of the wide-ranging find-spots of griffin protomes, and the Salamis cauldron (illus. 12), dated circa 700 BCE, was refashioned several times, but its exceptional level of preservation allows us to understand how impressive these objects likely were to their initial audience.[3] The eight pairs of cast griffin protomes, alternating with single sphinxes (a common pairing), were an original part of this ceremonial cauldron containing funerary food and drink in the tomb where it was discovered.[4] Including its iron base, the Salamis cauldron stands 51 centimetres (30 in.) high, but some were considerably larger, which we can surmise from both extant larger protomes and written descriptions.

Griffin protomes almost always survive alone, without their original cauldron, a pattern so consistent at sites such as Olympia that a single protome was possibly kept as a kind of relic after the cauldron was no longer used.[5] We will return to these protomes in Chicago later, but here, note these features, seen across most surviving examples: eyes inlaid for emphasis; an open, raptorial beak; an arching tongue mirroring the curve of the jutting, sharply pointed ears (illus. 13). A body part of neither lions nor eagles, on an intuitive level these almost knife-like ears might amplify the way a griffin signalled ferocity. In the famous silver fox domestication experiment, begun in Siberia in 1952, foxes were selected for breeding based on which animals were most 'friendly', defined by the researchers as 'most willing to approach them'. In addition to gradually yielding foxes who were inordinately comfortable around their human observers, successive generations of fox offspring began to manifest physical changes from floppy ears to curly tails, and their head shape in time became shorter and broader.[6] The cluster of physical characteristics that emerged in these foxes appear across other domesticated 'cute' animals, and it is notable that an invented being, the griffin, comprises a set of body-part forms found at the opposite end of the spectrum of shapes. Griffins' often spiky silhouette – including emphatically non-floppy ears – intensifies the way they visually read as predators.

Perturbing both now and likely to their original viewers, these objects from Panhellenic centres reflect how enthusiastically the griffin motif was adopted in Greek art. The West Asian derivation of these winged hybrids disconcerted earlier scholars, who defensively rationalized that 'both griffins and handle ornaments, therefore, are excellent examples of the way in which early Greek artists borrowed from the art of the East, but very rapidly improved upon their models'.[7] Griffin and sphinx imagery was so shared in visual and material culture between Greece

13 Pair of griffin protomes with bone or ivory inlay, from a cauldron, possibly from Samos, Greece, c. *600* BCE, *bronze.*

14 Bowl said to be from Kourion, Cyprus, c. *700* BCE, *gilt silver.*

and West Asia that sometimes only technical analysis clarifies where a specific protome was made.[8] Art historians continue to debate exactly how this process of assimilation of the griffin and other 'orientalizing' forms occurred, and recent studies have revealed these protomes were refashioned by often subtle and sometimes more intensive reworking, even through the Roman period. Even the term 'orientalizing' poses its own problems, so is used here advisedly.[9] Rather than view this as a kind of haphazard grafting of alien forms onto Greek root stock, the choice to adopt the griffin motif represents the preferences and aspirations of eighth- and seventh-century BCE Greek artists and their patrons.[10] The prominence of griffins in archaic Greek art thus was not an aberration: it was an active, meaningful appropriation serving to 'naturalize' this creature alongside sirens, sphinxes and the like.

The Griffin-Fighter Motif

This process is seen unfolding in a petite silver gilt bowl from the Cypriot Kourion Treasure, dated to 725–675 BCE, where griffin imagery plays upon signature Egyptian, Phoenician and Assyrian design elements (illus. 14). The bowl's multiple griffin types serve as an index of the complex cultural interactions in the eastern Mediterranean where it was made.[11] Stately 'heraldic' griffins, sphinxes and palmettes adorn the outer band of decoration alongside two griffin combat scenes, part of the shared visual language of the eastern Mediterranean. In one, a kilt-clad hero asserts his dominance, grasping a griffin's comb and thrusting his sword into the chest of the creature as it rears up. This vignette has been interpreted as drawing from either Egyptian or Assyrian art – the very ambiguity illustrates the imagery's diffusion.[12] The griffin-fighter motif's ubiquity in the Iron Age eastern Mediterranean perpetuates their Bronze Age popularity.[13] In the bowl's other griffin combat scene, a kilted hero, now atop a mountain, shoves his sword into a cowering griffin's beak. There are so many griffin combat scenes from this period that numerous artworks show specifically a hero vanquishing a griffin from above with a long sword, including an ivory found at Fort Shalmaneser.[14] Savour for a moment the eclecticism common at the time: that example offers a Levantine-style rendering of Egyptianizing motifs on a griffin-fighter ivory found in Assyrian territory. The griffin-fighter motif on objects exchanged across the eastern Mediterranean set the stage for the classical Greek understanding of this hybrid as intrinsically ferocious and eternally in conflict – but what else could one expect from an amalgam of two apex predators?

15 Kotyle (a Greek cup type), griffin with a lion and panther (with a harpy and sphinx on reverse side), attributed to the Giessen Painter, c. *600–575* BCE, *terracotta.*

As on the singular Kourion bowl, relatively mass-produced pottery at this time pairs griffins with unusual or fictive creatures. Frequently, these animals parade in a row, as on this early sixth-century BCE cup by the Giessen Painter, its particular shape a favourite of Corinth's potters (illus. 15).[15] Processions of exotic fauna, adopted from eastern imports, are so pervasive on Greek pottery of this period that they anchor characterizations of 'orientalizing' Greek art.[16] The currency of griffins on traded luxury goods – almost working like a prestigious logo – illuminates why in Herodotus' *Histories* and other classical Greek texts griffins figure so often on precious objects.

Griffins versus Arimaspi

In ancient Greek tales of griffins as beasts – rather than their use as images – griffins inhabit the fringes of the known world. In the tragedy *Prometheus Bound*, often attributed to Aeschylus and likely from the early fifth century BCE, griffins populate a strange and perilous landscape to the east. The fearsome creatures guard a river of gold: 'Beware of the sharp-beaked hounds of Zeus that do not bark, the gryphons, and the one-eyed Arimaspian folk, mounted on horses, who dwell about the flood of Pluto's stream that flows with gold. Do not approach them.'[17] In this baleful warning, one of their earliest mentions, griffins possess the attributes subsequently recycled into the early modern era: they are vicious, their identity is constituted in their role as guardians of gold (especially, as here, against the Arimaspi), and they dwell in an imprecisely defined hinterland.[18] The connection with the gods Zeus and Pluto made in *Prometheus Bound* is more unusual. Pluto's name in ancient Greek resembles the word for wealth so it may be that the griffins in a sense guard 'wealth's river' or even – considering Pluto's role presiding over the underworld – griffins' later association with death explored in chapters Ten and Eleven may be intimated here, though that seems less likely.

There is an earlier brief fragment mentioning griffins that is linked to Hesiod (traditionally, *c.* 700 BCE, but now placed 580–520 BCE with his authorship disputed), but it is Herodotus who has ossified into the main standard-bearer for classical Greek perceptions of the griffin.[19] Herodotus' account of the Persian Wars incorporates five mentions of griffins: in two, griffins are motifs on objects and the others double down on the *Prometheus Bound* characterization of gold-guarding, Arimaspi-fighting, foreign-dwelling beings.[20] Herodotus hedges about whether the creature really exists, and the question becomes part of their tantalizing and persistent connection to precious rarities: his first reference to griffins concludes with, 'it is probable, however, that the ends of the earth, encompassing the rest of the world as they do, and bounding them in, do possess things which strike us as exceptionally beautiful and rare' (III. 116). Herodotus' intricate dance around the credibility of his sources has engaged many classicists. Writing in the fifth century BCE, he claims that his source about griffins is a seventh-century poem by Aristeas of Proconnesus, *Arimaspea*, recounting a journey to the remote northern lands of Hyperborea. The existing fragments of the *Arimaspea* in later authors don't include griffins. Tellingly, a first-century CE work on aesthetics quotes it merely as an example of pompous writing tics to avoid, and the Byzantine John Tzetzes references the *Arimaspea* only to question its author's existence.[21] Herodotus typically cited earlier authorities to bolster faith in his own historical account but may have had a different rationale in presenting Aristeas as a source. By incorporating odd details such as Aristeas returning as a phantom centuries after his death, and as a crow no less (IV. 14–15), Herodotus might be setting up the *Arimaspea*'s contents, including griffins, to be viewed as similarly in the realm of the fantastic.[22]

Their role as guardians of gold against their ceaselessly acquisitive adversaries, the one-eyed Arimaspi, grounds Herodotus' first three mentions of griffins. Arimaspi largely share griffins' textual lineage, with *Prometheus Bound* and *Histories* also being their earliest Greek appearances. Violence saturates their landscape: Herodotus notes that where griffins exist, the human inhabitants 'are perpetually attacking their neighbours' (*Histories*, IV. 13). The aggression at the heart of their identity is manifest even in the Greek word for griffin which conveys the hooked or curved aspects of aquiline birds.[23] This Greek word may have Semitic language origins, with possible source words ranging from Hebrew to Akkadian, sharing that semantic range. Their name thus distils them down to beaks and talons, the hard body parts used in predation. Herodotus additionally marks out griffins on resplendent architecture and metalwork. Griffins coupled with sphinxes betoken the splendour of a 'large, luxurious' house (IV. 79), just as griffins and sphinxes often appear together on extant artworks such as the Salamis griffin cauldron. Herodotus' description of a fine cauldron dedicated to Hera as a 'bronze mixing-bowl . . . with a rim that featured protruding griffins' heads' (IV. 152) conveys how the cauldrons that often survive only through now-isolated griffin protomes were once regarded.

Accounts from Herodotus and others of griffins recursively fighting Arimaspi over gold contrast the richer narratives surrounding other mythic beasts. Classical Greek texts accord the winged horse Pegasus, for example, a broader narrative range, but the griffin's playbook remains tightly circumscribed around the perennial Arimaspi conflict – a pretty threadbare story. The equivalent in our time might be a TikTok rolling through its endless loop every few seconds, compared to a feature-length movie. Perhaps, though, its very simplicity – griffins guard gold from Arimaspi – contributed to its adaptability and ongoing usage for centuries to follow.

Representations in textual and visual culture are not always in sync, of course. Thanks to Herodotus, it is certain the Arimaspi story was in circulation by circa 430 BCE, but the scene only emerged on Greek vase decoration several decades later (*c.* 400 BCE).[24] Although a little late to the game, the motif of griffins battling Arimaspi quicky became popular in fourth-century vase painting, with enough instances to warrant a distinct category of red figure vase scholarship, 'Group G' – 'G' standing for 'griffin' (illus. 16).[25] The Arimaspean here wears the conspicuously foreign clothing used in Greek art to 'other' certain kinds of warriors, most typically Persians and Amazons. Athenian potters and painters conducted a brisk business

16 'Group G' *(for Griffin) pelike (a Greek jar type) depicting an Arimaspean fighting a griffin,* c. *350–325* BCE, *terracotta.*

exporting vases with this battle to a region where the scene would have played especially well to the local audience: the Group G vases are part of late fourth-century BCE 'Kerch style' vase painting, named after the abundance of these wares found on the Crimean Kerch peninsula, a place linked to the fictive Arimaspi and historical Scythians. As with the at times tepid assessment of earlier, orientalizing Greek art, the eminent art historian John Boardman belittled the Kerch wares as 'numerous but rarely ambitious, some are much given to colour and ornament, others are grossly repetitious'.[26] It would be intriguing to know how the purchasers of these vessels in Kerch interpreted such combat scenes; it certainly suggests ancients didn't view griffins as 'real' since their Black Sea owners would presumably notice if eagle–lion hybrids were fighting one-eyed warriors outside their city walls. While the battle scene follows a predictable type, it is also compelling. This griffin rears up, a formidable agonist, fully the height of the horse. The griffin's component parts are emphatically incongruent, the white body contrasting wings rendered in the same warm red tones of the horse and its rider. Indeed, Greek depictions of hybrid creatures in many cases accentuate their constituent parts (we will see how, conversely, the Renaissance artist Leonardo da Vinci sought to create 'seamless' composite creatures).[27] Representations of griffins fighting Arimaspi continue as a theme long after the fourth-century BCE Kerch vases, extending into medieval examples, such as the Hereford Mappa Mundi (*c.* 1300 CE), with other reimaginings far too numerous to list here. Much prior discussion of griffins lays stress on classical texts rather than visual culture and the wider spheres of influence shaping it, but my goal here, instead, is to tease out the larger pattern of the interpolation of the griffin motif from art into texts.

Dismantling the Fossil Theory

The habits of thought that tried to explain away external influences on Greek art and culture – and that considered the pervasive reworking of griffins into archaic art a troubling feature to be dismissed as an aberration – have not disappeared. A recently proposed theory about the origin of griffins as a novel invention of Greek culture has gained widespread acceptance, eliding North African and West Asiatic cultural influence on ancient Greece altogether. The folklorist Adrienne Mayor proposes that 'the griffins of ancient Greco-Roman narratives and art must certainly reflect reports of fossil remains of the beaked dinosaurs of Central Asia,' namely *Protoceratops* fossils.[28] Mayor's highly enjoyable book on this topic, *The First Fossil Hunters*, makes a persuasive case for fossils being curiosities that were collected and marvelled at in the classical world, and she carefully marshals Greek and Roman written sources. But the facts don't support her argument about griffins. While some ancient Greeks encountered dinosaur fossils or heard accounts of such remains – and while this might conceivably have reinforced for some the existence of the fantastic beasts they saw on objects in elite homes – fossils are not the inspiration for the notion of the griffin in ancient Greece. We have already seen that eagle–lion hybrids were depicted for thousands of years before they appeared in Greek art, and the examples examined above clarify that this composite was absorbed from broader eastern Mediterranean visual culture, alongside several other popular hybrids.

The rich antecedents of earlier griffin imagery are summarily dismissed in a single sentence that doesn't make clear that Mayor was even aware griffins were part of the menagerie commonly depicted in Bronze and Iron Age eastern Mediterranean visual culture.[29] Similarly, nothing in *The First Fossil Hunters* acknowledges the existence of the robust art-historical scholarship on archaic Greek art's influx of orientalizing motifs such as the griffin, siren and sphinx from those sources. Her book's idiosyncrasies might reflect the field of folklore's orientation towards the verbal over the visual, but the lack of critical response to these lacunae is remarkable: only a single review I encountered even raised the question of how thousands of years of ancient West Asian and Egyptian griffin imagery is at odds with the premise of the Greeks independently inventing the idea of a griffin as a result of inspiration from dinosaur bones in Central Asia.[30] Mayor's theory is now close to ubiquitous in public-facing sources (specialists of archaic Greece have largely ignored it), from a children's book reprise and television shows to museum labels in collections as venerable as those of the Art Institute of Chicago for the griffin protomes earlier in this chapter: 'Belief in a griffin ... was probably inspired by the fossilized remains of dinosaurs with beaks that once roamed Central Asia.'[31]

The shaky foundation of the fossil hypothesis relative to its facile acceptance suggests how ingrained certain interpretive biases towards Greek culture still are. To accept the *Protoceratops* hypothesis, thousands of years of ancient West Asian and Egyptian art must be conveniently forgotten, along with the ample scholarship detailing specific demonstrated patterns of the griffin motif entering Greek art from these sources.[32] Then one must be willing to attribute greater influence to the observation of fossil remains unearthed thousands of miles away, which don't even correlate particularly well to Greek griffins in art or literature. A small dinosaur, *Protoceratops*, possessed a distinctive neck frill, a fragile element of fossils that often disintegrates. This neck frill, the suggested inspiration for griffins' wings, doesn't especially resemble ancient depictions of griffin wings. Wings are such a popular feature of Greek composite creatures that even the version of the sphinx preferred in Greek art incorporates wings, despite Egyptian sphinx images having none.[33] The real insight this material offers is how culture can be forged in the richly productive process of appropriation. The lineage is certain: the griffins in archaic Greek art represent a redoubtable conjunction of predators, with even the paltry backstory to their conflict with the Arimaspi only a small step away from the generic images of kilt-wearing griffin fighters on Iron Age luxury goods.

Another challenge to Mayor's fossil hypothesis comes from griffins' ascribed home in a faraway place not being a distinctive geographical reference for this composite creature; rather, it is a routine ingredient in premodern formulations of fantastic beasts. The fact they are reflexively described as inhabitants of remote regions at the edges of the known world provides a ready excuse for not having seen these creatures at first hand – alive or fossilized. Herodotus wrote about griffins at the intersection of the realms of mythology and history, and just as he situates huge gold-digging ants in India, griffins, for him, live in far northern lands. Classical writers' sense of griffins' habitat remains fluid. Fifth-century BCE Ctesias – a Greek physician in the Achaemenid Persian court – places them in India, as does the third-century CE Philostratus of Athens, who reports:

> As for the gold that griffins dig up, there are rocks that are speckled with flakes of gold as if with sparks, and this creature quarries them by the force of its beak. These animals do exist in India, and are considered sacred to the Sun. Indian artists who portray the Sun god show his statue drawn by four of them. In size and strength they resemble lions in size, and attack even them thanks to the advantage of their wings, and also prevail over elephants and dragons. They do not fly far, but as far as birds of short flight, since they are not feathered as birds customarily are, but have scarlet webbing on their feet. When they whirl their feet they can fly and fight from the air, and only the tigress, which its speed makes equal to the wind, can escape them.[34]

Philostratus' characterization of it as one of many 'mythological wild animals' in India in the *Life of Apollonius of Tyana* (III.45) combines familiar details such as griffins' role in pulling the Sun's chariot, an unfamiliar habitat, their desire for gold and their ferocity and strength. Some texts mention them mostly through artworks depicting griffins, again hinting at the primacy of these visual works in constructing the concept of the griffin.[35] Another third-century author, Aelian, opines that to see a griffin is to know one, affirming that the griffin looks 'just as artists portray it in pictures and sculpture'.[36] His description lingers on the varied palette of the griffin's plumage: the feathers on its back are black; on its front, red; on its wings, white; and on its neck, blue. This colour combination of black, red, white and blue appears in griffin descriptions as early as that of Ctesias, and the specific Greek words deployed are used by that author to evoke rare, precious materials like cinnabar, which he typically used to describe fantastical phenomena, so that even their palette expresses the notion of griffins as a wondrous contrivance.[37] Aelian situates the griffins' habitat in Bactria and India, suggesting these remote places were to some degree interchangeable to his readers – as stand-ins for faraway locales.[38] Pliny the Elder and other writers place them in Scythia, while Pomponius Mela and Solinus (largely derived from the prior two authors) locate the griffins more specifically in the Scythian Riphaean Mountains, taken to be the world's northern boundary in antiquity.[39] Griffins' home shifts among ancient authors, but it is always at the remote fringes of the known – mostly sharing a name with real places, but so distant from readers that they were, in effect, mythical.

Chapter Three

Sacred Griffins:

Divine Partners and Symbols

But if Phoebus [Apollo] is there, Phoebus returned from Scythian climes to his Delphic tripod, guiding thither his yoked griffins . . .

Claudian, *Panegyric on the Sixth Consulship of Honorius*, 404 CE

One of the ways the griffin motif continued to be repurposed in ancient society was as a partner to the divine, or even as a stand-in. Standard reference works for ancient studies report griffins possessed a startling agglomeration of associations, such as the venerable *Paulys* encyclopaedia listing the creature's linkage to classical deities including – but not limited to – Apollo, Artemis, Dionysos and Nemesis.[1] Looking beyond the classical world, griffins can be seen variously on one of the earliest existing Buddhist stupas in India, pagan ceremonial vessels from Iron Age Scandanavia and in the pre-classical world with an unnamed Minoan goddess.

A Minoan Goddess' Companion

In the Bronze Age, a Minoan griffin perches next to a goddess in a seventeenth-century BCE wall painting from Xeste 3, a large building excavated at Akrotiri in the Aegean (illus. 17, 18). The griffin wears a collar, tethered by a red leash to a window post; the so-called 'Mistress of Animals' dominates the scene. She receives an offering of crocuses – the flower from which saffron is harvested – from a blue monkey standing on two legs. This vignette could be part of a larger festival celebrating girls' initiation into adulthood.[2] Saffron was ingested to alleviate menstrual pain, and crocuses' vivid yellow stamens dyed women's garments, so both the plant derivative's traditional medical and textile uses potentially reinforce the way griffin imagery seems particularly associated with women in Minoan as well as Mycenean art.[3] The bent wings, the whorl pattern on the body and the sleek aquiline head are common to Minoan griffins, though the Xeste 3 image doesn't sport the crest they also often have. A marker of the supernatural, the griffin at this female deity's side might also play a guardian role, as a particularly vicious – and magnificent – pet. Gaining the submission of this composite predator, which is signified as 'tamed' by the collar, offers a visual testament to the goddess's power (something seen already in illus. 3, 4, 5, 6).

17 The Great Goddess/Mistress of Animals, a griffin and a monkey in an offering-of-saffron ceremony, fresco from Xeste 3 structure at Akrotiri, c. 1650–1625 BCE, reconstruction drawing.

18 Griffin, Xeste 3 fresco from Akrotiri, c. 1650–1625 BCE, reconstruction watercolour detail of 17.

19 Reconstruction of Minoan 'throne room', c. *1700 BCE, Knossos, Crete.*

Likewise, in the modern reconstruction of a room in the Minoan complex in Knossos, Crete (illus. 19), a pair of griffins flank the 'throne', while another one protects the north door; griffins are frequently portrayed in this protector role, or the aggressor role of a hunter, from the Middle Minoan II period onwards.[4] Although not differentiated in the current reconstruction, the north wall griffin (but not those flanking the throne) likely possessed the Minoan-style 'bent' wing.[5] Griffins are more prevalent at Knossos than at some other Minoan sites such as Kato Zakros, where the assortment of composite creatures is so wide-ranging and fluid that the cohort from that site has been characterized as 'distinctly random'.[6] Given griffins' particular connection to female deities in Minoan and Mycenaean art, debate persists about whether this space at Knossos was devoted to the worship of a goddess or was the ruler's throne room. In fact, the former seems more likely.[7]

Oracular Griffins

Following their Bronze Age role as the companion to the Minoan divine feminine, by the sixth century BCE, griffins at the side of Apollo were more associated with the Sun and other light-bringing forces. Griffins were sometimes said to reside in the far northern Hyperborean realms (that is, beyond the north wind), where Apollo was 'honoured among them above all other gods', according to ancient writer Diodorus Siculus.[8] The late classical Temple of Apollo at Didyma, whose renowned oracle attracted people from across the ancient world, showcases griffins in the architectural ornament of its circa 300 BCE rebuilding (illus. 20). Although large-scale griffins appear on a ninth-century ancient Syrian building, it was only around the time of the Didyma temple that griffins began to adorn Greek architecture on the grand scale of projects such as that complex, despite their prior use on many smaller-scale objects.[9]

Griffins accompany Apollo elsewhere. Among the hybrid's many depictions on ancient coins, some of the most interesting are those from what numismatists call the 'animal series' issued during the tumultuous years of the Roman emperor Gallienus' sole reign (r. 260–68 CE) following the death of his father and co-emperor Valerian. This group of coins seems intended to evoke the protection of nine popular deities with traditional Greek religious rites during exceedingly difficult times, and griffins appear on the reverse of many of the Apollo coins, which, along with those of his sister Diana/Artemis, are disproportionately represented in the animal series, and may have been thought to possess a special potency against the plague.[10] Griffins also partner with Apollo in sculpture, as in the famed *Augustus Prima Porta* in the Vatican Museums, where the emperor's breastplate unobtrusively illustrates Apollo being transported through the air by a griffin. This scene also turns up in the Late Roman Claudian's writing – 'But if Phoebus [Apollo] is there, Phoebus returned from Scythian climes to his Delphic tripod, guiding thither his yoked griffins . . .' – and persists into medieval Christian sources, as we will see.[11]

Griffins were also linked to Artemis to an extent. Many versions of the cult statue of Artemis of Ephesus include griffins, though not prominently, and although the mistress of the hunt is more typically accompanied by birds and lions, the sheer

20 Sculptural fragment, c. *300* BCE, *Temple of Apollo, Didyma.*

abundance of material means numerous griffin depictions have been catalogued from her cult sites.[12] A few other hints of a tie exist. Thus Strabo's *Geography* mentions an 'exceedingly notable' painting, *Artemis Carried Up by a Griffin*, at the Temple of Artemis Alpheionia.[13] Griffins used for divine transport carries forward a pattern seen in ancient West Asian precedents, and Chapter Nine explores later iterations.

Ruled by a Solar God

This first-century CE altar, pairing Palmyrene solar gods with griffins, was made at the behest of warehouse workers labouring in the southern districts of Rome (illus. 21). On the pictured side, four griffins rear up with their front legs raised, as if poised to soar heavenward. The griffins' chariot carries Malakbel, and the Palmyrene inscription offers the altar as a tribute to 'Malakbel and the gods of Palmyra' from its people. The Latin inscription on the altar's adjoining side extols 'the most holy Sun', omits naming him as Malakbel and adds the reference to the *Horrea Galbana* (the Palmyrene patrons' Roman neighbourhood) – these differences make the Palmyrene and Latin texts complementary rather than exact translations of each other.[14]
The Roman-made altar aligns with other Palmyrene visual traditions, for at the Syrian city's Temple of Bel, griffins frame the sun deity, Malakbel, in a set of reliefs depicting the god in four celestial positions.[15]

21 Altar to the Palmyrene gods, c. 50–100 CE, marble.

22 Statue of Nemesis in the form of a griffin, Egypt, c. 100–200 CE, *faience.*

Nemesis: Griffins of Retributive Justice

The workers who were the patrons of the Palmyrene altar would have seen griffins in many other places around Rome, including through their recurring connection with the goddess Nemesis. Textual sources from the past can dominate scholarly accounts, but there are important ways in which griffins in Roman visual culture offer fresh insights. Archaeology has taught us that the goddess Nemesis was honoured in and near many civic arenas across the empire, a practice that for the most part was beneath the notice of the elites, who wrote the lion's share of surviving sources.[16] Sometimes used as the abstract concept of retributive justice, more typically Nemesis was a vengeful personification of that notion, with one ancient author describing her as 'an actual guardian presiding with universal sway over the destinies of individual men'.[17]

While the cult of Nemesis originated in ancient Greece, only in the Roman period did the griffin become a routine companion for the goddess – so much so that it eventually became a visual proxy for her in many works.[18] Like her antithesis, Fortuna (random chance), Nemesis could possess a wheel of fortune, and many renderings of griffins with a wheel survive. The pairing is first attested in the first century CE, then becomes increasingly common in the second and third centuries, even marking relatively quotidian items such as a Roman bread stamp that shows a griffin with a paw resting on top of a wheel.[19]

This lovely faience statue of a griffin was filled with interpretative possibilities for its initial viewers (illus. 22).[20] The griffin by this point had become fully identified with the goddess Nemesis, and the creature's paw rests on the wheel of fortune. The hollow-cast figurine's vivid blue glaze, the little touches of yellow and the marks on its base place its origin in Roman Egypt, where this depiction is especially common, most likely the second century CE. Its Egyptian context might have given this griffin-as-Nemesis another specific set of meanings, though: for in earlier Egyptian art, the griffin could signify the pharaoh (see illus. 31). Thus an Egyptian griffin with a wheel of fortune might have evoked multiple strands of meaning at once: the Roman goddess Nemesis, the Egyptian ruler and even, some scholars argue, Egypt's god of fate, (P)shaï.[21]

The Gundestrup Cauldron

The griffin motif was just as enthusiastically deployed beyond the boundaries of the classical world. One remarkable example is the largest silver vessel that survives from Iron Age Europe, conventionally called the Gundestrup cauldron, though 'container' is probably more apt (*c.* 150–1 BCE), which shows griffins in its now-mysterious imagery (illus. 23). Discovered in a Danish peat bog in 1891, dismantled but largely complete, its lively and complex iconography has attracted many would-be decipherers. A prevailing interpretation is that the silver plaques depict a Gaulish version of the *Cattle Raid of Cooley* (*Tāin bó Cúalnge*).[22] An inner cauldron plaque portrays a female figure flanked by two griffins, an aggressive-looking quadruped and a pair of delightfully nimble-looking elephants. Griffins don't feature in that epic or in surviving Gaulish inscriptions, so if the hypothesis holds true, their role on the cauldron would be to embellish the visual imagining of the narrative, perhaps as a nod to griffins' common presence on precious imported metalwork.[23] Alternatively the griffins could symbolize forces of chaos and evil being fended off by the beneficent Great Goddess, who was invoked in new-year rituals by the

23 Inner panel, Gundestrup cauldron/container, Iron Age Europe, c. 150 BCE–1 BCE, silver.

Celtic-Thracian elites who once were its original audience.[24] Others have interpreted the cauldron cosmologically, with the central female representing the Moon and the five animals, including the two griffins, standing for half of the months of their ten-month year.[25]

Further striking evidence of the dispersal of griffin imagery in sacred contexts comes from its appearance on an Indian Buddhist monument created at roughly the time of the Danish cauldron. The second- to first-century BCE renovations to a southeast Indian stupa's railing highlighted griffins in a procession of fictive and real animals interspersed with young men (illus. 24). Winged hybrid creatures within early Buddhism may have been viewed through the concept of *adrsta* (the unseen), the griffin being the means through which this understanding was transmitted through the air.[26] This imagery and its symbolism represent influence from Achaemenid Persian West Asia, with the first Indian instances appearing at Sanchi's Stupa 2. Masons' marks on the stupa are in the Kharosthi language, which was used at the time in the Gandhara region – the Indian region most in contact with classical style and imagery – suggesting a potential pathway that led to the griffin motif coexisting with scenes from the Buddha's life in the sculptural programme. Later Indian renderings include a gold coin showing a griffin being slain by a fourth-century CE Gupta emperor, as a mark of his prowess even against foreign

24 Sculptural relief, stupa railing, 2nd–1st century BCE, *Amaravati, state of Andhra Pradesh, India, limestone.*

(or supernatural) creatures.[27] These griffins in India lead us towards a connection to the divine investigated in the next chapter, that to Dionysos. Across the startling diversity brought together here, ranging from Minoan Akrotiri to Iron Age Denmark to post-Mauryan India, the role of griffins is often as literal or figurative transport between realms (heavens and Earth; chance and necessity), and perhaps their hybridity allows, or reinforces, that kind of significance.

Chapter Four

Drinking with Griffins

A griffin's claw I am called; in Asia, Arabia I am well-known . . .

Inscription on a sixteenth-century drinking horn

Across the centuries, griffins have appeared on countless drinking vessels as well as in spaces associated with social drinking. So-called 'griffin horns' were likewise used for an extensive period. Objects and places linked with griffins in either imagery or name have had an ongoing, important role in the social experiences in which they were used, showing that notions of the griffin could align with the pleasure and dignity of these shared moments at the table (or, in classical times, at the dining couch). We will see, too, how griffins' association with the ancient god of wine, Dionysos, continues to inform how we see these works, long past the eclipse of the era when he was venerated.

Renderings of Dionysos incorporate griffins from at least circa 400 BCE. It has been suggested that the griffin motif was transferred from Apollo to Dionysos at the oracular site of Delphi, but that kind of linear genealogy is somewhat misleading and countered by what we saw with the griffin cauldrons found at eighth to seventh-century BCE Greek sites dedicated to a range of gods and goddesses (see illus. 13).[1] A specific breadcrumb trail traceable to a particular location is necessary to understand neither the absorption of griffins into the rich vocabulary of Dionysian imagery redolent of eastern luxury, nor the shape-changing god's strong tie to hybridity.[2] Ancient authors impart a decidedly fierce edge to Dionysos, on display in his military conquest of India (though that enterprise's main goal by some accounts seemed to involve Dionysos getting Indians to drink wine), mentioned by Arrian as an antecedent for the efforts of Alexander the Great, another figure paired with griffins, to seize India.[3] Sharing connections to martial success and riches, it is hardly surprising that griffins feature in Dionysian imagery. Many ancient vessels depict scenes akin to this one of Dionysos riding a griffin-drawn chariot on a southern Italian, fourth-century BCE wine decanter attributed to the Lycurgus Painter (illus. 25). Spikily contoured griffin silhouettes provide a visual foil to the sensuous curves of the god of wine they transport. Below the wine god's chariot, an old satyr gamely refills his jug from a large wine container, a *krater*, while fauns and maenads join the revelry.

As the god of the vine, Dionysos, or his griffin minions, often decorate floor mosaics of spaces for entertaining in ancient Greek homes, especially the *andron*.

25 Situla (a Greek wine decanter) depicting Dionysos in his griffin-drawn chariot, attributed to the Lycurgus Painter, c. 360–340 BCE, *terracotta.*

26 Pebble floor mosaic from House of Mosaics, c. 375–350 BCE, Eretria, Greece.

This was a room set aside in the grandest homes for men to socialize, often with wine; an *andron* from the Greek city of Eretria showcases griffin imagery typical of these rooms, which served as a kind of early version of the 'man cave' (illus. 26). Men, reclining on couches encircling the room, could see the mosaics as they fraternized, and griffins have pride of place in the centre of the floor; in other examples of pebble mosaics, pairs of griffins frame the threshold. Griffins are, in fact, the most common kind of imagery in fourth- to third-century BCE pebble mosaics, appearing in 36 extant pavements.[4] A clear pattern emerges in how these spaces were used: a striking 65 per cent of the rooms containing these floors have the distinctive raised borders used for drinking couches, and a further 15 per cent directly adjoined drinking spaces.[5] The Eretria floor, where scenes of griffins battling with Arimaspi alternate with lions attacking horses, is characteristically pugilistic in tone. Marking spaces for gender-specific communal drinking, the wild and fantastic beasts populating the floors of these rooms may have resonated with the participants' sense of their own masculinity, in the classical era constructed through attributes such as power and aggression.[6] As these pebble mosaics became popular in Greek homes, they replaced woven carpets from places like Phrygia to the east, and it is likely that the canon of images used was adopted from the textiles – not least the griffin, which as we have seen was a mainstay on exotic luxury objects, signalling the prestige connected with them.[7] For their late classical audience, griffins and other orientalizing motifs could also evoke the cherished antiques crafted by their archaic Greek forebears, rather than the West Asian objects that had once inspired those heirlooms.[8]

Griffins' connection to social drinking spaces continues; it is easy to find bars and pubs around the world today with variants of griffin/gryphon names, ranging from a jazz bar in Seoul, Korea, to a sports bar in Modena, Italy. At the time of writing, one can readily order a commercial neon sign of a griffin holding a cocktail, as found at a hipster bar in Las Vegas that doubles down on its imbibing-griffin signage (illus. 27). The bar's interior envelops its patrons in a set-designed version of the past, with faux irregular columns and brick arches, along a street of quirky establishments, including an Evel Knievel-themed pizza pub across the street. While griffin representations can convey many meanings, perhaps this instance comes the closest to offering a cheekily ironic spin on the off-putting severity of the creature's typical public image?

In addition to appearing in social drinking spaces, there is a long tradition of griffin imagery on drinking horns.[9] An example is a second-century BCE ivory drinking horn, a rhyton, that terminates in a powerfully articulated

27 Neon signs for The Griffin bar in Las Vegas, Nevada.

28 Rhyton with horned griffin, Parthian, c. 100 BCE, ivory.

horned griffin (illus. 28). Excavated in the Parthian Persian fortification of Old Nisa in Central Asia, this was one of about fifty ivory drinking horns found at the site. In the lineage of earlier, Achaemenid Persian drinking horns crafted from precious metal, often embellished with senmurvs (a mythical bird somewhat like a phoenix), griffins and other creatures, this ivory horn's skilful carving imparts to the griffin a sense of dynamic energy with the slightly flexed forelegs and extravagant curl of the horns.[10] The creature is so visually compelling that the ivory even featured on a Soviet postage stamp from 1969.

The drinking horn's connection with griffins persists, with a fascinating twist – the creature was not only part of the visual lexicon of drinking vessels but came to also be referenced in the name of the object. So-called 'griffin claws', namely the medieval example from the Treasury of Saint-Denis, functioned as sumptuous drinking vessels (illus. 29). Today more commonly termed 'drinking horns', they often feature, since their nineteenth-century romantic revival, as a key accoutrement in pop culture of any self-respecting Viking. But medieval and early modern sources call them griffin horns, or griffin claws, even when they had no griffin imagery.[11]

29 'Griffin claw' of Saint-Denis, c. 1125–50, bison horn, gilded copper and amethyst.

The early thirteenth-century gilt copper adornments on this 'claw' (actually a bison horn) include a disquieting bird-leg base that riffs on the griffin's identity by having the four talons characteristic of raptors.[12] Every year in Saint-Denis, a town on the northern outskirts of Paris, following the feast of the Ascension four priests would bring the griffin claw to each of the local taverns to calibrate measurements to the 'pinte de Saint-Denis'. Holding a generous 1.464 litres, the 'pint' was almost twice the volume of a modern wine bottle.[13] Given the ancient association of griffins with the wine god, and the fact that the medieval French name *Denis* is linked to the very same ancient god Dionysos, it is tempting to speculate that ancient connotations somehow played a role in the medieval use of the Saint-Denis 'griffin claw'.

When in the sixteenth century a griffin claw was crafted for Mainz's noble winemaking family von Greiffenclau – whose name deriving from the German for griffin claw is attested as early as 1211 – the vessel's German inscription played on the creature's exotic origins, proclaiming, 'A griffin's claw I am called; in Asia, Arabia I am well-known.'[14] However frequently depicted, the creature retains a paradoxical sense of being exogenous, constitutive of its identity and allure. Later examples can perpetuate the association with men's communal drinking, among others a large German drinking horn used by the Firemens Guild in Büsum, tipped in 1604 with a finely wrought griffin head.[15]

30 Wine holder with griffin appendages made in Nevers, France, 1680–85, faience.

Griffins remained a popular motif in European decorative arts for centuries, part of a visual lexicon lush with fantastical details. A search in the collection database of many North American and western European museums usually turns up a fascinating array of objects of this nature, with scores of items in particular that were used for lavish entertaining. A large wine vessel made in late seventeenth-century Nevers, France, captures how the griffin could be part of a visual language that now seems at once imposing and outlandish (illus. 30). The mythological scenes on the exterior of this vessel were drawn by the artist Michel Dorigny, who so suited the tastes of the time that his works decorated numerous high-end Parisian homes.[16] Thus it is not surprising to see his Dionysian scenes used here, but the juxtaposition with griffin body parts makes this vessel unique among what survives from this major centre of faience (a fine tin-glazed earthenware) production. The griffin-head handles and the clawed feet that support the large bowl – used for storing wine on a grand banquet table – punctuate this vessel, our final and most exuberant example of griffins gracing objects destined to be viewed while inebriated.

Griffins' classical associations with the wine god, Dionysos, probably inspired the pairing here, which follows other slightly earlier wine coolers with leonine feet as a base, as well as the bird feet of objects as in the Saint-Denis griffin claw.[17] Designers in Nevers adopted the fanciful 'grotesques' of Italian maiolica wares, especially those from Urbino, and the griffin details work on those terms, too. Dragon-shaped handles and other figures in that vein dramatically accent other French faience, sometimes also combined with more scenes from Dorigny's *Bacchanales* or similar source material.[18] The Nevers wine cooler's luxuriant excess exemplifies the reign of Louis XIV, when such decorative flourishes were features of the Baroque style fashionable under his rule. The exceptional technical skill required to produce this large a vessel would have impressed viewers aware of the rarity and cost it implied, intensifying the impact on its well-heeled initial audience.[19] The griffin's head and claws amplify this saturation of visual experience, and thus the creature further offers an entry point to a kind of escapism for its viewers that we will explore in upcoming chapters. By this same token, whether on a Baroque wine holder, a medieval drinking horn or an ancient decanter, this half-way beast also signals the possibilities of transformation and social bonding intrinsic to the communal experiences in which they were used.

Chapter Five

The Art of War:

Griffins on Weapons and Armour

Shields . . . blazoned with griffin-eagles

Aristophanes, *The Frogs*, first performed in 405 BCE

Griffins, a formidable fusion of two predatory beings, have been strategically employed for millenia to enhance the visual impact of both ceremonial and battle-ready armaments. Upcoming chapters explore how griffins play a role on coats of arms and for prominent military figures such as Alexander the Great; here, we investigate other dimensions of griffins' place in the visual culture of warfare. Amid the vast array of potential examples, this selection purposefully showcases a diverse array of militaristic griffins ranging from a Roman god of war's chestplate and gladiators' helmets to United States Air Force imagery and an ancient Egyptian battle-axe.

The Pharaoh as Griffin

In New Kingdom Egypt, a griffin could signify the pharaoh as warrior, as on a sixteenth-century BCE gem-encrusted copper battle-axe found in Thebes within the tomb of Queen Ahhotep (illus. 31); her son, the pharaoh Ahmose, is rendered on this ceremonial weapon as a griffin on one side and as a sphinx on the other. Ahhotep, regent while her son was young, likely had a role in Thebes' military success, so her burial with this ceremonial axe, along with a dagger, carried extra weight. The axe blade's griffin as pharaoh exemplifies how eclectic Egyptian visual culture was at the beginning of the New Kingdom, for while the body and bent wings seem inspired by Bronze Age Aegean griffin imagery (see illus. 18), its long beak reprises earlier Egyptian animal composites that mix the lion with different birds of prey, for instance a vulture. Egyptian griffins tend to have more hawk-like heads than their eagle-based West Asian contemporaries, but the big picture is that their depictions range as you would expect from a society famed for the rich multiplicity of its animal composites. The inscription beside the axe's griffin claims the creature is 'beloved' or 'begotten' of the falcon-headed war god Montu, associated with military victories by the pharaoh.[1]

Later, on the interior panel of a war chariot, the fourteenth-century BCE pharaoh Thutmosis IV is depicted in the form of a winged lion functionary of Montu, trampling vanquished enemies from multiple territories. Still more griffins

31 Pharaoh as griffin on head of ceremonial axe from tomb of Queen Ahhotep, Thebes (d. c. 1530 BCE), copper alloy with semi-precious stone and gold.

as familiars of Montu adorn New Kingdom warships.[2] These ties are long-standing: pharaohs appear as falcon-lion hybrids in Old and Middle Kingdom images, including Fifth-dynasty renderings on the causeway of the funerary complex of Sahure near Cairo (2491–2477 BCE).[3]

'Shields . . . blazoned with griffin-eagles'

In the classical era, griffins frequently emblazoned Greek and Roman shields, helmets and breastplates, creating a reciprocal loop: their reputation for ferocity made them seem appropriate in that context, and appearing on implements of war reinforced that aspect of their identity. Even classical Greek comic writing takes the association for granted, as in Aristophanes' offhand reference in *The Frogs* to 'shields . . . blazoned with griffin-eagles' (l. 929). Likewise, Athena's helmet on her cult statue in the Parthenon is described by Pausanius in his second-century CE tour of Greece as having a sphinx flanked by griffins (1.24.5). A fourth-century BCE gold-and-enamel pendant disc featuring the head of the goddess Athena Parthenos, now in St Petersburg, shows leonine griffins on her helmet, but mortals could also wear griffin-adorned helmets in Greece and Rome. Thus a griffin's head topped the helmet crest of the *thraex* (Thracian) type of gladiator – a use surely inflected by griffins' exotic allure, as Thracians were stereotyped as lacking 'civilization', that is, as being decidedly non-Roman.[4] On the most detailed *thraex* helmets a feather

32 Thraex *gladiator's helmet, Roman, 1st century* CE, *bronze.*

pattern covered the crest, making the individual fighter further embody the griffin – indeed, sometimes actual bird feathers were also attached to the helmet. A first-century CE *thraex* helmet with griffin foreparts protruding from the top (illus. 32), discovered in the gladiatorial barracks in Pompeii, follows late Republican Roman helmets in its general form, which in turn echo Greek griffin-crested helmets.[5] The *thraex* gladiator type originated in the early Roman Republic, when enslaved people were forced to fight using their traditional weapons. By the time we encounter the *thraex* in visual culture, though, like so much else that went on in Roman spectacles, this gladiatorial identity was just part of the showmanship. The storied gladiator Spartacus came from Thrace, yet he fought not as a *thraex* but as a heavily armoured *murmillo* – a gladiator armed as a Roman legionary soldier. Conversely, the emperor Caligula, with no particular connection to Thrace, fought as a *thraex* in the arena, as part of his energetic and successful campaign to scandalize his fellow Roman elites.[6] The most common adversary for a *thraex* in the arena was a *murmillo* – and so these fights would enact a fictive mini-war of Rome against its foreign griffin-adorned adversaries. The *thraex* as a fighting persona also connoted pride, wealth and cunning. A dream-interpretation manual of the time informed its male Roman readers that dreams (and even nightmares) of fighting a *thraex* signalled that the dreamer 'will marry a woman who is rich, crafty, and fond of being first'.[7] The inclusion of the griffin on the *thraex* helmet implies layers of meaning: while the hybrid creature conventionally adorned armaments, its connotations when paired with the *thraex* gladiator in particular dovetailed with other elements of the griffin's identity, namely its suggestion of riches and the foreign.

Mars the Avenger

Cuirassed sculptures – statues of powerful armour-clad men and gods – punctuated public spaces throughout the Roman Empire. We've already noted the griffin carrying Apollo on the famous *Prima Porta Augustus* sculpture now in the Vatican Museums. Ceremonial armour represents a glamoured-up version of battle equipment, communicating complex messages on armaments several removes away from the gore of combat. Various forms of griffin imagery are present on these statues, occasionally in proud pairs, while at other times assuming more supporting roles, quite literally.[8] These sculptural griffins on armour tapped into associations already centuries old by the time the Roman cuirassed statues were carved, but also anticipate the griffin's later use in heraldry.

In the brawny statue of Mars Ultor (the Avenger), the pair of griffins on the torso-covering muscle cuirass resonate with other less prominent animal imagery, including *pegasi*, wreaths of elephants' and rams' heads (illus. 33). The heavily restored colossal statue found in two pieces is likely a Flavian-era copy of a statue from the temple of Mars Ultor in Rome's Forum of Augustus, a temple that has been characterized – only with slight hyperbole – as 'the supreme architectural statement of the ideology of the Augustan regime'.[9] The original placement of the statue within or near the temple is debated, but what matters for our understanding is the project's significance for Augustus, who in building this temple brought a plan that Julius Caesar had initiated to completion.[10] The programme's imagery would have been especially charged following Augustus' return of the Roman legion standards captured by the Parthians, a diplomatic triumph through which the emperor symbolically reversed a humiliating defeat, accruing enormous political capital in the process. As such, the statue of the god of war, with griffins featuring prominently on its cuirass, may have symbolized to some viewers retributive justice – a connection that resonates with griffins' links to Nemesis or their symbolism within ancient Egyptian astrology, discussed in Chapter Seven.

33 Mars Ultor, Roman, c. 100 CE, marble.

Forum of Trajan

Part of the language of triumph, griffins made a compelling choice for the decorative programme executed for the Forum of Trajan (106–12 CE), funded by imperial order with booty from the Dacian Wars (illus. 34).[11] The friezes recycle seven groupings drawn from the visual repertoire of Roman imperial public art, and it's noteworthy that four of the Forum's seven repeated motifs contain griffins: eagle-headed griffins with vases and candelabra, tripods or cupids; and lion-headed griffins with both cupids and vases.[12] The pictured frieze fragment shows the first type, with a griffin framed by a candelabrum and a *kantharos* vase, and was excavated in 1927 at the behest of Italy's Fascist government, for whom ancient Rome's visual language of power served their own political rhetoric. The Forum's visual components were so widespread in Roman imperial public spaces that they likely evoked a general sense of gravitas for the original viewers rather than activated specific recollections related to death and its commemoration, a prior interpretation. This sculptural griffin was perched 11 metres (36 ft) above ground level as part of the entrance area of the square in Trajan's monumental complex, making its details hard to discern. The candelabrum, a rarer inclusion, potentially alludes to Roman ritual or the concept of *lux perpetua*, but, in the end, the funerary connotations of winged creatures and 'eternal light' are difficult to reconcile with the triumphalist messaging of a frieze

34 Fragment of griffin between candelabrum and vase from Trajan's Forum, Rome, 106–12 CE, marble.

whose overriding goal was the projection in urban space of Trajan's military prowess and power, a ready fit for griffins.[13]

Iron Age Soldiers

Moving beyond the confines of the classical realm, we find that during the La Tène I and II periods (approximately spanning from the fourth to the second centuries BCE), griffins not only held a significant presence on artefacts like the Gundestrup cauldron (see illus. 23), but had a place on European Iron Age belts and swords. In certain instances, these depictions may have conveyed a sense of collective identity, for griffins on belts seem associated particularly with foot soldiers.[14] During the La Tène II period, griffins are abundant on sword scabbards; however, they are less prevalent during the La Tène I period.[15] That said, the creatures are often very loosely rendered by La Tène metalsmiths: on one belt hook, for example, the decorative figures have alternately been viewed as a pair of griffins or a pair of herbivores.[16] While we don't have the same indicators of a specific tie to warrior groups, the reach of this imagery at that time is evident from roughly contemporary belt buckles in quite a few variations of griffins (all in combat) excavated in Siberia and to its south, and, additionally, fourth- to third-centuries BCE Chinese jades deploy griffin motifs.[17]

The Nagyszentmiklós/Sânnicolau Mare Hoard

Early medieval art offers many examples of warlike griffins, with some particularly intriguing instances on the gold vessels from a hoard found in Nagyszentmiklós (now Sânnicolau Mare, Romania), likely created by early eighth-century Avar metalworkers. We will focus on a jug from the hoard, one that leads us into strange new lands of representation in its smorgasbord of violent imagery (illus. 35, 36). So alluring that a reproduction was even included in the hoard – alongside the *Mona Lisa* – of time bandits loot in the 1981 movie by that name, its shimmering gold body is encircled by four large medallions, one depicting a victorious knight atop a horse, holding a lance and resting a hand on a much smaller captive walking alongside him. The discrepancy in scale emphasizes the knight's military ascendancy, punctuated by the severed head that lolls from his saddle. Avar art offers some parallels to this kind of scene, but many more are found in Byzantine and Roman art, as a bombastic proclamation of victory.[18]

The next medallion renders an eagle-headed griffin felling a deer, the side illustrated here. By now the predatory tableau of a mythical griffin on the attack might almost seem 'natural', but how does this familiar scene resonate with the vessel's other medallions? The medallion to its left shows an archer on top of a human-headed winged steed. His prey, a panther, is poised to receive the tip of the arrow directly in its mouth, like many Sasanian images of a ruler on horseback shooting arrows at a large feline.[19] But the most striking aspect of this medallion – the bearded human head of the creature that the archer rides – remains mysterious, having no equivalent within Avar culture. It does serve to remind us, however,

35 Embossed gold jug from the treasure of Nagyszentmiklós (Sânnicolau Mare), Avar, c. early 8th century CE*, gold.*

36 Multiple views of the embossed gold jug from the treasure of Nagyszentmiklós, illustrations by József Hampel, 1894.

that the griffin was just one of many composite beasts in their visual repertoire. Rotating the jug another quarter turn, in the next medallion, an aquiline creature rears behind a nude woman who holds little branches in her upraised arms. The hybrid has griffin-like attributes, with its protruding ears and a ruff-like lock of hair grafted onto a predominantly avian form. Initially, the woman might appear to be dancing, but the scene shows the beast abducting her, its claws grabbing her back and belly, adding sexual violence to the list of predation scenes depicted on the gold jug.[20] Scholars grandly label this abduction scene as a *Himmelfahrt* (Ascension), but that term obfuscates the horror of what's rendered, the first phase of an assault. Comparable images come from sources as remote as ancient Gandharan art; it may have some distant relation to scenes of Ganymede's abduction or the Hungarian turul bird legend, but the most likely origin of the image is Central Asia.[21] The brutality of a familiar scene, a griffin's attack on a herbivore, gains more frisson from these juxtapositions. The modality might vary, the imagery might draw from sources ranging from Central Asia to Constantinople or even Rome, and each medallion has its own distinct aggressor, but the four images cumulatively offer a singular message of bellicose power and subjugation through violence.

Griffins with curvilinear patterns likewise adorned Avar belt buckles (illus. 37), yet as noted recently: 'The late Avar griffin is a near-universal symbol; however, when, why and from whom it was adopted is open to discussion.'[22] While a

37 Belt ornament with griffin motif, Avar, late 7th–early 9th century CE, *copper alloy and tinning.*

Byzantine griffin belt buckle has been excavated from an Avar site, limestone moulds used to create griffin belt buckles with the lost-wax process have also been discovered at Avar sites showing local production occurred alongside the import trade. Late Avar metalsmiths innovated too, for example, creating a visual formula in which two griffins attack a single herbivore.[23] Decorated belts held particular importance in this horse-loving culture, noted for its invention of the iron stirrup, with Avars even sometimes wearing more than one belt at a time. We have no recourse to their own texts, for the few remnants of Avar language to survive have not been deciphered. Nonetheless, suggestions have been offered as to the significance of the many Avar griffins. Earlier Avar belts display *tamga* clan symbols, and the griffins on later Avar belts might be seen as more embodied *tamgas*, with griffins representing an ancestral clan.[24] Conversely, because griffins were the very first motif to appear across the Avar community, it could be that the creature symbolized unity.[25] It is telling that the nomadic Avars embraced the griffin motif so extensively: highly fungible, the composite carried weight as a recognizable image among the many societies they interacted with.

A Griffin that Roared: Recontextualizing the Pisa Griffin

The Pisa Griffin (illus. 38), which long topped that city's cathedral, demonstrates another way an object's meanings can shift profoundly through war, for the most likely theory is that the bronze came to Pisa as booty from Al-Andalus, the Muslim Iberian Peninsula, and boldly memorialized that triumph. Standing just over a metre tall, the sculpture represents a dazzling technical accomplishment as the largest surviving example of medieval Islamic metalwork. Carbon-14 analysis of organic matter taken from inside the wings confirmed the griffin was fashioned in the eleventh to mid-twelfth century.[26] Earlier conjecture as to its original purpose ranged from its surmounting a fountain to being an incense burner.[27] Its Arabic inscriptions convey good wishes to an unnamed owner, in a phrasing and script style that points to the object's creation in Caliphal Córdoba.[28]

Recent scientific analysis has further revealed the Pisa Griffin was a noisy medieval automaton: when its bellows were blown, its metal shell echoed and amplified its sound.[29] Automata are widely attested in descriptions of medieval courts, particularly in the eastern Mediterranean. Byzantine and Islamic rulers alike seemed to delight in deploying these proto-robots to amaze visitors with their ability to move and make sounds.[30] While the setting is very different, the way this griffin seems crafted to elicit a sense of wonder is a theme we've noticed before, such as with the archaic Greek griffin head protomes (see illus. 12, 13).

But how did a noisy griffin end up on the Pisa Cathedral's roof? Exactly where the bronze creature was made and how it arrived in Pisa continue to be debated; this murkiness illustrates (again) how the griffin motif crossed geographical boundaries and inhabited many visual languages. Earlier scholarship leaned towards an eastern Islamic place of manufacture like Iran, or plunder from a raid of the

Fatimids in 1088.[31] Some consider it a product of an Italian workshop in the south, in nearby Genoa or even in Pisa itself.[32] More recently, consensus has emerged around this extraordinary example of medieval metalwork being captured as booty during the Pisan military's Balearic campaign of 1113–15, then placed as a trophy on the victorious city's cathedral's gable.[33] However important to art historians, the provenance might not have mattered much to the medieval Pisans who won it in battle – their writing from the time tends to focus on the material value of plundered objects.[34] The exigencies of war make small, precious objects especially enticing booty – another way the relatively large Pisan griffin was conspicuous. Its appearance, in all of its gorgeously stylized forms, made the object the epitome of both luxury and triumph, for the extent to which medieval viewers considered it specifically Islamic is debated.[35] Eleventh-century Pisans selected a cathedral architect whose name (Busketos, adapted to Buscheto) indicates he was Greek, so even before the arrival of the Pisa Griffin, this medieval city sought to project a cosmopolitan image.[36] *Spolia* – fragments from ancient buildings – were incorporated into the structure of

38 Pisa Griffin, c. 1100, bronze.

39 Gryphon Warrior *99–01 exercise, Camp Mackall Army Air Field, North Carolina, 1999.*

the cathedral, yet certain repurposed elements were showcased.[37] An Al-Andalusian column capital accented the north end, and wooden doors from Majorca the western end. The Pisa Griffin received particular pride of place perched above the hallowed eastern end of the cathedral. From this vantage point the automaton emitted eerie sounds, according to Pisan sources, as the area's strong maritime winds blew through its bellows, before it was taken down in 1828. Now the Pisa Griffin has slipped into the role of an artwork displayed in the cathedral's museum, with a replica taking its place above the cathedral.

Griffins' connection to the visual language of war continues. One of many recent instances would be this griffin on a United States Air Force aircraft that took part in the *Gryphon Warrior* exercise (illus. 39). The training was part of preparations as a division-ready brigade (DRB), a mission that resonates with the long-standing connotations of the griffin, for the DRB designation is for units that are constantly vigilant, poised to deploy on short notice.[38] Similarly, in 2023, Ukrainian forces were keen to get use of the Swedish Gripen (meaning griffin) fighter aircraft. The griffin's martial identity makes it easily accessible as a symbol of military prowess, and modern uses tend to be applied to air-based fighting, perhaps a distant echo of the griffin's avian roots.

Chapter Six

Griffins on the Move:

Depictions in Nomadic Central Asia

While most prior scholarship gravitated towards griffin imagery of the classical world and ancient West Asia, the many examples from Central Asian nomadic societies are illuminating – at times aligning with the prior chapter's case studies, but also manifesting some very distinctive qualities. Artistic exchange spanning this vast region has long been multidirectional, as demonstrated by this remarkable shaft-hole axe head, probably fashioned around 2000 BCE in the region of Bactria and Margiana, which illustrates the early extent and flexibility of this hybrid creature's forms (illus. 40).[1] The quadruped on the left couples a leonine body with aquiline claws and wings, an unnerving amalgam of raw predatory power. Sometimes labelled a dragon, it can just as readily be characterized as a winged lion griffin. The central figure, with its human body defamiliarized by a double bird head and taloned feet, most resembles the upright 'griffin demon' from West Asian art of the first millennium BCE (see illus. 7). Gold foil picks out salient features such as the avian heads and wings on both sides of the silver axe head. This formidable being's roots are likely in prehistoric Central Asia, where the features possibly reflect a mask used in shamanic rituals.[2] Moving to the eastern edge of Central Asia, specifically the Altai region in the second millennium BCE, societies, particularly in the Karakol, used ever-morphing bird imagery, often combined with antlers. Their art likely influenced the region's later societies, with the result that when the so-called 'Persian' horned griffin diffused eastwards into this area, it encountered an existing tradition of bird-composite imagery.[3]

Pazyryk Culture of the Altai Mountains

We are drawing closer to Herodotus' mythical ends of the Earth, where griffins were reputed to roam. Let's now try to untangle some of the strands of myth and history related to this region, for Herodotus' account has moulded some of the scholarship in ways that now warrant reconsideration. In the Altai Mountains, cutting across China, Mongolia, Russia and Kazakhstan, griffins were ubiquitous in the visual language of the nomadic pastoralist society now referred to as the Pazyryks. The Pazyryks lived at the eastern edge of the Scythian world, though defining the wider

40 Shaft-hole axe head with bird-headed demon, boar and dragon, Bronze Age, Bactria-Margiana, c. 2000 BCE, *silver and gold foil.*

cultural category of Scythians and the subgroup of the Pazyryks both pose their own conundrums. Being nomadic, Pazyryk remains largely come from human and horse burials, not settlement sites. The long-standing regional tradition of hybrid imagery and the rendering of bodies poised in the process of transformation, seen in the Bronze Age axe head pictured above, carries over to Pazyryk imagery, where a dazzling array of composite creatures adorned both the bodies of buried individuals and the trappings of their horses. The imagery of griffins and other winged composite creatures found across the region have stimulated scholars to posit their meanings – including, but not limited to, celestial mythology, the hunt, cannibalism, the cycle of seasons and funerary beliefs.[4] Evidently much work remains to resolve this question.

A Pazyryk 'chieftain'

Archaeologists have uncovered remains of seven bodies with tattoos from the Pazyryk sites, including three whose tattoos can be seen with the naked eye and four recently discovered to have tattoos using infrared imaging.[5] Pazyryk tattoos' twisting, complex patterns incorporate many hybrids, especially griffins (illus. 41, 42). No texts survive from this society, and the disputed dating of the graves hinges on whether the evidence from art-historical comparisons, dendrochronology, radiocarbon dating or topography is privileged, yielding suggestions from the sixth to third centuries BCE.[6] The 'chieftain' from Burial Mound/Kurgan 2 in the Pazyryk Valley is likely the earliest of the tattooed bodies, probably dating from circa 300 BCE, while others, namely the young soldier and 'Ice Maiden' with griffin tattoos, from sites on the Ukok plateau, about 200 kilometres (125 mi.) from the Pazyryk type site, were buried slightly later, circa 277 BCE.[7] The chieftain was also the first tattooed person excavated, in 1948. His age at death – fifty to sixty years old – the lavishness of his grave and his being interred with a woman and seven horses implies elevated status, thus explaining his modern appellation. The careful preparation of his body for burial included removing his internal organs and applying wax to the skin. Mummification, along with the local environmental conditions and the structure of the mounds

41 Close-up of the Pazyryk chief's hoofed griffin tattoo, the sixth found on his body, from Pazyryk Kurgan 2, c. 400–300 BCE.

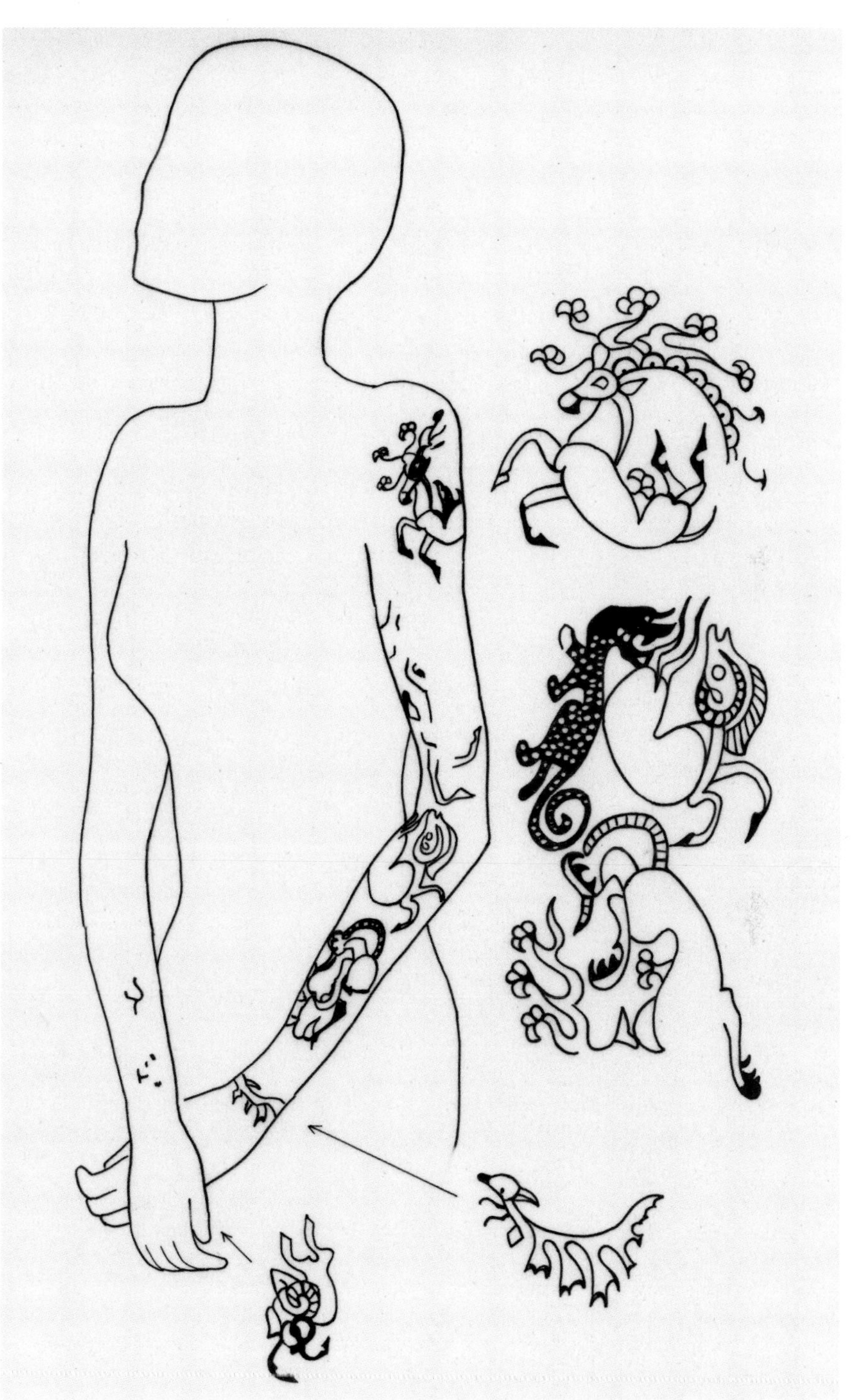

42 Tattoos on so-called 'Ice-Maiden', Ak-Alakha 3, Kurgan 1.

43 Finial in the form of a large griffin's head with a stag's head in its beak from Pazyryk Kurgan 2, c. 500–400 BCE*, wood and leather.*

above burial pits, which filled with water that quickly froze, allowed his and other Pazyryk remains to survive to an unusual degree. In all, the chieftain had at least six griffins inked into his skin. Most of his tattoos were visible even to the site's excavator back in 1948, but later infrared imaging revealed still more, including a hoofed griffin on his left foot.[8]

The Pazyryk 'hoofed griffin' has a tenuous place within griffins' 'family resemblance', because it integrates into the lion–eagle composite features, like hooves and antlers, which seem inspired by the red deer, *Cervus elaphus*, prevalent in the region.[9] Pazyryk visual culture is defined by fluidity: depictions of humans and other animals share attributes freely, and these shapeshifting forms may have held particular significance within a shamanic belief system. Indeed, Pazyryk individuals with tattoos may have been thought of not so much as adorned by these creatures but in some way as 'merged with, or accompanied by, subsidiary beings or spirit selves'.[10]

A consistent visual syntax underlies the recombining animal elements of Pazyryk visual culture. This griffin-shaped finial from a headdress came from the chieftain's burial site (illus. 43), and it's worth taking a moment to envision it worn on the head of a person tattooed with the same vocabulary of forms. The griffin opens its rapacious beak to reveal a stag's head with elaborate antlers, each terminating in a miniature raptor or griffin head with its own antlers.[11] This recursive layering can be seen almost as a 'frame narrative' in objects from Pazyryk society gravesites, and the same aesthetic of transformation is found in the griffin tattoos, where antler tips can metamorphose into heads.[12]

A Soldier, an Ice Maiden

Earlier assumptions based on the chieftain's burial theorized that tattoos were a prerogative of Pazyryk high-status men; however, newly discovered tattoos brought to light that body art was more widespread. The mummified remains of a woman who died in her late twenties, excavated in 1993 in Kurgan 1 of Ak-Alakha 3, bears a hoofed griffin tattooed on her left shoulder (illus. 42). Her tattoo captures the fractal quality that structures Pazyryk imagery: the griffin is rendered with antlers, each of which, in turn, terminates in its own small stylized griffin head.[13] In popular culture this woman is known as the 'Ice Maiden', and she has achieved sufficient fame to be the subject of both a BBC/Nova documentary and a book-length poem.[14] She was buried with six horses; griffin composites decorate her horses' cheek guards, and other imagery from the woman's tattoos is shared with that on her grave goods.[15] Her grave's isolated location, as well as the honours afforded to her burial, hint that this young woman may have held a special status – archaeologists speculated that she may have been a soothsayer or healer.[16] Opium and cannabis were both found in her grave, which might relate to shamanic practices. Alternatively, these substances may have more pragmatically offered this young woman relief from ailments such as the dislocated and damaged joints she had already suffered by the time of her death.[17]

44 Representations of griffins decorating Pazyryk horse harnesses, from Kurgan burials of the Altai region, c. 5th–3rd century BCE.

A young man, whose remains were excavated from Kurgan 3 of the Verkh-Kaldezhin II site, was tattooed in a similar fashion to the so-called chieftain and the Ice Maiden, with griffin heads included in the curving compositions on his body.[18] His burial goods – only one horse and modest weaponry – suggest he was an ordinary soldier, intimating that tattoos weren't exclusive to Pazyryk elites.[19] Of the seven tattooed Pazyryk individuals, he seems to have been the youngest, and since his tattoos are the simplest, it's tempting to speculate that tattoos were gradually acquired throughout a life, perhaps even earned.[20]

Though seven bodies make for a small sample – potentially not representative of Pazyryk tattooing customs – certain patterns emerge. The tattoos' placement suggest they were not likely to be covered by clothing, and the main difference between the tattoos on men versus women was that the women weren't tattooed on their legs.[21] Apart from the chieftain's foot tattoo, their griffin tattoos were all found on these ancient people's upper bodies, adorning their upper arms and particularly shoulders.[22] The chieftain, the Ice Maiden and the young soldier all had the hoofed griffin tattooed prominently on their shoulder, and infrared imaging has revealed the same griffin tattooed across the left shoulder of the woman buried

45 Horse saddle from Pazyryk Kurgan 1, c. 5th century BCE, *felt and horse hair.*

with the chieftain in Kurgan 2.[23] Both women, the Ice Maiden and the chieftain's companion, also had deer antlers tattooed on their left wrists.[24] Such similarities hint at a syntax for the placement and significance of their tattoos. Figurative tattoos may have been a distinctive, or at least unusual, feature of the Pazyryks: other ancient societies with tattooing traditions for which we have remains – as in those from the Tarim Basin in neighbouring Xinjiang – inked only abstract geometric patterns.[25] This is all the more noteworthy given that the griffin motif appears on contemporary metal objects from Xinjiang.[26]

Of Horses and Griffins

It is worth noting that the griffin motif, in all of its fecund variety, was equally pervasive on Pazyryk horse trappings (illus. 44). Horses had many roles in Pazyryk society. Burial goods suggest their military purpose, and wealth came from trading horses, but they were also part of the hunting and gathering activities of daily life.[27] While much of the excavated horse equipment can seem ceremonial, wear from extensive prior use indicates these objects weren't made specifically as grave goods.[28] One particularly intriguing detail is that, in light of the horse masks that formed part of the buried equipage, it is possible that some of the human tattoos' composite hoofed 'griffins' could, in fact, render the masked horses that also formed part of local beliefs connected with shamanism and shapeshifting.[29] In Pazyryk tombs, each horse was equipped with unique gear. This individualization is evident at the Berel grave site, located on the Kazakhstani side of the Altai Mountains, which is notable for its array of widely sourced, opulent burial items.[30] Amid that variation, an underlying visual syntax emerges across the horse gear in Berel. Images of predation and transformation, both of which often included versions of the griffin, are mirrored on each side of the animal's body.[31] At Al-Alakha 3 Kurgan 1, bridles on five of the six buried horses likewise carried a griffin motif. This spectacular felt saddle cover from Pazyryk Kurgan 1, excavated in 1929, shows the characteristic mirroring of a nearly identical predation scene on each side (illus. 45).[32] In this image, appliquéd on felt, each side's ibex beneath the griffin contorts in pain, its helplessness emphasized – a visual formula seen in other images of griffins ravaging large herbivores. This griffin is pure predator, lacking the deer-like antlers and hooves seen elsewhere in Pazyryk art, intensifying the visual message of dominance.

Of course, objects buried with Pazyryk individuals were not necessarily made within that culture; many may have been acquired via the flows of gift exchange, trade and booty that coursed across the Eurasian steppes, and the fungible quality of griffin imagery suited this setting well. An interesting parallel is a later first-century CE felt carpet from the Mongolian site of Noin Ula, decorated with a similar repertoire of griffins and other creatures found frequently on Pazyryk items.[33] The appliquéd felt saddle cover's imagery is, though, congruent with that used in Pazyryk tattoos, so is usually taken to be a local work.

Mythic Distortions

An interpretative lens through which these images have again and again been viewed is the writing of Herodotus. At Berel, for instance, thousands of kilometres from Greece, the bronze griffins found decorating a fourth- to third-century BCE Pazyryk tomb lid has been likened to Herodotus' gold-guarding griffin.[34] Herodotus suggested the name of the Arimaspi was Scythian in origin, and in the nineteenth century, before the discovery of the Pazyryk remains, it was hypothesized that the legendary Arimaspi had lived in the Altai Mountains.[35] The fact that the idiosyncratic Pazyryk hoofed griffin is referred to as a griffin at all testifies to the ongoing influence of Herodotus: since hooves characterize herbivores, adding them to a combination of apex predators 'dilutes the brand', one might say today, and if it weren't for the eagerness to link Pazyryk material to Herodotus, these hoofed composites might well not be categorized as griffins. Given the indigenous traditions of shamanism – which blurred the boundaries between creatures through ceremonial transformations – and the interpolation of characteristics of local fauna (in particular, the red deer), a direct link between the Pazyryk 'hoofed griffin' and classical Greek griffins seems improbable.[36] Another interesting component of the Pazyryk hybrids being labelled as griffins is that, while wings are taken as a hallmark attribute of griffins from, for example, classical Greece, within the context of the cultures of the Central Asian steppe, other bird attributes are privileged, such as the beak or feathers; wings come into the mix largely due to the influence of Achaemenid Persian imagery.[37] Scholars have even used the narrative of the griffin motif coming from a specific Western source to justify a certain dating of the Altai material: the Pazyryk use of horned griffins, it was argued, meant the dendrochronological evidence should be ignored, with the burials then dated to the fifth to fourth century BCE.[38] (This assumption is all the more questionable given the longevity and dispersal of horned griffin imagery.)

Such interpretations of the Pazyryk griffin motif set the stage for the identity politics that inflect our current understanding of the Altai region's archaeological record. The griffin-tattooed Ice Maiden illustrates how stories shape the world: her name in English, shared with a character created by the Danish author of fairy tales Hans Christian Andersen, seems calculated to evoke a world of fantasy. Meanwhile, her find-spot happened to be in territory contested by Russia and China. Soon after excavation in 1993, her remains were transferred to the Siberian city of Novosibirsk. Protests by the people living in the Altai region – an ethnic republic of Russia – for whom the woman and her hoofed griffin had become symbols of regional identity, demanded her return. The body was repatriated in 2012, an event celebrated with shamanic ceremonies. The Gazprom-funded museum built to showcase the Ice Maiden styles the models in its displays with Asian features resembling those of current inhabitants, contrary to Russian archaeologists, who posit the Ice Maiden was ethnically Caucasian.[39] Just as writing about ancient Pazyryk societies' use of the griffin has often been preoccupied with a putative classical origin of the motif, much debate about human remains such as those of the Ice Maiden focuses on ethnicity, concerns inflected by power dynamics between contemporary Indigenous Altaian peoples and the Russian state.

The griffin motif became part of the contested identity of the Altai, a place long seen as a gateway on many levels, not least between East and West.

46 Coat of arms of the Altai Republic.

It was here that the early twentieth-century mystic Nikolai Rerikh sought Shambala, the entrance to the land of enlightenment in Tibetan Buddhist writings, and it remained a destination for New Age travellers. Following the collapse of the Soviet Union, the Altai gained titular nationality within the Russian Federation, along with its own coat of arms (illus. 46) and other trappings of independence. During this period of the Altai Republic's self-fashioning, the ancient Pazyryks were embraced as ancestors, and thus a griffin came to emblazon the republic's coat of arms.[40] The coat of arms adopts ethnographic motifs in a self-consciously folkloric style; other projects by its designer, Ignatii Ortonulov – including a book documenting traditional Altai folk costumes – demonstrate a wider interest in asserting a local visual cultural identity, something also seen in other former Soviet regions.[41] The griffin on the republic's coat of arms does not especially resemble the hoofed griffin decorating Pazyryk remains; rather, Ortonulov has rendered a largely straightforward lion–eagle hybrid in a folkish style (the wonderful little head emerging from the end of the tail, however, is one distinctively Pazyryk-looking detail, as in illus. 43). We might say that, even here, on the Altai's coat of arms, the classical world's rendering of a griffin – privileging an academic discourse anchored to Herodotus – has edged out local visual culture.

47 Modern recreation of Pazyryk tattoos from body of 'chieftain' on Dave Mazierski, 2012.

Neo-Pazyryk Identities

The griffins tattooed on these ancient nomads continue to be repurposed outside of Altai regional politics. Within contemporary tattoo art communities, numerous trade publications have delved into both Pazyryk tattoo technique and imagery.[42] There have been some particularly fruitful intersections of scholarship and lived practice in this area: in the 1960s a Danish archaeologist had the Pazyryk chieftain's tattoos reproduced on his body; and, more recently, a Canadian medical illustrator has replicated the full set of tattoos over the course of a decade (illus. 47). Given his profession, he was able to carefully locate and size the tattoos on his body to correspond to those on the ancient Pazyryk man. When Russian researchers involved in the infrared imaging project discerned additional tattoos, notably the griffin on the right foot, he had them added too.[43] The photo of his tattooed body, far more eloquently than the line drawings plotting out body art on excavated remains, captures the way the tattooed creatures form a dynamic system of symbols in tandem with the body – we can see, for example, the way the horned griffin on his near bicep looks across to its counterpart on his other arm. Such fluid transmissions from past to present make clear the tenacity of griffins as a visual motif, and the way in which the insistence on foregrounding the textual tradition – most often the work of Herodotus and a small cluster of classical authors – has obscured and flattened its meanings.

Chapter Seven

Guardian Griffins

We have come that we may extend our protection around
the healthy child Minhotep, alive, sound, and healthy,
born of the noblewoman Sitsobek, alive, sound, and healthy.
Spoken by griffin and other protective figures, ancient Egyptian magic wand/birth tusk, Middle Kingdom era

Pugnacious and imposing, griffins have guarded many settings, including the countless doorways they have framed throughout history. This role is revisited in subsequent chapters, shedding light on the wide array of objects that griffins embellish. Chapter Eleven considers their role in more symbolic transitions, such as in funerary arts. Similarly the initial transition in life, childbirth, has at times been safeguarded by griffins, as in a group of 'magic wands' from ancient Egypt. We even have representations of vigilantly maternal griffins doting on their young. Griffins also populate a fascinating array of objects intended to protect in other ways, through cleansing rituals, as with medieval pitchers called aquamanilia.

Ancient Egyptian magic wands offer an especially interesting example of how the image of griffins might offer protection to the object's owner. Some scholars prefer the term 'birth tusks' or 'amuletic knives' over the eyebrow-raising name 'magic wands', though the latter remains more commonly used. During the Middle Kingdom period, hippopotamus tusks were carved with images and texts to fortify the vulnerable, and almost half of the surviving examples of these magic wands include some version of a griffin.[1] Many of their inscriptions avow 'protection from day' and 'protection from night'.[2] Most, if not all, of these wands held the specific purpose of safeguarding mother and child, overt in one wand's message: 'We have come that we may extend our protection around the healthy child Minhotep, alive, sound, and healthy, born of the noblewoman Sitsobek, alive, sound, and healthy.'[3] Current thinking emphasizes their protective role in childbirth, but earlier scholars speculated the wands might have been used to draw warding circles around sleeping or deceased people, for many have one side of the tip worn down.[4] Griffins stood sentinel too on sleeping headrests, especially from the New Kingdom. Sharing much imagery with the Middle Kingdom magic wands, these protective figures in Egyptian sources such as the *Coffin Texts* and the *Book of Two Ways* are gatekeepers, requiring arcane knowledge of spells and secret epithets before allowing passage to the farworld.[5]

48 Magic wand/birth tusk, Egyptian Middle Kingdom, c. *1880–1700* BCE, *incised hippopotamus ivory.*

On a wand carved circa 1880–1700 BCE (illus. 48), the griffin strides across the tusk's surface with the deities Tawaret and Bes, both possessing feline attributes and proffering protection during childbirth. The battalion of predominantly feline and leonine composite creatures, all dedicated to saving mother and child from the perils of childbirth, also appear on Egyptian infant feeding cups from the same era.[6] Many of these supernatural beings hold knives, intensifying the atmosphere of threatening menace. A pharaonic-looking figure emerges from the griffin's back, which is a fairly common feature on these wands.[7] A wand from Thebes depicts a griffin with a similar pharaonic figure above its wings, and its inscription promises, 'I have come to extend [protection] . . . I am he who carries over both wings of the griffin.'[8] The name of the figure emerging from the griffin's back, 'he who carries over' of the inscription, might be interpreted as Inheret/Onuris, the divine force of restorative justice who reinstated the eye of the solar deity in an ancient Egyptian cosmogony tale, *The Myth of the Solar Eye*.[9] Ancient Egyptian scripts had several characters corresponding to 'griffin' in English: the *Solar Eye* text uses the term transliterated as *sfr* or *sfrr*, which may correspond to the winged type of griffin; while another term, transliterated rather intimidatingly as *s3(w)g*, may indicate the unwinged type.[10] The *Solar Eye* griffin, associated with light, is heavily hybridized: the desert creature sports a hawk's beak, human eyes, lion's legs, a snake's tail and a fish's gills. It is a fascinating creature in its own right, albeit one without correlate in visual culture.[11] In this text, a vulture whose job is to see everything transpiring on Earth proclaims,

> Behold, a griffin smelled them [a series of animals including a lion and catfish], and he has already dug his claws into both of them while carrying them under the light of the rays(?) of the sky. Behold, he has already left them down, he has scattered them on the mountain before himself while feeding on them. If (you think that) I am lying, come with me to the mountain and I will show to you how they are scattered and putrefying before him while he feeds on them.[12]

The text's griffin is remorselessly aggressive, instinctively focused on keeping safe intimate, domestic spaces. Beyond what is implied in the *Solar Eye* myth, it has been suggested the wands' ancient users may have recognized in griffins another layer of astral symbolism, for the creatures were also linked with the stellar groupings used in ancient Egyptian astrology, called decans. Specific decans were seen as narrating the cosmic war waged by protective forces such as the griffin and pharaoh against dangerous foes. This grand battle of retributive justice against evil gives a backdrop to the more immediate aim of protecting mother and child at the perilous time of childbirth.[13]

Griffin Parenting

Other ancient griffins impart a parental spin to their broader protective role, for example a seventh-century BCE bronze revetment that covered a metope from a building at Olympia, a site important across the Greek-speaking world (illus. 49). Here, an eagle-headed griffin looms over another so small it can snuggle between its parent's front and back legs, a visual formula of a kind with other animals safeguarding their young in Greek art.[14] Later parallels revisit the theme of their fierce protectiveness of young, but this bronze griffin and her nestling show an early expression of the trope in the visual arts. Usually written about as a mother griffin, this behaviour would accord with typical raptor behaviour in which the female broods offspring, and female lions are most involved in care of cubs.

Yet earlier, Mycenaeans rendered several versions of griffins with their chicks, on seals as well as a small ceramic container, and those examples are also intriguing for a potential connection between griffins and women in early Aegean societies (see illus. 17). The Late Bronze Age alabastron (illus. 50), a container probably used for honey or perfume, excavated at Lefkandi in Greece, features an unusual scene: adorable little griffins in a nest between their large griffin parents, matched by a goat family on the other side. This phase of pottery painting rendered many novel images, which some have seen as a deliberate pushback against preceding norms, but in any event this scene offers one of the few instances of cute griffins before the modern era's 'domesticated' creatures in some children's literature.[15]

49 Metope cover depicting adult griffin protecting baby, archaic Greek, c. *700–600* BCE, *bronze.*

50 Alabastron (container for perfume or honey) depicting griffin family, Xeropolis-Lefkandi, Mycenaean (Late Helladic IIC *period),* c. *1200–1050* BCE, *terracotta.*

51 Pair of griffins for guarding a doorway, originally from northern Italy, c. 1100–1200, pink limestone.

Guarding Entrances

Their custodial role consequently takes many forms, whether as a zealous ward for its young, protecting gold against the Arimaspi, or in a more general way through their frequent safeguarding of doorways. Griffins secure entrances, places potentially of symbolic as well as physical transitions, whether in an ancient Greek drinking space, a medieval French church or a Las Vegas casino (see illus. 26, 70, 102). A formidable pair of twelfth-century CE limestone griffins once kept watch over the entrance to a chapel on the Piazza di Porta Ravennate (now Porta Ravegnana) in Bologna (illus. 51).[16] Whereas in the Olympia metope the griffin loomed protectively over the baby griffin, these figures under the griffins are captured prey: a calf and a knife-bearing man. The hapless victims correspond to the beings savaged by griffins in medieval bestiary illuminations discussed later, part of the pattern of griffins handily vanquishing any adversary a narrative might offer.

Griffins guard the entrances, but also can imply protection within buildings. At the Spanish monastery of Santo Domingo de Silos, griffins are introduced into the iconography of the medieval cloister next to scenes of Christ's Annunciation and Ascension and thus frame the symbolic boundaries of his arrival on Earth and his leaving of it (illus. 52).[17] Twelfth-century carvings of griffins appear on the southwest and southeast piers of the cloister, part of a rich vocabulary of monstrous creatures including dragons, centaurs and sirens that embellished this monastery. Silos was by no means alone; other Romanesque church sculptural programmes such as that of Saint-Michel-de-Cuxa include griffins – imagery likely repurposed from imported textiles.[18]

Almost a thousand years later, the 9/11 attacks on New York City's World Trade Center yielded a twenty-first-century example of griffins being seen as having protective agency. Cass Gilbert's early skyscraper at 90 West Street incorporated a lavish programme of neo-Gothic gargoyles on its terracotta exterior, including numerous griffins. Immediately to the south of the World Trade Center, debris from the twin towers rained down on the exterior for days as fires raged throughout the interior of Gilbert's 1907 building. While damaged, surprisingly the structure largely survived, with some attributing its status as the 'miracle building' to the mystical protective qualities of its guardian griffins (more prosaic souls saw it as a triumph of the fire-resistant properties of its terracotta cladding), and one of the original exterior griffins now looms large in the restored lobby of the building.[19]

Aquamanilia

The composite's protective function can follow other routes, as in the use of aquamanilia, vessels used for hand washing as part of both religious and secular medieval rituals. An aquamanile could assure cleanliness, sometimes itself a virtue, and often linked to values such as propriety and godliness. Though initially used liturgically, by the twelfth century in affluent homes people would pour scented water from these vessels to wash their hands (illus. 53). Quite a few griffin-shaped examples survive. The usual forms for medieval aquamanilia were part of the visual vocabulary of court culture, with lions the most popular choice.[20] This fifteenth-century copper alloy example represents a type produced from the prior century, and it is exceptionally well preserved, with even the original spout protruding from the chest.[21] Details of the 'flame tail' (*Flammenschweif*) suggest a Nuremberg workshop, since others from the period integrate the same flourish.[22] This griffin's aquiline front

52 Capital no. 47, southwest pier, lower cloister, c. 1100–1200, Santo Domingo de Silos Abbey, Spain.

53 Aquamanile in the form of a griffin, Nuremberg, c. 1425–50, *bronze.*

talons are carefully differentiated from the leonine rear paws. The endearingly doleful expression created by the pronounced upper beak might seem unique to this object, but two more griffin vessels – one housed in Paris, the other in Kraków – share almost exactly the same look.[23] These vessels for hand washing otherwise vary widely. In the Louvre's aquamanilia collection alone, there are several different types of griffin, such as an oddly barrel-chested one from lower Saxony produced circa 1200.[24] This range of ways that griffins are part of a visual language of safeguarding, even in courtly spaces, carries over to some of their associations in our next case study: their role in eastern palatial settings.

Chapter Eight

In the Halls of Power:

Griffins in Byzantine and Sasanian Palaces

O friends, it is an awesome sight. A griffin's breath projects a blazing jet, terrifying the mortal nature of those present.

Byzantine poem, describing the imagery in a building for Emperor Leo VI (r. 886–912)

Griffin imagery is prevalent in an array of official artwork, part of the public communication of numerous historical leaders, including the inaugural Roman emperor, Augustus. While he (or his functionaries) might include a griffin on his cuirassed statue from Prima Porta in Rome, and on an oversized Mars the Avenger (see illus. 33), the reverse of some of the first Roman emperor's coin issues keeps alive the tradition of griffins on Roman Republican and earlier Greek coins going back to the sixth century BCE. Likewise Emperor Trajan incorporated griffins in some of his most important public building (see illus. 34). Early Byzantine and Sasanian Persian rulers continued using the motif. The very name the East Roman Empire, more commonly known today as the Byzantine Empire, suggests its complicated relationship with antiquity, and analysing griffins' place in this visual culture casts light on a larger set of questions. Some associations of the griffin start to be shed in favour of new ones, but many of the earlier meanings of the griffin motif – allying it with Nemesis, Dionysos, power and domination, luxury and protection – persist. Sources, notably the Greek *Physiologos* and a poem exalting a Byzantine palace, align griffins with fiery radiance, a familiar theme from ancient representations and one that suffuses Sasanian depictions, too.

Griffins in the Great Palace Mosaics and the Hippodrome

The sprawling complex now called the Great Palace of the Byzantine Emperors served as the administrative heart of the empire, especially early on. Many emperors sought to leave their mark by updating its buildings during their reigns, and its archaeological record is complex, so dating many parts remains controversial. The lavish floor mosaics of a palace courtyard near the hippodrome have been assigned to the fifth to seventh centuries, but their most likely patron is the early seventh-century emperor Heraclius.[1] Most the courtyard's four griffins follow patterns

54 Griffin devouring a deer, Byzantine, c. *600, floor mosaic, Istanbul.*

55 Griffin devouring a lizard, Byzantine, c. *600, floor mosaic, Istanbul.*

explored already, including one with a nastily sharp beak, attacking a deer (illus. 54).[2] By this point, we've witnessed millennia of griffins doing what griffins do best – perpetrate violence – and this attack on a herbivore offers a succinct visual shorthand of that combative lineage. Gory details such as the rivulets of blood and the way the griffin's claws sink into the flesh of its prey impart an extra measure of savagery. Elsewhere in the mosaic programme, another winged griffin, this one with horns and a leonine face, tears into a hapless lizard (illus. 55). Here, too, runnels of blood accentuate the demise of its prey, and the sleek silhouette of this griffin erupts with spiky protuberances: horns, teats and some over-large claws that convey its aggressive energy. The overall theme of this resplendent mosaic floor defies easy categorization, encompassing many ferocious battles among various human and non-human animal combatant combinations, sometimes adjacent to children at play, Dionysiac imagery, and possible folktale scenes. This multiplicity in itself could intimate the sprawling extent of the early Byzantine realm, showcasing its abundance.

Pagan Images of Luxury and Status

To see how these different strands of meaning might intersect, let's step back and look at broader cultural trends happening around the time the mosaics were laid. Heraclius' reign was defined in many ways by conflict with Sasanian Persians. He led Byzantine armies before becoming emperor in 610, and his years of combat culminated in his decisive victory and the Byzantine destruction of Khosrow II's palace at Dastagird in 628. In the Great Palace mosaics, the inclusion of the horned leonine griffin with the lizard may suggest that even in the midst of their ongoing war, the long-standing enemy of the Byzantines was simultaneously a site of desire. This griffin may have struck Byzantine viewers as to some degree 'Persian-looking': the Sasanians continued the earlier Persian tradition of griffins sporting prominent curving horns (see illus. 11, 28), though the curved horned griffin type is actually quite widespread. Griffins may have functioned almost like the equivalent of a designer label in modern consumer culture, indicating aspiration and luxury. The creature's lustre persisted from Greek and Roman antiquity, an easy way for a writer like the third-century Athenaeus to illustrate the ostentation of a banquet guest, who is derided with, 'This guy? From nowhere, I'm sure of that – except one nice embroidered rug with Persians and some damned Persian griffins on it.'[3] Griffins, with their long-standing association with gold and luxury, could mark wealth, culture and excess – or arriviste attempts to brand oneself with such status – and the horned type seems to have done so most emphatically.

The alluring lizard-eating griffin may also have hinted at Dionysos.[4] Visual culture, but not texts, includes lizards among the animals of the Sabazios cult.[5] The tenth-century Byzantine encyclopaedia, the *Suda*, flatly asserts, 'Sabazios . . . is the same as Dionysos,' and the two deities are conflated elsewhere, so the lizard being consumed might have a whisper of Dionysian ties, too. Elsewhere, the palace courtyard mosaics incorporate unambiguous components of a Dionysiac procession, including Pan carrying a Bacchic child, along with other commonly represented procession figures such as an elephant and a woman with a vessel of wine.[6] The ongoing enthusiasm for pagan allusions in a Christian milieu is exemplified by the fifth-century poet Nonnos, who intermixes biblical commentary into a poem unwinding over 20,426 lines of Homeric diction glorifying Dionysos. His *Dionysiaca* highlights griffins' connection with retributive justice: 'Round her [Nemesis'] throne flew a bird of vengeance, a griffin flying with wings.'[7]

Untangling the meaning of these pagan concepts to Christian Byzantine audiences has made for a lively debate among scholars. One perspective, in a quick snapshot, uses the fact that prominent individuals in the sixth-century court of Emperor Justinian were singled out as pagans for persecution to argue there was a coterie of crypto-pagans at the top of early Byzantine society.[8] Countering that view, Justinian's motives for targeting wealthy opponents as pagans could have had more to do with political expediency.[9] While indeed there were anti-pagan crusaders such as John of Ephesus, most evidence points to early Byzantine elites appreciating classical culture more as a marker of high status than an indicator of religious belief.[10] Thus the mosaic's Dionysian elements express a wider appetite for classical culture and might have furthermore projected a sense of worldly abundance.[11] If the griffins of the Great Palace mosaics seemed redolent of the classical past, that would have only enhanced their appeal, rather than stir controversy. With little basis, it's even been proposed that both griffin and lizard are Christian symbols, it's more compelling to, instead, situate the mosaics' griffins as the rethinking of classical antecedents in a medieval milieu.[12]

The spectrum of meanings seen in earlier griffin images largely continues through the early Byzantine period, including their place in the environments for the emperor and public spectacles and competitions. A pair of early Byzantine column capitals discovered near the hippodrome conjoin griffin heads and the figure of Nike, goddess of victory, holding up a monogram.[13] The connection of the griffin motif with Nike near the hippodrome suggests the creature's place within the games continues; griffins also appear on Byzantine bronze rein guides used for horse racing in the hippodrome.[14] Moreover, a Merovingian source claims the emperor Heraclius, perhaps the mosaics' patron, himself fought lions and boars in the arena – a suggestion that's all the more interesting given that competitions in which a combatant squared off against an animal opponent had, for centuries, been prohibited.[15] Later in this chapter we will see how Heraclius, in addition to his curious fondness for participating in the gory spectacles, was preoccupied with other matters that may be reflected in the Great Palace mosaic imagery.

Fragmentary Stories

No single overarching interpretation offers a fully satisfying framework for parsing the meaning of the griffins within the Great Palace mosaics. Some past explanations – including those drawing on the ideology of Heraclius, a classical hunting treatise

56 Striding griffin with aquiline beak, Byzantine, c. 600, floor mosaic, Istanbul.

or an allusion to the emperor's African origins – account for some features but omit the presence of griffins.[16] The floor's scenes, which might now seem maddeningly disconnected from each other when we impose the expectation that everything has to come together into a tidy package, express the preferred aesthetic of their time. Choricius of Gaza reports early sixth-century pantomime dancers performing fragmented vignettes, shifting identities and even genders over the course of one performance.[17] Similarly these mosaics showcase independent scenes rather than a continuous narrative.

Given the way early Byzantine spectators savoured elements of discontinuity and variety, the exuberant heterogeneity of the four griffins in the Great Palace mosaics might be, in fact, expected; indeed they could seem linked merely because all four have received the label 'griffin' in art-historical discussion. Regarding the other two griffins in the mosaics, one is powerfully leonine – and in that way is alike to the beast eating the lizard – but with an aquiline beak and wings (illus. 56), a type most often seen on Late Roman precious portable goods.[18] We will never know what its head turns to consider, for that portion of the mosaic has been destroyed. On the other side of this solitary creature is the most discussed image of the Great Palace mosaics, an eagle fighting a snake writhing in its talons, and this leonine griffin may have resonated with the eagle and snake's long-standing status as a symbol of sovereignty.[19]

The fourth creature usually labelled a griffin from the courtyard mosaics is missing much of its body, and is distinctive for its horn (illus. 57). Positioned just

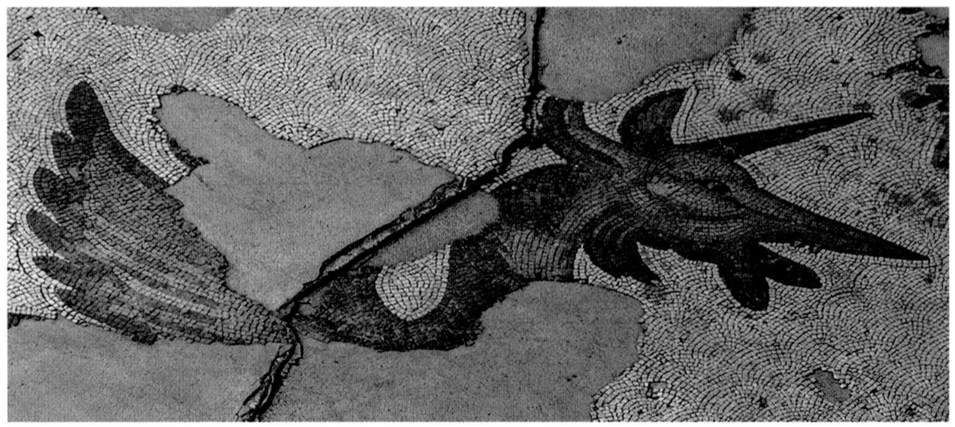

57 Single-horned griffin, Byzantine, c. 600, floor mosaic, Istanbul.

above and to the left of the griffin eating a lizard, this fragment has been variously described as an 'okapi-headed' griffin or a 'winged unicorn'.[20] The okapi identification derives from its long face, gaping mouth, long horn and hairy ears, though some details – namely the sharp teeth and wings – are not features of the ruminant okapi.[21] Okapi, part of the giraffe family, don't otherwise make an appearance in Byzantine art or writing, though there are possibly okapi in ancient art, such as at the Persian site of Persepolis. The mosaic's peaceful-looking creature doesn't particularly resemble classical art's griffins, but its alterity may have given it a certain titillating glamour. This seems the case in other early Byzantine mosaics lingering on the 'exotic' and the rare, as in the roughly contemporary mosaic at Haleplibahçe of a zebra led by a person appearing to be from sub-Saharan Africa.[22] That said, we will see in Chapter Ten how Byzantine writers used the Greek word for griffin for combinations in art that no longer survive – or may have never been depicted – including a donkey griffin. It is possible, therefore, that the strange okapi-headed creature would have, to a seventh-century viewer passing through the corridors of the imperial palace and summarily glimpsing it, been thought of as a griffin – if, indeed, it were even given that much focused consideration.

An Imperial Bath and Its Fire-Breathing Griffin

Prior chapters noted many examples rendering these winged hybrids as heavenly creatures. While some medieval texts give an overtly Christian gloss to the celestial realm, the linked classical intellectual traditions of astrology and astronomy also continued into the Byzantine period. Extolling the decoration of the bath of Byzantine emperor Leo VI (r. 886–912), an intriguing medieval poem praises Leo's astrological knowledge, then immediately follows with a description of a fire-breathing griffin in the bath's decor: 'O friends, it is an awesome sight. A griffin's breath projects a blazing jet, terrifying the mortal nature of those present.'[23] It is hard to say when the decorative features the poem describes date from; sometimes literary confections such as this were produced to commemorate renovations, not *de novo* constructions, but the poem is a sign of a Byzantine audience associating these winged hybrids with the sky.[24] Having griffins epitomize an emperor's knowledge of the 'axis of heaven' would have made sense to Byzantine readers because of the creature's ongoing connection with the heavens generally and the Sun specifically – explored further in the next chapter. In the context of the astral connections of Leo's bath, the medieval Greek *Physiologos* tradition offers a graceful, even reverent example: two griffins, who dwell in remote eastern realms, greet the morning Sun, and one stays with the Sun until dusk. The griffins' vast wings shield Earth from being scorched by the Sun's incandescent glow, which the author likens to the way the Virgin Mary and Archangel Michael intervene to protect humanity from God's wrath.[25] Leo's bathhouse fire-breathing griffin drives the celestial connection home, though in the imperial setting it seems more fearsome than the gently protective image in the *Physiologos*. Breath of fire is not a consistent griffin superpower, but it appears as far back as some of the composite's depictions from even the third millennium BCE (see illus. 3, 4), an attribute shared with dragons. Fire and water could seem like a counter-intuitive mix, but imagery of the radiant fire-breathing griffin suited the imperial bath setting, where the water features would have been expected to offer up a glittering luminosity, for just such an aesthetic vocabulary is deployed to describe the buildings and the person of the emperor alike.[26] This tissue of interconnected meanings might seem precisely tuned to Byzantine sensibilities, but many elements were shared with the neighbouring Islamic patrons.[27] Astrological subjects adorned other early medieval bathing spaces, and we can imagine the griffin in Leo's imperial bath as part of that repertoire. The fire-breathing griffin, and the way it signalled the emperor's knowledge of the firmament, was part of a larger tradition of writing about Leo as a master of arcane knowledge, deserving of his sobriquet 'the Wise' – a word, it is worth remembering, etymologically connected to 'wizard'.[28]

While study of astronomy had revived somewhat in the Middle Byzantine period under rulers like Leo – which contributed to his moniker 'the Wise' – the same interest in the early Byzantine period only magnified Heraclius' (the likely patron of the Great Palace mosaics) reputation for eccentricity.[29] Although ancient Roman emperors rationalized even momentous decisions with astrological portents, no evidence links other early Byzantine emperors with pursuing these interests to such an extent. Heraclius' absorption in astrology is attested in sources written both west and east of his empire, for both the seventh-century Merovingian Fredegar (Chronicle, IV.65) and the eighth-century Kitāb al-Maghāzī report that he cast a horoscope in 621 that predicted his empire's defeat by a circumcised people. In that year Muhammad's nascent religion was still largely unknown outside of the Arabian peninsula, so the story goes that Heraclius apparently incorrectly assumed the circumcised enemy of the Byzantines would be Jewish forces.[30] Additionally, four medieval manuscripts credit Heraclius with writing all or part of the first astronomical treatise based on the city of Constantinople's celestial coordinates.[31] Inconsistencies among the manuscripts mean that just how extensive his role was ultimately remains unclear, but Heraclius likely had some involvement with the section calculating Easter's date.[32] Unusual in many respects, Heraclius attracted notice as an early Byzantine emperor-cum-astronomy-writer, so it is possible that the relative abundance of griffin imagery in the Great Palace courtyard mosaics hinted at his interest in the heavens, especially given that a fire-breathing griffin mosaic had that association in the emperor Leo the Wise's bath.

Sasanian Griffins

While some connotations are shared, a closer look at how the griffin was used within Sasanian Persian visual expressions of power on its own terms is in order. In an investiture scene on a late fourth-century Kushano-Sasanian gilded silver plate, two griffins flank the throne (illus. 58).[33] Beaked with pointed ears and positioned about knee-high to the human figures in the scene, the griffins face outwards with

58 Investiture scene, Kushano-Sasanian, c. 300–400, gilt silver plate.

their front paws raised. In fact, if it were not for their context in a scene fraught with ceremonial significance, the image might today read as the griffins being adorable pets. The plate's heavily worn details testify to its use over a considerable time. Note, too, that these creatures don't have the curved horns of what is stereotyped as the 'Persian griffin', going to show that eagle–lion hybrids had fluid morphology within the Persian art tradition as well. The plate's imagery raises interesting questions related to iconography and point of origin: the clothing and weaponry resemble Sasanian royal iconography and its find-spot is reputed to be Rawalpindi, Pakistan, the modern eastern edge of the ancient Sasanian world. It compares with another piece from a related cultural milieu, a fifth- or sixth-century Sogdian wall painting from Temple II at Penjikent, Tajikistan, which shows an enthroned goddess similarly flanked by composite creatures. The latter are only partially preserved, but they have sometimes been identified as griffins, with both leonine and aquiline elements visible.[34] While the conceptual space around terminology for animal hybrids habitually blurs boundaries, in this specific cultural context the ambiguity between griffins and the mythical bird known as a senmurv keeps arising. In the visual culture shared by the Penjikent painting and Sasanian art, as in the Sasanian rock reliefs at Taq-i Bustan in Iran, griffins and senmurvs

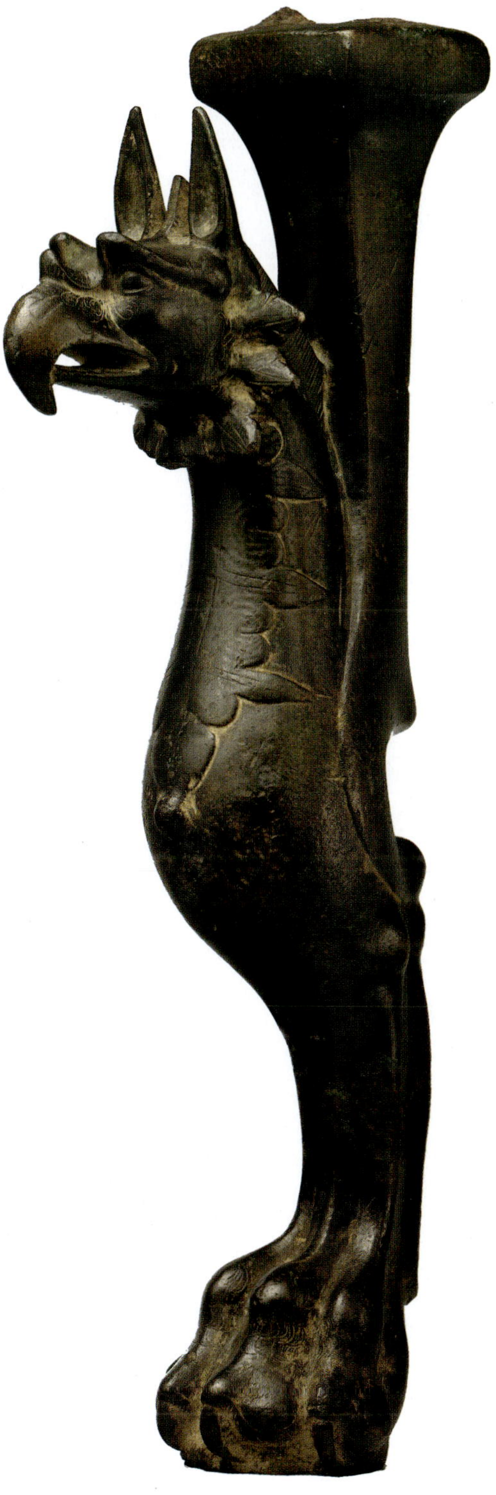

59 Furniture leg, Sasanian, c. *700, bronze with ceramic core.*

both possessed a specific and highly potent form of charisma tied to royal glory, denoted by the Pahlevi word *Xwarrah*.[35]

Furniture was another way griffins had a place in Sasanian material culture, through the composite creature's place in the tradition of furniture legs inspired by animal leg shapes (lions are especially common). This leg comes from western Iran in the late seventh or early eighth century, shortly after the fall of the Sasanians, and other Sasanian griffin furniture legs survive (illus. 59).[36] The leg is emphatically leonine, down to the curve of each razor-like claw. A griffin head erupts above, with the hooked beak of an eagle and its cuspate ears creating a sense of keen and perpetual vigilance. Its bronze exterior, with stretches of finely incised decoration, is cast around a ceramic core. Much of the writing about griffin-shaped legs like this one suggests they were the base of Sasanian thrones, although given that griffin imagery appears on many luxury goods, a bona fide regal connection is not certain.[37]

Returning to the Kushano-Sasanian silver plate, we might wonder if the griffins we see render the legs of a throne. Another possibility, given that the silver plate shows the full bodies of the griffins rather than the elision of leg and head used for the furniture legs, is that early viewers inferred the creatures were motifs on a hanging or wall painting framing the ruler (for a much earlier example of this arrangement, see illus. 19). Whatever the specific associations conjured within its original context, what is clear is that Sasanian Persians incorporated griffins into their regnal spaces, following the Achaemenid tradition. Furthermore, within the Sasanian cultural sphere, the conjunction of eagle and lion may have evoked the divine light of Ahuramazda, and equated the griffin to solar symbolism more generally.[38] In the next chapter, we'll unlock other ways this creature signified radiance.

Chapter Nine

Griffins Aloft:

Griffins as Luminous, Flying and Heavenly Creatures

Quickly, the griffins bore him up into the air so high that Alexander thought all the earth no more than a floor where men thresh corn and the sea like a dragon upon the earth.

***Alexander Romance*, translation of the Middle English Thornton's prose version**

Previous chapters detail how griffins are portrayed in depictions of the heavens and the deities residing there. However, this rich vein of subject-matter has still other, very widespread expressions, which we explore here. It's easy to find examples of lamps from antiquity through the modern era adorned with these perennially light-bearing creatures. Correspondingly griffins are celestial transportation in stories of Alexander the Great's chariot yoked with griffins, and appear in this mode across medieval societies from France to Central Asia. This creature can also coexist in a heavenly sphere with a stern array of holy figures on an Armenian church facade.

Griffin Lamps

With griffins' persistent association with the heavens and golden radiance, numerous variations of their image populate Roman lamps – one type with a sprightly little griffin on top was made throughout the first and second centuries, with examples found in diverse locations, from a Colchester lamp factory to Sardis, Turkey.[1] Some designs see griffins paired with figures including dolphins, Apollo or Mars.[2] Griffin lamps being so commonplace is in keeping with the motif's use on all manner of small Roman bronze objects, from razors to chariot ornaments.[3]

This abundance continues beyond the classical era, with a recent study documenting 22 early Byzantine griffin lamps found at different sites.[4] Yet even that careful catalogue overlooked examples, such as this previously unpublished fourth- to sixth-century Byzantine hanging lamp, now in the Chrysler Museum of Art in Virginia (illus. 60).[5] Its form echoes earlier griffins as well as introducing details that become more common later. The neck ridges, for instance, resemble those on some ancient Greek and Roman griffins (see illus. 25, 34), but its closest published corollary is the sixth- to seventh-century griffin lamp now in the British Museum, though the London lamp is slightly larger.[6] A Christogram surmounts the head, seamlessly

60 Lamp with griffin-head handle, Byzantine, c. *4th–6th century, bronze.*

blending Christian meanings with the pagan past. Poised in the elegant curve of its beak is a small globe, a feature found more commonly in later griffin representations (see illus. 67), and in Asian dragon imagery, as explored in Chapter Eleven. Their variety suggests that Byzantine griffin lamps were produced in a range of workshops, with some adding details like a little bird, dolphin or inscription.[7]

The classical linkage of Apollo with griffins lingered in some circles, as we saw with the Late Roman author Claudian, but for most viewers, any connection to Apollo was by now likely attenuated to the point where there was just a loose sense of griffins being appropriate for illuminable objects. Meanwhile, the use of more overt Christian iconography, first seen on lamps towards the end of the fourth century, became widespread in the mid-fifth century. Returning to the question of how pagan and Christian elements were interwoven in these times, it's worth noting that archaeological finds such as the deposit of Late Antique lamps excavated in Corinth, including objects with overtly Christian imagery, were found in a subterranean context that suggested they were left as pagan offerings.[8] As in the case of the Great Palace mosaics (see illus. 55), griffins – ever motile – readily bridge distinctions between Christian and pagan, between worldly and religious.

The Flight of Alexander

A ubiquitous image in medieval art is the *Flight of Alexander*, in which the winged creatures pull the Macedonian ruler's chariot through the sky. The incident appears in a group of related medieval texts of which the *Alexander Romance* is best known, but the flight's image gains a life of its own, turning up in many places beyond the confines of a manuscript page. Medieval reworkings of Alexander the Great's deeds have their own complicated textual history going back to the Greek third-century CE Pseudo-Callisthenes, with the Greek *Alexander Romance* translated into a long list of languages including Mongolian and Ge'ez, and, in the tenth century, Latin. The surprising twists taken by its lineage include the likelihood that the Greek *Alexander Romance*'s mention of the general's flight came from a fourth-century CE Talmudic text.[9] The focus of earlier historians, such as Arrian, on Alexander's battles shifts to a recounting of improbable, exciting escapades in sync with the cadence of medieval romance writing. Therein the Macedonian king, aware of the griffin's terrifying skill set thanks to a prior skirmish, uses meat as bait to ensnare and chain griffins to his chariot (the number of griffins varies). Dangling more meat above the griffins, the beasts' rapacious appetite for flesh propels Alexander's chariot into flight. The exhilarating moment as Alexander soars into the air pulled by griffins became the visual token of the entire *Alexander Romance* corpus: 'Quickly, the griffins bore him up into the air so high that Alexander thought all the earth no more than a floor where men thresh corn and the sea like a dragon upon the earth.'[10]

Since antiquity, griffins have been shown powering aerial transportation (see illus. 25), with many depictions of griffin-drawn chariots, not least those featuring Apollo or Dionysos.[11] The latter tie is particularly salient – Alexander was compared with Dionysos, styled a fellow conqueror of India, by ancient writers such as Diodorus Siculus. The many precursors to the images of Alexander the Great borne aloft by a griffin-powered chariot eased the way to its medieval preeminence, with Alexander's flight seen in art from medieval France to Türkmen courts.[12] A twelfth-century Byzantine ivory box, now in Darmstadt (illus. 61), exemplifies the way in which Alexander's status as a ruler is often emphasized in *Flight* scenes: he is depicted wearing a diagonally draped *loros*, a ceremonial garment distinctive to the Byzantine emperor.[13] On either side of Alexander a griffin leashed to the chariot rears up, with a little winged figure above each, echoing classical personifications of victory.

The prevalence of the *Flight of Alexander* with griffins is all the more interesting given the wider variety seen in textual accounts; large white birds, not griffins, propel him in the Greek *Alexander Romance*, and eagles in the version known to Chaucer.[14] Other birds – mythical or not – such as the roc or phoenix carry rulers through the air in related works including the Persian epic *Shahnameh* (*c.* 977–1010). Kaikaus' throne is lifted into the sky by eagles whom he has tricked using mutton as bait – a clear analogue of Alexander's ploy with the griffins. Further evidence of these creatures being semantically clustered is seen in one term in medieval Arabic that can be translated as griffin, phoenix or sphinx.[15]

61 Flight of Alexander the Great, Byzantine, c. 1100–1200, side panel of ivory casket.

62 Flight of Alexander, miniature from Le livre et le vraye hystoire du bon roy Alixandre *(The Book and True History of the Good King Alexander)*, c. 1420.

A lavish French manuscript further illustrates this keenness for Alexander imagery by those who ruled (illus. 62). Six griffins pull a cage, with Alexander, his royalty confirmed by his crown, hunched over slightly inside the uncomfortable-looking contraption. This manuscript's 86 illuminations of Alexander's adventures, executed in vivid colours and exacting detail, were painted in Paris circa 1420–25. Its scale and the extraordinary skill displayed in the work suggests a royal patron may have commissioned the manuscript, and it attracted the acquisitive eye of another monarch, King Henry VIII, reflecting the enthusiasm of late medieval and early modern rulers for the *Alexander Romance* cycle. Further, the *Flight*'s broad-based popularity in visual culture did not slacken until the sixteenth century.[16]

Models of Rule

Medieval scenes of Alexander's flight were earlier viewed as embodying the sin of pride or *superbia* (*Ubermûtecheit* in medieval German sources, where this reading seems particularly common). Then scholars differentiated the various medieval vernacular traditions broadly in terms of their positive or negative stance towards the Macedonian general.[17] In this vein, Alexander is scrutinized for a perceived lack of moderation – one characteristic of his that everyone can perhaps agree upon, even if not all condemn him for it. For the detractors, his heavenly ascent with griffins evidences a prideful hunger for knowledge, his *hybris* manifest in incriminating details, such as his griffin-powered aerial exploration motivated by his *curiositas*.[18] Perhaps some original viewers of this Flight of Alexander from the Basel Münster saw it through this censuring lens (illus. 63), a likelihood supported by the column's adjacent scene of Adam and Eve, but the vast popularity of the *Alexander Romance* corpus across the medieval and early modern world doesn't seem to depend on reading his far-off adventures as moral tutelage.[19]

In outlier instances, for example the Strasbourg textual redaction, where Alexander is maladroitly reformulated into a Christian monarch, this transformation tellingly involved editing out griffins and other marvels of the East from his adventures.[20] Given the *Flight*'s appearance in so many medieval times and places, a uniform meaning can't be imposed on the motif. We have western medieval versions that seem to liken the moment to Christ's Ascension, and in the medieval east, in Byzantine and Ottoman sources, Alexander reliably provides a positive example for rulers, a trend that begins in the tenth century, only to later intensify.[21] In the Byzantine historian Sphrantzes's first-hand account of the Ottoman siege of Constantinople in 1453, Alexander comes up as the ultimate role model for Mehmet the Conqueror.[22]

An enamel dish now in Innsbruck but originally from the medieval eastern world extends the *Flight of Alexander*'s scope (illus. 64). The central medallion of this *champlevé* and *cloisonné* enamel dish shows the crowned ruler seated in a griffin-drawn chariot or throne within a dense visual field, richly coloured and intricately patterned. The concentric composition echoes how the Ptolemaic

63 Flight of Alexander, column capital from church interior, late 12th century, Basel Münster.

64 Artuqid plate, c. 1100–1150, gilt copper with enamel.

planetary system was represented, which may resonate with griffins' long-standing solar connections and, in turn, parallels long-established ruler symbolism.[23] Roughly executed inscriptions in Arabic and Persian connect it to the mid-twelfth-century Artuqid dynasty of eastern Anatolia and northern Mesopotamia.[24] The inscriptions are to some degree unique – making them both fascinating and harder to interpret – for this plate is the only medieval enamel object bearing the name of a Muslim ruler. Most plausibly it was either made at the behest of the Artuqid leader Ruk al-Dawla Da'ud bin Sukman or received by him as an exquisite gift from the Byzantine ruler. It could also, however, come from medieval Georgia, and still further possibilities have been suggested.[25] The uncertainty around who made this enamel work derives in part from how very often Alexander's flight with griffins was represented in medieval art.

Heavenly Creatures

These scenes were part of a wider sensibility within ancient and medieval visual cultures in which griffins readily pair with heavenly figures. Thus, while multiple manuscripts attest to an Armenian tradition of the *Alexander Romance*, which often manage to make even Alexander's horse look griffin-like with avian heads and claws in their illuminations, the same hybrid beast accompanies much more staid Armenian iconography, appearing alongside martyrs at Aghtamar's Church of the Holy Cross in what is now eastern Turkey.[26] Here the griffin, accented with rosettes and other shapes that also embellish their medieval textile depictions, is juxtaposed with a martyr in the portrait medallion above, one of the holy men rendered on the church exterior who also happened to be an ancestor of the building's patron, the ruler Gagik Arcruni (illus. 65).[27] Just as this griffin is positioned next to the entrance to the king's gallery at the church in Aghtamar, the necklace-like band on its wings and other jewel-like adornment also connect it to Sasanian Persian visual traditions, signalling their divine essence or even belonging in the royal paradise.[28] The spread of certain kinds of stylized visual language in the eastern medieval Mediterranean likely drew some inspiration from the revival of Sasanian Persian artistic tradition under the Abbasids, a process that also informed the depiction of the proud griffin striding across the south facade of the tenth-century Armenian Church of the Holy Cross, as well as the inclusion of other fabulous beasts such as the senmurv. This backdrop informs our next topic, some patterns of diffusion for another type of griffin across the medieval Mediterranean and the surprising puzzles they present.

65 South facade of the Church of the Holy Cross, Aghtamar Island, Armenian, c. 915–21.

Chapter Ten

Encircling Griffins:

Mapping the Influence of a Motif

A marvellous surcoat sprinkled with gold, purple silk with a white triple border and ornamental griffins.

***Digenis Akritas*, *c.* twelfth-century CE Byzantine epic poem**

Across wide swathes of medieval art, one encounters the visual formula of a griffin encircled by a medallion. Echoic circular frames had long offered an organizing visual schema; ancient floor mosaics are just one antecedent.[1] The griffin medallion functions in a similar fashion in other neighbouring societies, finding its way into sometimes markedly different settings and formats. Looking eastwards, a similar visual language appears in contemporary Chinese textiles from the Liao dynasty (916–1125) in the use of dragons on even imperial textiles. By the eleventh and twelfth centuries, griffin textiles were circulating widely around the Mediterranean, and the earlier heterogeneity seen in settings such as the Great Palace mosaics had been honed to a few beloved types. The stylized form of an encircled griffin in profile marks countless medieval luxury goods and noteworthy buildings.

Ivory Oliphants

Portable goods like textiles and carved ivories served as a medium for transmitting specific kinds of griffin imagery, communicating in a visual lingua franca of sorts. Artisans using these medallions as a compositional framework often combined griffins with other courtly animals, as when they carved oliphants – the ivory horns used across much of the medieval Mediterranean for hunting and military signals (and maybe a bit of drinking). The Borradaile oliphant shows the standard way medallions encircle griffins and other beasts in profile, with an ensemble of imagery so common it has been ascribed to an Islamic, Byzantine, southern Italian and, in a by-now-familiar curatorial move, a generically eastern Mediterranean origin (illus. 66).[2]

A 'Donkey Griffin' at an Umayyad Reception

That said, textiles likely were an even more frequent conduit, as seen in the reception of the Umayyad caliph from Cordova in 946–7, within the Byzantine imperial palace's *Chrysotriklinos*, 'the golden reception hall'. It sets the scene with a silk

66 Borradaile oliphant, c. 1000, ivory and silver.

dignified with a lion griffin and possibly another small griffin.[3] Courtiers stand next to 'reddish-purple curtains of . . . griffins and asses'.[4] The translation 'griffins and asses' conveys the single Greek word γρυπόναγροι (*grypónagroi*, donkey griffin), raising the possibility that the palace curtains bore a sort of a winged donkey rather than two distinct creatures. Wings were appended to many different creatures in ancient and Byzantine images, conveying in a quick visual shorthand a momentary transcendence of the banalities of earthbound existence – a later text as it happens describes winged dogs as part of imperial palace decor in Constantinople.[5] While some Byzantine apocalyptic writing mentions a donkey, no winged donkeys survive in Byzantine art, hence the *Book of Ceremonies*' typical translation of the term as two distinct creatures rather than a single intriguing composite. In any case, the *Book*'s account of the encounter between the Byzantines and the Umayyads – whose foreign identity is insistently affirmed with the repetition of the term 'Saracen' – reinforces griffin-adorned textiles' weight to both sets of medieval viewers. Griffin imagery works especially well in these moments of contact across cultural spheres. Other textiles are described with words used for courtly garments, such as *chlamys*, suggesting an overlap in use – a gorgeous piece of silk could serve as both garment and wall hanging – as well as imagery.[6]

This early fourteenth-century *History of Niketas Choniates* manuscript illumination (illus. 67) likely renders the emperor Alexios v Doukas, whose brief, tragic rule ended with the conquest of Constantinople by the Fourth Crusade in 1204.

67 Emperor in robes woven with griffin medallion pattern, from De rebus post captam urbem gestis *(History of Niketas Choniates), Byzantine,* c. *1240–60.*

White griffins stand out against the deep purple background of the emperor's long robes; two large medallions cover his torso and legs, and two more are glimpsed on the sleeves. A band of smaller indistinct animals, also in white, encircles each griffin. Since the Byzantine court could be, indeed, byzantine in its finely calibrated hierarchies, that the man at the apex was emblazoned with huge griffins stridently signals the motif's status.

Eastern Cloth for Western Saints

Numerous griffin medallion textiles survive, though displaced from their original eastern context. Often arriving in western Europe as diplomatic gifts, these valued fabrics could be at some stage transformed into altar cloths and coverings for precious saints' relics.[7] It has been argued that using eastern medieval griffin silks to wrap the relics of western European saints derived from their role in ancient funerary arts, as seen on Roman sarcophagi (see illus. 72), though a looser association seems more plausible.[8] As with many of the artefacts in this book, the current chapter's case studies represent a much larger group. An eminent textile scholar parsed this abundance of medieval silks with griffin medallions into six categories based on subtle differences in posture, ornament and features such as the inclusion of panthers.[9] These relocated Byzantine and Islamic silks were not novelties; rather, they were a well-established type of luxury good that had been imported for many years. The *Liber Pontificalis* records an increase during the seventh and eighth centuries of papal acquisitions of animal-patterned textiles, including ones featuring griffins. Eudoxia's *titulus* of 795–6 CE records a fabric with 'great griffins and two gold-studded wheels with a cross and a purple- and gold-studded border'.[10] Other attributes could have been mentioned, including weaving technique or monetary value, so this emphasis on the colour and the griffin design articulates the priorities and the appeal of these elements to the medieval owners of these silks.

The cathedral treasury in Sion, Switzerland, houses a silk patterned with medallions containing pairs of griffins who rear up, their heads turned back towards each other (illus. 68). This majestic Byzantine silk was used as an ecclesiastical garment, a dalmatic, though possibly this was repurposing; it is noteworthy as one of the few surviving purple Byzantine textiles. Its purple dye has degraded to now appear almost brown, but chemical analysis confirms that murex – a purple dye restricted to Byzantine society's highest echelons through an imperial monopoly – was used.[11] Liudprand of Cremona reports in his tenth-century account of being an emissary in Constantinople that his purple fabrics were confiscated since he lacked the proper rank to own such rarefied items.[12] The Sion griffins' leonine claws are especially pronounced, their taper echoing the shape of the tail's terminus. Rosettes on the haunch, teardrop shapes on the leg and a filigree-like reticulation across the neck all contribute to the creatures' integration into the abstract decorative language of the textile. This blending transfers to other media, such as sculpture (see illus. 73), offering another instance of how griffin imagery calls into question

68 Once-purple medallion patterned silk, c. *10th–11th century, cathedral treasury, Sion/Sitten, Switzerland.*

conventional distinctions made in art history that parse out the subject separately from surrounding 'decoration'.

The large twelfth-century Byzantine silk now in the cathedral treasury in Sens, France, wrapped St Siviard's remains (illus. 69). Its threads were dyed with a comparatively restrained palette: a largely monochromatic white-on-white scheme, highlighted with touches of gold and purple. This silk makes remarkable use of the lampas technique, with the griffin largely woven from the same light thread as the background, but protruding slightly from the main surface. These features all serve to create a work of remarkable subtlety, for the griffin is surrounded by vegetal ornament and an encircling medallion also woven using the lampas weft. Brocading with delicate gold thread wound into the fabric's silk base illuminates the griffin, imparting to the silk a resplendent materiality.[13] Documents show that medieval textiles with gold threads, in some instances anyway, could cost four to twenty times more than those without.[14] The gold, the exquisitely wrought textural variation and the use of silk, whose crystalline molecular structure refracts light in myriad directions, attest to the way the interplay of light and movement were cherished aesthetic traits.[15] This chapter's epigraph from Digenis Akritas (a suitable context for griffin imagery as its titular character embodies porous boundaries, as the Two-Blooded Border Lord) and a Byzantine *ekphrasis* of a joust showcase the same sensibility when describing the clothing of the jousting emperor, its griffin medallions resplendent not only with gold, but 'many pearls'.[16] The jewel's radiance tightly aligns with the splendour of the emperor's person as 'he performs great and wonderful deeds'.[17]

Lines of Transmission

Degradation over time, and modern display practices, often make it hard to discern the original lustrous qualities of medieval silks. We are further removed from these objects' complicated histories by earlier collecting habits, as in the trimming away of irregular edges from centuries of use or deterioration.[18] Likewise, the silk enshrouding the relics of St Siviard took a convoluted path to its current location, with relics arriving in Sens from the Abbey of Saint-Calais in Le Mans during the ninth-century Viking incursions.[19] St Siviard had earlier led that monastic community, and his remains were wrapped in the griffin silk before being tucked away in a casket reliquary. Different provenances have been suggested for the Siviard textile, which is common to a scenario where both the weavers and products routinely cross borders. Tenth-century Byzantine civic commercial regulations allow Syrian weavers working in Constantinople a special elevated status.[20]

69 Medallion patterned silk, so-called shroud of St Siviard, 10th–11th century, cathedral treasury, Sens, France.

Medieval French texts conflate Byzantine and Islamic textile workmanship under terms related to 'Saracen' that mostly seem to indicate the premium quality of the fabrics.[21] Thus, to the Siviard silk's medieval audience, the distinction in potential workshops of origin was likely moot. Most scholars judge the Siviard's shroud to be Byzantine, but a medieval Iraqi workshop has also been posited; the Sion griffin silk is generally given a Byzantine provenance as well, but others have opined it is Syrian.[22] That art historians who have devoted decades to studying these textiles hold such differing opinions about whether the Sion and Siviard silks were made by Byzantine or Islamic weavers is significant – it's a telling indicator of the extent to which composition and technique were shared between Byzantine and Islamic textile workshops in the eleventh and twelfth centuries. As such, I would argue, the controversy about the silks' origins isn't a problematic distraction so much as it can be considered – more fruitfully – to be the story itself.

The griffin motif worked exceptionally well on this highly portable medium, destined for transmission across borders. The medium energizes the griffins with rich patterning, sheen and stylized forms. These silks, as with instances such as the Avar griffin belt clasps (see illus. 37), testify to the varied ways in which medieval peoples adorned their bodies with this creature, a durable symbol within the changing currents of exchange and influence. We now turn to a very different set of griffin representations, shifting our focus from peripatetic textiles to the stone carvings on a building. This ease of migrating across artforms surely was an important factor in the longevity and dispersal of the griffin motif.[23]

Crusading Griffins

Griffin imagery can be spotted on quite a medley of medieval churches, yet the creature does not have a particularly robust Christian hermeneutic tradition. The griffin motif here often seems to be largely inspired by luxury goods, though inflected by contemporary events. Thus, in Aquitaine, several churches with ties to the Crusading movement incorporate griffins in their sculptural decoration. On the south facade of Parthenay-le-Vieux's church of St Pierre (illus. 70), from circa 1100, a sculpted ribbon of this motif frames the left tympanum, the half-circle over the doorway.[24] The repeating pattern of symmetrical pairs is likely a direct appropriation from textiles. The griffins' proudly upright stance echoes the tenor of the scene of conquest in the middle, where a crowned man mercilessly tramples a pitifully small opponent beneath his horse – business as usual for griffin-adjacent imagery. The man is often interpreted as Constantine the Great, but other possibilities include a lord of Parthenay, a biblical king (David) or a triumphant allegorical figure.[25]

A ribbon of rampant griffins, comparable to those around the rider tympanum at St Pierre, also appear across town on another church, Sainte-Croix, on the south portal. These, in turn, inspired the use of the same motif at nearby buildings as in Lamairé, where a very familiar-looking griffin graces a west portal column capital.[26] These griffins in Aquitaine correlate with the local church

70 Carved area above the door, tympanum, encircled by band of griffins with rider in the middle, south facade, c. 1100, Church of St Pierre, Parthenay-le-Vieux, France.

decorative programmes' emphasis on the Crusading movement – a conduit through which luxury goods arrived in this area of France. We might look at this as griffins' long-standing connotations with precious materials and the exotic being deployed to articulate a powerful message – that Crusaders could transfer the griffin's alien allure and bravery onto their own mission. Texts influential for the Crusading movement position griffins in the intimidating landscape of eastern lands, such as Fulcher of Chartres' history of the Crusades, in which a brief description focuses on griffins' savagery and their being 'mad beyond all insanity' (*ultra omnem rabiem saevientes*).[27] Other telling instances of griffins constituting part of the visual messaging of medieval Crusades include English examples, for instance, the twelfth-century Clunaic capital from Lewes priory, and a set of thirteenth-century wall paintings from the nave of the Church of St Mary in West Walton. This cycle emulates luxurious imported wall hangings, replete with griffin medallions painted in a rich red hue. The church's patronage has been connected with the Crusading aspirations of King Henry III, a monarch tied to Aquitaine via his formidable grandmother, Eleanor, with the griffin motif reinforcing the visual expression of this conquest-oriented, militarized vision of medieval Christianity.[28]

Chapter Eleven

Griffins in the Realms of Death and Transcendence

Just like the sun within a mirror, so
the double-natured creature gleamed within,
now showing one, and now the other guise.
Consider, reader, if I did not wonder
when I saw something that displayed no movement
though its reflected image kept on changing.
Dante, *Divine Comedy, Purgatory*

The repurposing of griffin-adorned Byzantine silks, as wrappings for revered saints' relics in western medieval churches, points to the image's association with liminality and transcendence. Indeed, griffin imagery at the site of a famed ancient oracle such as the Temple of Apollo at Didyma (see illus. 20) can suddenly seem a not-so-remote antecedent. The ache of grief maybe found some relief in the promise of transcendence to the afterlife, hinted at by the griffin's in-between status. As we consider the trajectory of their image in funerary arts, and their use in paradisical iconography, Adam naming animals or of the Fountain of Life, it becomes clear they pointed to a world beyond for many of their viewers. These dual-natured creatures symbolically bridge realms, whether in William Blake's reimagining of Dante's *grifone* or the ultimate passage from life to death on an ancient tomb.

Ancient Egyptian Tomb Paintings

At Beni Hasan, a vast Middle Kingdom necropolis, several types of griffins are rendered. Some follow forms we've already explored, as in Tomb 3's wall painting for Khnumhotep II (*c.* 1922–1874 BCE), where a pharaonic figure, like those seen on Egyptian magic wands (see illus. 48), erupts from a griffin's back. In the twenty-first-century BCE Tomb 15, a griffin walks in a row of desert animals, sharing the visual cadence of West Asian animal procession scenes, reworked centuries later in 'orientalizing' Greek art (see illus. 15).[1] The most intriguing creature from Beni Hasan described as a griffin, though, might be the one painted on the north wall of Tomb 17 (illus. 71), the resting place of the regional governor Khety (*c.* 2125–1985 BCE).

71 Griffin with Horus- and Seth-like features, on the south wall of the tomb of Khety, Egyptian 11th dynasty, c. *2125–1985* BCE, *Beni Hasan, modern reconstruction drawing.*

The tomb painting shows Khety overseeing a desert hunt with a griffin whose composite nature almost seems colour-coded, for the vivid blue of its feline back contrasts with the yellow-and-white patterned wings snugly folded against its torso (a not uncommon habit in the depiction of hybrids of using colour to accent the 'seams' of constitutive parts). Typically for Egyptian art, its head is closer to a Horus-like falcon, in fine points such as a beak shorter than an eagle's. Some of this composite beast's attributes are more unusual; the spiky terminus of the tail might come from images of the asinine god of chaos, Seth. A row of pointy teats distends down from its torso, full as if of a nursing mother, providing another example of a maternal griffin (see illus. 49, 50). The griffin's collar and leash, though, might tell us the most about the tomb's hunting scene, for the collar's chequerboard pattern attracts the eye, making a profound and obvious statement of domestication. Inscribed above the creature is the label *Saget* [*sgt*], and since the same word is used above the griffin in the tomb of Neheri I at El-Bersheh (*c.* 1985–1795 BCE), it could denote a tamed griffin type – though perhaps not one with much popularity, since those are the only two known instances of *Saget*.[2] However, instead of playing a docile role, it has also been suggested this composite could have been construed similarly to the fearsome protective griffins of the Middle Kingdom magic wands (see illus. 48), its pronounced teats connecting it to the same symbolic space of physical birth and spiritual rebirth to the afterlife.[3] While these examples of griffins from the Beni Hasan tombs are intriguingly varied, griffins are relatively uncommon within the relative abundance of surviving Egyptian art. It is in classical Greece and Rome that this hybrid beast becomes consistently part of the visual language commemorating death.

Children's Sarcophagi

Starting in Greek and Etruscan art, griffins and other winged creatures frame a visual anchor, often as a vase or fountain, on sarcophagi and tomb paintings. Many ancient Roman ash chests and grave altars render griffins, sometimes shown adjacent to objects such as incense burners.[4] Based on their size, it seems that almost all the Roman sarcophagi with griffins on the front side were crafted for children, which to a modern eye anyway tinges the imagery, however fanciful, with particular pathos (illus. 72).[5] The front panel of this Roman sarcophagus positions griffins around a female torso with acanthus leaves instead of legs and a fruit basket perched atop her head. The children's sarcophagi with griffins, mostly made around 130–150 CE in Rome, are part of a larger shift to burial with a sarcophagus rather than the previously preferred ash chests, so may indicate shifting attitudes towards death and burial, with cremation becoming viewed as too traumatic following the loss of a child.[6] The most common way griffins appear, though, is a little later as ever-vigilant guardians on the end panels of adult-sized Roman sarcophagi; this use peaks in the third century CE.[7] Griffins are of a kind with the other winged figures populating these objects, and part of a visual field filled with details such as garlands that have long been dismissed as 'decorative'. More helpfully, they can be seen as one element of many perceived as an integrated visual message (with the hybrid animal not compartmentalized by its audience into the tidy categories earlier favoured in art history of 'subject' or 'ornament').[8]

72 Sarcophagus for a child, Roman, c. 100–125 CE, marble.

Pearl or Eye? A Byzantine Enigma

Griffins continued to feature in funerary arts throughout the Middle Ages.[9] This fine-carved Late Byzantine marble panel (illus. 73) has its closest comparison in a sarcophagus made for a thirteenth-century aristocratic woman, Anna Maliasene.[10] Anna separated from her husband in order to become a nun by 1274 and died shortly thereafter.[11] On her sarcophagus, in the Thessalian town of Ano Volos, griffins fill medallions alongside bird pairs and two-headed birds, perhaps because griffins – while visually constituted fairly equally from their two 'source animals' – are ordinarily written about as mostly avian in their behaviour. As with some griffin-shaped lamps (see illus. 60), its beak holds a small circle, which could

73 Panel likely from a sarcophagus, Byzantine, c. 1250–1300, marble.

be interpreted as a pearl, in keeping with the griffin's association with wealth. In Chinese art of the time dragons with such circles in or near their mouth are commonplace, and in that context the pearl signifies the sun or moon, its luminosity oftentimes amplified with flames coming from the disc. However, the round form could depict an eyeball plucked from a hapless victim of the griffin's ferocity, a scene replayed elsewhere in that era. For example, a twelfth-century ceramic bowl shows a griffin rending into a doe, a claw clamping the prey's eye socket and a telltale eye balanced in its beak.[12] An unsettling array of Byzantine rulers had their opponents blinded, the most notorious being Basil II, who in 1014 blinded most of a cohort of 15,000 Bulgarian prisoners. The tableau of a griffin with its prey's eyeball perched in its beak would have offered a rarefied version of violence actually witnessed in that society. In modern hunting, raptors are sometimes trained to aim for the eye of their victim (albeit not a common approach), and griffins' representation as intensely powerful birds might take cues from actual practices in training predatory birds.[13] Another way to view the object grasped in that powerful beak is to connect the disc with the protruding diagonal lines that extend above the mouth, in which case the griffin might be grasping a bone (bones are consumed, to varying degrees, by different species of predatory birds, suggesting another way that a highly stylized medieval conception could be distantly inspired by observed animal behaviours).

The panel follows a visual cadence that is familiar by now: the funerary griffin's circular frame echoes the griffin medallions on luxury items circulating around the Mediterranean. So, too, the patterning of the background and the treatment of the creature's wings blur the boundary between figure and decoration. Some areas of the body are embellished, as with the elegant curvilinear lines on its rear haunch and the teardrop with a budding form on its front one, its pose angled to fit its circular frame. None of this is really new, though. A small cross inset along each edge is all that advertises the Christianity of its patron. There is no distinctive griffin motif for a medieval funerary context: it resembles the highly portable images that, as we have seen in the previous chapter, readily travelled vast distances on medieval works. The extent of funerary griffins is suggested by far-flung examples; from the other side of medieval Europe, in the Bayeux Tapestry's (*c.* 1070) mention of the death of King Edward, a text memorializing the monarch's passing is bracketed by a griffin.

Griffins at the Fountain of Life

Griffins also can inhabit paradise as when one joins a centaur around a vase on the facade of an eighth-century Umayyad 'desert palace', Mshatta (illus. 74). The Mshatta complex was never completed, but the south wall was extensively carved before construction halted, and large fragments of the architectural sculpture were taken to Berlin from their original site near Amman in the nineteenth century. It may have welcomed pilgrims returning from the Hajj to Mecca, while also functioning as a commercial hub. A gorgeous interlace web envelops the surface; distinctions

74 Animals drinking from fountains, griffin and centaur pair on right, originally from Mshatta, Jordan, Umayyad, c. 750, limestone.

blur between creature and decoration, the animate and the abstract. Medallions fashioned of loose vegetal fronds encircle the animals. In the pictured area of the Mshatta exterior, the left pair of animals bend their heads to drink from the vase between them, usually taken to symbolize the Fountain of Life, a Qur'anic and biblical motif with a rich exegetical tradition. In the right pair, the griffin inclines to drink from the life-giving water, a particularly captivating sight for observers in a desert environment.[14] The Fountain of Life, the carved tendrils enveloping the facade's lower surface and the fantastical animals together convey the notion of paradise to the original viewers at Mshatta.[15] So often shown on the attack, both the Mshatta griffin and centaur are notably at peace, for the medieval sagittarius normally carries a bow. At Mshatta, creatures are limited to the sculpted surface on the stretch of south wall to the left of the entrance. The suggestion has been made, which seems reasonable, that a mosque was located, or planned, on the interior of the 'uninhabited' right-hand section, for living beings are rarely portrayed in Islamic art, but with more instances within secular Islamic art.[16]

Portraying a griffin alongside a fountain is fairly common in medieval settings, ranging from the ninth-century choir screen from Sorrento's Old Cathedral to Byzantine manuscript illuminations, recalling countless ancient griffins flanking vessels (see illus. 34). In a manuscript made circa 1200 in Constantinople for the Georgian Queen T'amar, griffins at a Fountain of Life recall a theme mentioned

75 Grammar treatise by Theodore Prodromos, Byzantine, 12th century.

in Psalm 36:9 and refigured in the Book of Revelations 21:6.[17] An especially exuberant rendering of the griffin at a fountain (illus. 75) occurs in a twelfth-century manuscript for another aristocratic woman, Irene, whose literary patronage was floridly eulogized – her generosity likened to that of the gold-gushing river Pactolus.[18] The illumination of the grammar treatise written by Theodore Prodromos has touches perhaps intended to delight its learned female audience, such as a letter H(eta) on folio 50v fashioned from the figures of two women holding a book.[19] The remarkable fountain is on the other side of that same folio, concluding the chapter on Greek feminine grammatical forms. The Fountain of Life gushes six streams of water into a pool teeming with fish. The lion and griffin inject even more vitality: the griffin – a dreamy confection painted in pink and gold – springs towards the fountain, its aquiline head turned away. The captivating scene playfully details lively abundance, with the griffin amplifying the paradisical image.

Adam's Naming of Animals

Griffins are also present in diverse medieval depictions of the Garden of Eden, especially during the moment when Adam assigns names to various beings, including in an early medieval ivory, a fifth-century Syrian church floor mosaic and twelfth-century Italian frescoes of the Church of San Pietro a Valle in Ferentillo (illus. 76).[20] One inspiration for the Ferentillo griffin may be a third-century

76 Adam Naming the Animals, *c. 1175–1200, fresco, Church of San Pietro a Valle, Ferentillo, Italy.*

sarcophagus, now ensconced near the church's altar, showcasing a griffin closely resembling the creature painted on the upper wall. More symbolically, the dual nature of griffins in these *Naming* scenes may signify humanity's possibilities for transcendence, for spiritual advancement, and the inclusion among 'real' animals is set off by the additional griffin juxtaposed immediately above the *Naming* scene at San Pietro.[21] The naturalized status the griffin has in the painting is mirrored sometimes in writing, such as a seventh-century Byzantine poem about creation that eulogizes griffins' prowess right after that of lions and bulls.[22]

Dante's *Grifone* and Blake's Re-envisioning

Dante offers another way of thinking about how these winged composites could portray spiritual ascent. Near the end of the *Divine Comedy*'s *Purgatory*, the griffin leads the procession that Dante follows to the place where his beloved Beatrice appears:

> His wings – so high that they were lost to sight;
> his limbs were gold as far as he was a bird
> the rest of him was white mixed with bloodred.[23]

While the ostensible role of Dante's griffin involves the prosaic task of pulling a chariot, the creature has been interpreted variously as symbolizing Christ's two natures (the most common interpretation), the Virgin Mary's chastity and, more recently, as the final earthly emperor or a statement regarding the Florentine commune and imperial authority.[24] Considering the influence of the mythographic tradition on fourteenth-century thought might offer some insight.[25] Just as today's awareness of classical myths might begin with popular compilations – like Edith Hamilton's *Mythology*, or modern Internet sources reliant on those collections – rather than from direct engagement with classical writers such as Ovid, throughout the Middle Ages mythographic works that gathered excerpts of classical writings proliferated. One such twelfth-century compiler, referred to as the Third Vatican Mythographer, associated griffins with a position in the middle – chthonic – realm when describing the god Apollo's accoutrements: 'the lyre, which shows us the image of celestial harmony; the griffin, which shows him [Apollo] to be an earthly deity; and arrows, by which he is shown to belong to the lower regions'.[26] This placement of griffins in the terrestrial plane of a tripartite scheme parallels Dante's installing the beast within the in-between *Purgatory*.[27] Looking at his beloved Beatrice, Dante the pilgrim sees the griffin reflected in her eyes, where its two natures (lion and eagle) alternate, while the griffin remains immutable in his direct vision:

> Just like the sun within a mirror, so
> the double-natured creature gleamed within,
> now showing one, and now the other guise.

Consider, reader, if I did not wonder
when I saw something that displayed no movement
though its reflected image kept on changing.[28]

Beatrice's perception starkly differs from that of Dante the pilgrim, as she is able to discern the individual elemental components of the composite. Labels such as 'double-natured' repeat, yet the creature's hybrid nature does not make it 'monstrous' in the sense in which other creatures in Dante warrant the term in a pejorative way.[29]

Dante has inspired many artists, and the griffin-drawn procession acquired an enduring visual formula shortly after his death.[30] One of the most satisfying visual expressions of the *Purgatory*'s culminating moment comes centuries later, in William Blake's watercolour of the griffin's procession (illus. 77).[31] This work, conflating elements from several cantos, has been assessed as 'the climax of Blake's *Comedy*, and we might almost see it as the climax of his career as well'.[32] While capturing the visionary wonder of Dante's narrative, Blake inserts his own commentary

77 William Blake, Beatrice Addressing Dante, *illustration for Dante's* Divine Comedy, *1824–7, ink and watercolour.*

78 Gustave Moreau, Fairy with Griffins, *late 19th century, watercolour and gouache, with pen and brown ink.*

into this cycle from late in his career, made while bed-ridden from illness. The imposing griffin's head is haloed by a rainbow of colours, balancing Beatrice's mandorla of light. Clouds encircle the griffin's halo, echoing the nebular wisps partially surrounding the monstrous beasts, the Leviathan and Behemoth, in Blake's fifteenth engraving of the *Book of Job*. Through a nuanced interpretive move worthy of medieval hermeneutics, the halo resembling cumulus clouds around the griffin might establish a connection – similar to that around the two creatures depicted in his rendition of Job elsewhere – with a worldview that the artist absorbed from Milton's concept of the Mundane Shell.[33] Following this vein, Blake might be taken to diminish his *Purgatory* griffin as possessing a banally materialistic 'single vision', a theme Blake returns to time after time using the dismissive phrase 'Newton's sleep', reinterpreting Dante's text, where the griffin as seen by Beatrice embodies the rich dualities of two distinct beings.

Symbolist Dreaming of Griffins

Griffins betoken a more modern transcendence in a later nineteenth-century artist's work, namely the Symbolist painter Gustave Moreau's many depictions of the creature (illus. 78). He painted this watercolour, *Fairy with Griffins*, late in his career, around 1885–90, combining two of his favourite themes: indolent nude females and winged mythic beasts. Earlier, in a notebook begun around 1865, he listed 'woman in cave guarded by griffins' under his ancient and biblical theme category, and numerous griffin paintings and drawings by him are documented that no longer exist.[34] The watercolour's griffins might be imagined as protecting the sleepy fairy of the phantasmagorical scene, warding against the bright blue chimera in the painting's lower right area. The two griffins can also be understood in terms of Moreau's place in the Symbolist movement, a response to naturalism in which artists and writers turned inwards to produce work grounded in personal metaphors and individual imaginings. These approaches were carried forward into the twentieth century by artists such as the Surrealist André Breton, who was so captivated as a teenager by a painting of a woman with griffins on display at the Moreau Museum that he wrote of the lurid fantasies it inspired.[35] Moreau's 'splendid dreams' were esteemed by Breton and others even during the ascetic dogmatism of formalism in the 1950s, an indication of the appeal of content such as griffins and fairies, which would be disparaged by critics, notably Clement Greenberg, as mere 'literature'.[36] In that intellectual and artistic moment favouring the rigours of modernity, griffins would be decidedly categorized as kitsch, inverting their earlier association with transcendence.

Chapter Twelve

Moralizing Griffins

There are also . . . mountains of gold which men cannot approach because of the dragons and griffins and other huge monsters, set there to show us what sort of guardians avarice employs.

St Jerome, a letter from 412

Griffins have been used to teach strikingly contradictory lessons across the numerous sources that offer them up as an exemplar, even within, say, just looking at bestiaries, the popular medieval book of beasts. How, too, does the didactic purpose of the bestiary change in the early modern era? Looking at other instances ranging from a twelfth-century German Haggadah to a twenty-first-century Africanfuturist novel this hybrid beast presents a similarly nuanced and fascinating array of interpretations.

Bestiaries

Medieval bestiary manuscripts offered spiritual lessons drawn from a mix of actual and mythical creatures. The griffin, a relative latecomer to bestiaries' stable, joined the 'second family' of bestiary manuscripts in twelfth-century England; their content almost doubled with the addition of many new animals. The bestiary tradition grew out of the moralized animals in the *Physiologos*, discussed in Chapter Eight, with many differences among the many surviving manuscripts – substantial divergence between the Latin and Greek versions being just one. While griffins in the Greek *Physiologus* are light-capturing avian creatures associated with the Archangel Michael and the Virgin Mary, they are absent from the Latin *Physiologus*.[1] The hybrid appears in another bestiary predecessor, Isidore of Seville's *Etymologies*, a text so all-encompassing that it was the basis for Isidore being named patron saint of the Internet. The entry, as expected from the title, begins with an etymology, and a specious one at that: Isidore suggests that *grypes* (griffin) arises from combining the word for 'crane' with the term for four feet.[2] The rest of Isidore on griffins – from their habitat in the Hyperborean mountains to their insatiable appetite for humans and horses – follows the classical tropes explored in earlier chapters. Isidore's influence moulds the portrayal in the bestiary:

79 A griffin attacks a pig (top), from the Worksop Bestiary, England, Romanesque, c. *1185.*

> The griffin is so named because it is an animal with feathers and four feet. This species of wild beast is born in northern regions or in the mountains. In every part of its body it is similar to a lion, in wings and face it is similar to eagles. The species is extremely hostile to horses, and they tear to pieces the men they spot.[3]

Medieval artists often adapt visual formulae to local circumstances, with English bestiary manuscripts imagining griffin prey in terms of local fauna, and thus a design in the Worksop Bestiary, made around 1185, shows a griffin carrying off a piglet – an alarming development that seems of no concern to the pigs below (illus. 79). The illuminations dwarf the terse description of griffins squeezed between them on the page. The composition was later adapted, like many others from the Worksop Bestiary, in the Northumberland Bestiary (*c.* 1250–60), one of many such interconnections across this family of manuscripts. While griffin imagery varies stylistically from manuscript to manuscript, bestiaries invariably emphasize their aggression, with common prey being pigs, horses, rabbits and, alas, humans.[4] While the illuminations define griffins through violence, their descriptions often lack the moralizing lesson imparted by other bestiary entries – the one for an eagle encourages the reader to 'seek the spiritual fountain of the Lord'.[5] A few bestiary manuscripts add an ancillary text about gemstones, a lapidary, which in some versions reprises griffins' role guarding Scythian emeralds, likened to a diabolic envy for 'the pearl of faith', and some French bestiaries follow a similar tack.[6] That said, despite pairing two animals considered mightily virtuous in the bestiary tradition – the eagle and the lion – the English second family bestiary textual tradition typically writes about griffins as a formidable but morally neutral predator.

Down the Rabbit Hole with the Ripon Misericord

Ethical codes were communicated through other facets of visual culture of course, such as the church misericords from across western Europe, from which dozens of griffin carvings survive. Misericords offered standing clergy a place to lean during long church services, and their often playful carving nonetheless reinforced teachings for the faithful. A late fifteenth-century misericord from Ripon Cathedral (illus. 80) is especially well known, for the future author of *Alice's Adventures in Wonderland* was possibly inspired by its griffin and rabbit – with his father as rector at Ripon he paid many visits to this church. We explore his story more in Chapter Fifteen (see illus. 103–5). The carved griffin clutches at its prey, the rabbit, scrabbling for the rabbit hole just out of its reach. Not long before the Ripon misericord was carved, an anticlerical satire, *The Plowman's Tale*, was appended to *The Canterbury Tales*; here a griffin argues a pro-papist position with a pelican, offering another possible interpretative lens.[7] More likely though this griffin was a warning to avoid the perils of greed.

Negative depictions in early medieval sources likely inspired such treatments, as in a letter written by St Jerome in 412, which describes griffins in the wild:

> The ocean . . . takes nearly a year to cross before you come to India . . . this land is the home of the carbuncle and the emerald, and those gleaming pearls which our great ladies so ardently desire. There are also in it mountains of gold which men cannot approach because of the dragons and griffins and other huge monsters, set there to show us what sort of guardians avarice employs.[8]

This letter to the classically trained monk Rusticus leans heavily on Jerome's supposed knowledge of exotic lands, intended to broadcast the early Church Father's cosmopolitan purview.[9] Thus the griffins' habitat remains remote, for a year of travel is needed to reach this place where they guard their riches. Jerome is clearly conversant with the tradition going back to Herodotus of griffins as guardians of gold but their tenacity is recast, here, as a sin: avarice. Rabanus Maurus (*c.* 780–856) similarly maligns griffins, casting their struggles against the Arimaspi for emeralds as 'with unflagging effort, [they] struggle, not to possess and use spiritual riches, but to take them away from people'.[10]

This interpretative thread, situating avaricious, morally repugnant griffins as an integral part of the riches of certain remote landscapes, continued to have currency. Greedy griffins appear in a collection of fables very popular in the Middle Ages, *The Book/Mirror of Natural Wisdom* (*Speculum Sapientiae*), a kind of proto-self-help book (illus. 81). In this Austrian version, an old man counsels a young man to turn away from the temptations represented by gold mountains encrusted with emeralds, for the griffins guarding this tantalizing treasure in India will kill him. Instead, he's encouraged to follow the path of the wise Brahmins and seek true treasure, virtue, avoiding the disfigurement to his inner self caused by avarice embodied by griffins. Earlier German writers, such as the thirteenth-century Albertus Magnus, echo their role guarding both gold and emeralds, also bringing up that griffins placed in their nests agates, which Magnus connects with vivid dreams and robust physical strength (*On Animals*, XXIII.46).[11]

80 A rabbit trying to escape a griffin's clutches as another descends down a rabbit hole, misericord, late 15th century, Ripon Cathedral, England, wood.

81 Youth journeying to India to find a mountain of gold, but discovering it guarded by griffins, miniature from Spiegel der Weisheit *(Mirror of Natural Wisdom), Austria,* c. *1430.*

Griffins convey other negative meanings in medieval writing, including versions of the word 'griffin' designating hybrid identities that are being vilified. A twelfth-century chronicle by Richard of Devizes castigates Greek-speaking Sicilians with the terms 'grifons', 'grifonaille' and 'Griffones' in his description of their conflict with Richard the Lionheart.[12] The meaning of these overlapping terms are slightly different, but their semantic range centres on cruelty and pride, often associated with foreign, especially 'Saracen', persons.[13] He disparages those whose tongue and land are regarded to be not in sync, for there is some sort of pathetic 'two-ness' to them. With its role as a cultural crossroad, numerous griffins populate medieval Sicilian art, including mosaics from the Norman Stanza and a Monreale cloister capital. Other Anglo-Norman authors focus on the treachery of the medieval Greeks called 'grifons' in their accounts, while taking pains to differentiate them from their illustrious classical forebears.[14] Correspondingly in Milton's *Paradise Lost* (1667), immediately after the poem recounts Satan's hybrid nature, it segues to the 'Gryphon' (in some versions, 'Gryfon'), whose rapacity for gold matches Satan's hunger for entrapping humanity (II.943–4).

Encyclopaedic Systems of Knowledge

Encyclopaedic works perpetuate the pattern of emphasizing griffins' violence: when the *Book of Flowers* (*Liber Floridus*), the medieval text compiled by Lambert, Canon of Saint Omer, was copied circa 1460 by a Flemish illuminator, the prey of choice for the beautifully drawn griffin was a human. The victim hangs limply from its beak, echoing the bestiaries' admonition about griffins' aggression towards people. Indeed, the image is so striking that it was, in turn, chosen for the Getty Museum's marketing of its 2019 major exhibition, the 'Book of Beasts' (illus. 82).

82 Banner advertisement for Getty Museum's 'Book of Beasts' exhibition, featuring a miniature from Flemish manuscript of the Book of Flowers, *c. 1460.*

83 Griffin surrounded by other beasts in a grid, from a French translation of Bartholomeus Anglicus, De proprietatibus rerum *(On the Properties of Things), 1447.*

The bestiaries' organization served as a model for more encyclopaedic texts being written, such as the influential work by Bartholomeus Anglicus, or Bartholomew the Englishman (illus. 83), *De proprietatibus rerum* (On the Properties of Things, Books 12 and 18) of around 1242–7, which mentions, among other snippets, that a griffin's egg is an antidote to poison. Jean Corbechon translated Bartholomeus' Latin text into French, of which 46 manuscripts survive, this version made for King Charles v being the most lavish. Here the griffin holds pride of place in the centre of a grid and is by far the largest creature. Its compartmentalized animals, juxtaposing real and imaginary creatures but often emphasizing the latter, recall works such as the English *Aberdeen Bestiary* or the Spanish Rylands Beatus's *Noah's Ark* (both *c.* 1200) and had ancient antecedents as well.[15] The visual ordering in the Bartholomeus manuscript, though, also looks forward to shifting paradigms in the early modern era that frame and interpret the natural world in terms of empirical evidence and carefully researched taxonomic structures. The sceptical detachment of early modern times is even more striking when we look at medieval perspectives preceding it, when the question that mattered wasn't the existence of griffins, but their moral significance.

The *Bird's Head Haggadah*

Fewer medieval griffins possess a positive moral spin, and one such representation comes from a manuscript likely produced in Mainz circa 1300, conventionally called the *Bird's Head Haggadah* (illus. 84). Throughout the manuscript, Jewish identity is denoted by means of distinctive pointed ears on the birdlike heads, identified as griffin heads by scholar Marc Epstein, whereas non-Jews, rendered with faces devoid of features, acquire a null value.[16] The interpretative pathway leading to this use of griffin heads is quite nuanced but, to summarize: some rabbinic interpreters, writing about the curtain of the Holy of Holies, suggested the translucent curtain was layered so that the eagles and lions it depicted were mystically superimposed, becoming griffins in the eye of the beholder.[17] Earlier manuscripts as in the *Ambrosian Tanakh* (*c.* 1236–8) deploy full griffin figures to render the Jewish mythological figure the Ziz, and later, sacred objects such as eighteenth-century Torah Ark valences also rendered griffins.[18] Layered onto the hallowed status of the griffin on the ark's curtain, the overall positive attributes of lions and eagles in rabbinic literature may have possessed an especially poignant meaning for the Jewish population of Mainz: this city's victims of the infamous Rhineland massacres committed during the First Crusade were commemorated as being 'swifter than eagles and stronger than lions'.[19] The quietly domestic act shown in this particular illumination was, in fact, fraught with significance – for baking matzo was, along with other Passover preparations, the target of especially heated antisemitic vitriol, in which the unleavened bread was wilfully misconstrued as an evil inversion of the Eucharistic host. Placing this image in the physical, as well as symbolic, heart of the manuscript worked as part of a visual polemic; the figure busily baking matzo in his

84 Griffin-headed man placing matzo in an oven, illumination from the Bird's Head Haggadah, *c. 1300.*

domed oven normalized this activity, which countered the swirls of suspicion and hostility surrounding it in certain medieval Christian sources.[20]

That use of griffin imagery to offer an alternative positive set of values for Rhineland Jewish communities remains exceptional. Even recent literary uses of the griffin can absorb some of the earlier negative connotations, offering the hybrid creature up as a shorthand for various sorts of fakery. In Tade Thompson's Africanfuturist *Wormwood* trilogy of novels, the creature is the mental avatar for the psychic narrator. The dissonance between the character and this avatar is hinted at in its final mention in the first book where during a sleeping vision he finds himself to be his 'true self, not the gryphon'.[21] Correspondingly in Chapter Seventeen of George Eliot's novel *Adam Bede*, published in 1859, the griffin signals artful dissimulation:

> Falsehood is so easy, truth so difficult. The pencil is conscious of a delightful facility in drawing a griffin – the longer the claws, and the larger the wings, the better; but that marvellous facility which we mistook for genius is apt to forsake us when we want to draw a real unexaggerated lion. Examine your words well, and you will find that even when you have no motive to be false, it is a very hard thing to say the exact truth, even about your own immediate feelings – much harder than to say something fine about them which is not the exact truth.

What is perhaps most remarkable from this passage is that griffins create a kind of muddying backwash from the world of fantasy into the objective world. Indeed, it seems that once the hybrid form of the griffin has been touched upon, any depiction of its mundane parts will be unavoidably tainted – or, perhaps, augmented? – by style over meaning. Similarly, for Eliot, the modern writer's quandary is that, once fine style has hybridized with true content, the writer may never again be confident of speaking with pure honesty: it seems that, for her, tragically, words cannot serve two masters.

Chapter Thirteen

Making Their Mark with Griffins:

From Heraldry to Visual Branding

To bere a gryffyn in armys is a tokyn of a grete man and a strong fighter and double of condicions and maners, for that birde in the further partie is like an egle and in the hyndre partie like a lyon.

***Tractatus de armis*, treatise on heraldry, *c.* 1440–50**

The fearsome nature attributed to griffins made them a popular motif on armour throughout the ancient world, with examples ranging from the helmet of the *thraex* gladiator to the horse trappings and tattoos of a Pazyryk warrior (see illus. 32, 44). Likewise modulating the griffin's image could signal shifts in identities: when the sixth-century BCE Greeks of Teos fled the Persians' attack on Asia Minor and founded the colony of Abdera in Thrace, the griffin remained on their coinage, but its orientation shifted from right-facing to left-facing.[1] Medieval officials likewise deployed the griffin across a range of seals, and Chapter One explored ancient uses of griffins on ancient cylinder seals.[2] Seals – where the griffin motif attests to layers of individual and collective identity, often with a military spin – set the stage for understanding how and why griffin imagery would become popular in heraldry. Heraldic griffins provide a ready shorthand of aristocratic lineages while signalling specific conventional attributes. Moreover, this area of visual culture – with its tremendous economy of expression – also provides the vocabulary that undergirds griffins' ongoing use in corporate and academic branding.

'To bere a gryffyn in armys'

A treatise on English heraldry, *Tractatus de armis*, dedicated to Anne of Bohemia (d. 1394), adapts earlier tropes, subtly shifting the griffin's meaning. Whereas in the previous chapter we saw ways griffins are construed negatively (their love of gold being equated with avarice, for example), in heraldry our favourite composite creature is rehabilitated as a positive role model. Its appetite for violence and wealth, disquieting to medieval moralists, is reframed to align nicely with the normative

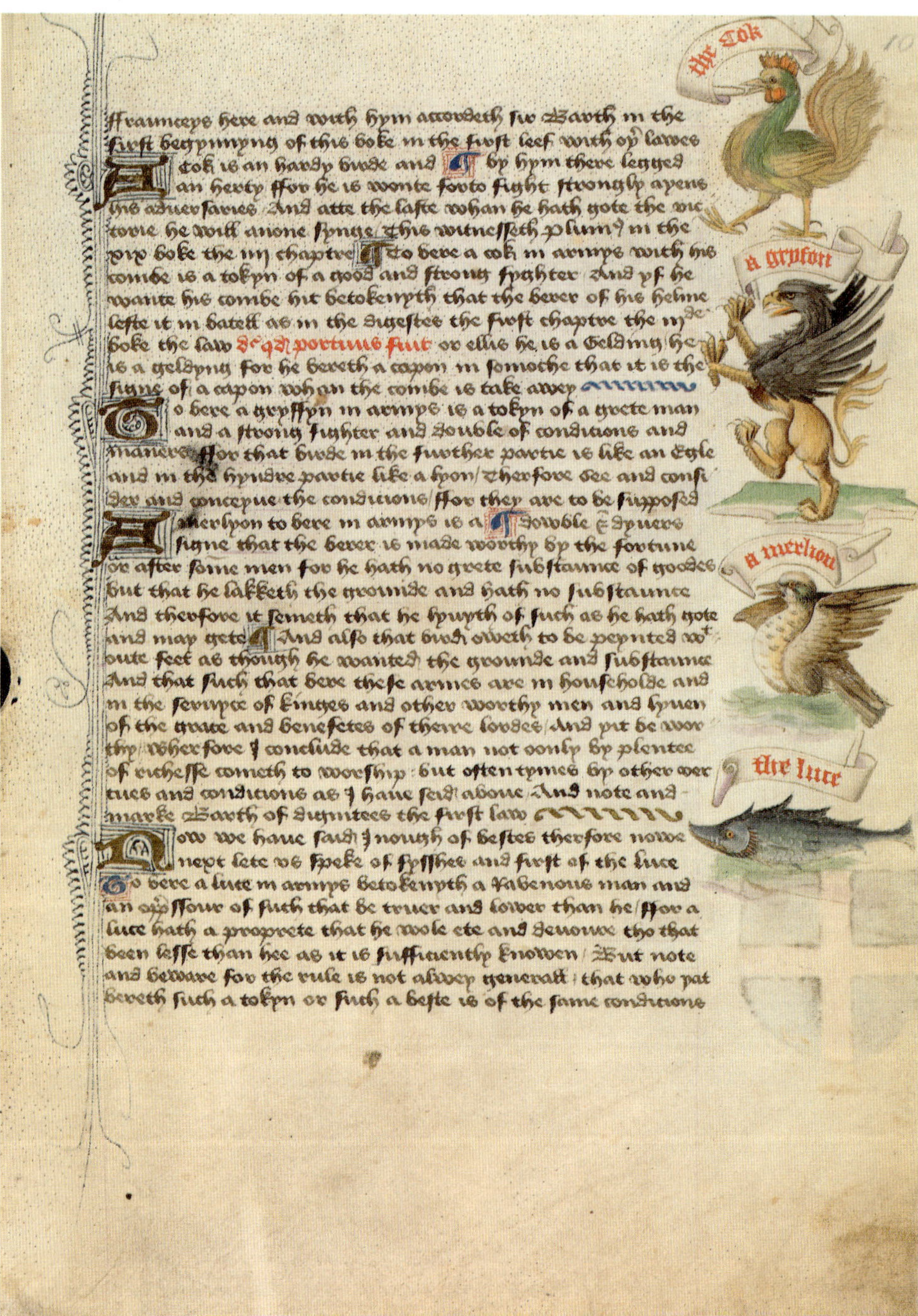

ffraunceys here and with hym accordeth sir Barth in the
first begynnyng of this boke in the first leef with oþ lawes
A cok is an hardy birde and by hym there legged
an herty ffor he is wonte forto fight strongly ayens
his aduersaries And atte the laste whan he hath gote the vic
torie he will anone synge this witnesseth plinn' in the
xix boke the iiij chaptre To bere a cok in armys with his
combe is a tokyn of a good and strong fyghter And yf he
wante his combe hit betokenyth that the berer of his helme
lefte it in batell as in the digestes the first chaptre the iij de
boke the lawe ff q̄ð portinis fuit or ellis he is a Gelding he
is a geldyng for he bereth a capon in somothe that it is the
signe of a capon whan the combe is take awey
To bere a gryffyn in armys is a tokyn of a grete man
and a strong fighter and double of condicions and
maners ffor that birde in the further partie is like an Egle
and in the hyndre partie like a lyon therfore see and consi
der and conceyue the condicions ffor they are to be supposed
A merlyon to bere in armys is a double & dyuers
signe that the berer is made worthy by the fortune
or after some men for he hath no grete substaunce of goodes
but that he lakketh the grounde and hath no substaunce
And therfore it semeth that he lyuyth of such as he hath gote
and may gete And also that birde oweth to be peynted wt
oute feet as though he wanted the grounde and substaunce
And that such that bere these armes are in housholde and
in the seruyce of kinges and other worthy men and lyuen
of the grace and benefetes of theire lordes And yit be wor
thy wherfore I conclude that a man not oonly by plentee
of richesse cometh to worship but often tymes by other ver
tues and condicions as I haue seid above And note and
marke Barth of dignitees the first lawe
Now we haue said inough of bestes therfore nowe
next lete vs speke of fysshes and first of the luce
To bere a luce in armys betokenyth a rabenous man and
an oppressour of such that be truer and lower than he ffor a
luce hath a proprete that he wole ete and deuoure tho that
been lesse than hee as it is sufficiently knowen But note
and beware for the rule is not alwey generall that who þat
bereth such a tokyn or such a beste is of the same condicions

85 *Johannes de Bado Aureo,* Tractatus de armis *(Treatise on Arms),* c. 1440–50 *manuscript of 14th-century text.*

values of heraldic texts. The *Tractatus* circulated widely, including a Middle English version (illus. 85), parsing out the meaning of the griffin in arms as:

> To bere a gryffyn in armys is a tokyn of a grete man and a strong fighter and double of condicions and maners, for that birde in the further partie is like an egle and in the hyndre partie like a lyon. Therfore see and consider and conceyue the condicions, for they are to be supposed dowble & dyuers.[3]

This passage encapsulates several signature attributes. The griffin on a coat of arms marks an especially skilled fighter, because the lion–eagle hybridity, rather than diluting each animal's capabilities, makes them 'dowble'. The illustration that accompanies the text fully asserts the griffin's 'dyuers' (archaic form of 'diverse') nature, for the eagle foreparts and lion hindquarters conjoin abruptly in vivid, contrasting colours. An earlier text from circa 1320, the Anglo-Norman *De Heraudie*, attributes to Alexander the Great a coat of arms with 'un griffoun d'argent'.[4] Griffins decorate Alexander's helmet going back even to Hellenistic coinage, and

86 Detail from coat of arms granted to Anne Boleyn in 1532 of 'a Male Griffin argent', the supporter, on right.

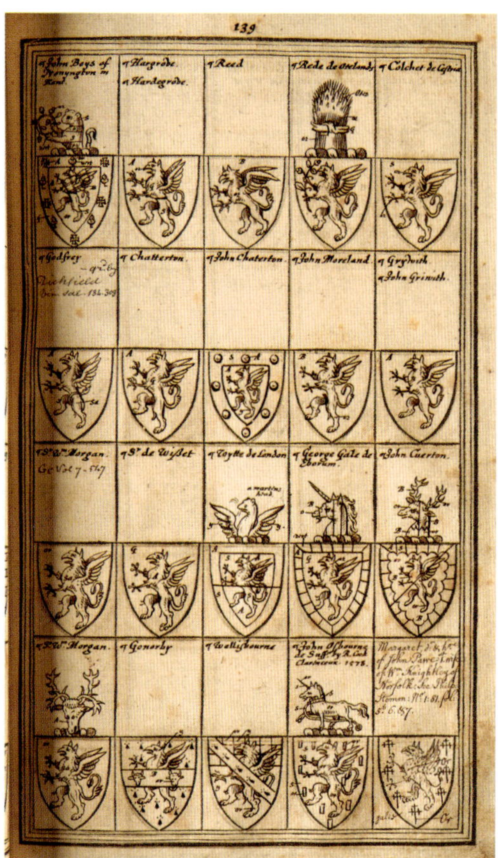

87 Catalogue of heraldic griffins, from Vincent's Ordinary *manuscript, early 17th century.*

medieval heraldic texts such as the *Eneas de heraldis* regard his reign as the beginning of armoury.[5] By the late fifteenth century, griffins had become a popular heraldic feature, as had fictive beasts more generally.

The language of heraldry is highly precise, and blazons – textual descriptions of arms – in both French and English rolls of arms, chart minute deviations that can seem quite rarefied: a herald quipped in 1696 that it is 'a study which loads the memory without improving the understanding'.[6] Thus, within its sometimes punctilious details, designated 'male' and 'female' griffins arose, and from there a sexual dimorphism is sometimes applied by art historians to other eras' renderings of the beast – with ancient wingless griffins, for example, anachronistically being labelled as male (it's not a distinction of concern for ancient writers). Within English heraldry, a male griffin is the more unusual variant: instead of wings, menacing spikes protrude from its body, as seen with the right 'supporter' animal for Anne Boleyn's coat of arms granted in 1532, where the griffin's crown-like collar attaches to a chain furling around its body, described in the sixteenth century as, 'a Male Griffin argent, armed and tufted or similarly gorged and chained' (illus. 86).[7] The early seventeenth-century

Vincent's Ordinary catalogues the minuscule variations of griffins on coats of arms: 62 griffins segreant (a 'rampant' or rearing-up posture for a quadruped, sometimes used specifically for the griffin), 24 griffins statant (with all feet on the ground) and 73 griffin heads – and all this without even including badges and crests. The superabundance of heraldic griffins on this page from the *Ordinary* (illus. 87) has the contours of a dictionary, mapping out slight semantic shifts within a visual stemma. Indeed, with its density of information and the rigid syntax structuring it, the process of absorbing the meaning of a specific heraldic coat of arms can seem more akin to practices of reading than viewing.[8]

King Edward III

Given this lineage of precisely constructed heraldic images, the adoption by an English monarch, Edward III (1312–1377), of the griffin as a special emblem was consequential. He likely acquired it from the aristocratic family of Montagu. When Edward granted William Montagu the right to use the royal eagle as his crest in 1335, Montagu reciprocated by giving the king the right to deploy his family's symbol of the griffin.[9] Thereafter Edward III used the griffin as his device on a range of objects, such as four brooches recorded in the official inventory, itemizing them

88 Privy seal of Edward III bearing the image of a griffin, c. 1335.

89 Edward III*'s griffin, illustration by Edward Bawden in* The Queen's Beasts *(1953).*

according to the number of pearls and diamonds encrusting each.[10] More interesting, though, is Edward's use of the griffin on a seal he began using in 1335 (illus. 88).[11] Seals guaranteed authenticity, and this one seems to have been used specifically for the king's correspondence regarding military matters, in distinction to his privy and great seals for communications about other topics.[12] Especially given this monarch's appetite for warfare, maybe the fourteenth-century significance of the griffin recalled the creature's ancient ties to armed combat.

The griffin became so intertwined with King Edward III's identity that centuries later, when Queen Elizabeth II was crowned in 1953, the medieval monarch was represented among the 'Queen's Beasts' as a griffin. These ten heraldic statues, sculpted in plaster by James Woodford, were commissioned by the British Ministry of Works to proclaim the young queen's lineage and were placed in front of a temporary annex of Westminster Abbey built for the coronation. The commemorative booklet sidesteps the more unsavoury implications of griffins to primly assert, 'In contrast with the dragon, a symbol of evil, the griffin was a beneficent creature,' representing 'guardianship and vigilance, combining the keen vision, alertness and swiftness of the eagle with the courage and strength of the lion' (illus. 89).[13] The booklet takes pains to describe the beast's august lineage, citing sources as eclectic as Bronze Age Cretan gold sculpture and the sixteenth-century *Accedens of Armory*'s discussion of griffin claws.[14] For the twentieth-century audience, this appeal to tradition was paramount – notwithstanding that some of the antecedents underlying the *Queen's Beasts* figures were actually very recent, such as the Windsor badge held by the griffin, adopted by King George VI only fifteen years earlier to bring the imagery in line with the family's newly adopted, more English-sounding name. Heraldry's reimagining of the past, by dispelling griffins' prior negative connotations, facilitates the seamless adaptation of the heraldic griffin into many contexts.

Medieval Badges

The griffin, in its heraldic profile, features on at least eighteen badges, akin to brooches, the small mass-produced cast lead tokens acquired in secular settings and by pilgrims at churches across western Europe.[15] Often dismissed because of their abundant, seemingly disposable quality, they were crafted with the explicit knowledge that they could be transported across cultural boundaries by the wearer. Some badge imagery is strongly localized, as in the scallop shell indicating the pilgrimage destination of St James at Santiago de Compostela, but – no surprise – that's not the case with the griffin badges. As seen on other small portable objects, the griffin motif here seems to be more metamorphic, a symbol that spoke fluently to international audiences – known find-spots include the Netherlands, Belgium, France and England. We don't know whether the individuals who acquired these inexpensive items thought of them in ways comparable to our modern sense of a souvenir or as something more like an amulet, or an admixture of the two.[16] Some scholars have focused on the possibility that griffin badges may have been intended to offer apotropaic force.[17] The find-spot of the original version of this particular fourteenth-century badge on a riverbank in London is typical, since many have been found on riverbanks (illus. 90).[18] While there is a long tradition of magical thinking around the act of placing amulets in and near water – for example, the apotropaic scrolls deposited in ancient Roman waterways – we don't have enough evidence of similar riverside finds of badges with griffins to confirm a meaningful pattern. Another possibility, not exclusive to the protective

90 Twenty-first-century replica of 14th-century badge or brooch, excavated from Billingsgate foreshore, London, lead–tin alloy.

ARRIANI
NICOMEDENSIS,
NOVI XENOPHON-
TIS, APPEL-
LATI.
De rebus geſtis Alexãdri Magni regis
Macedonum libri octo, ſumma dili-
gentia ad Græcum exemplar emen-
dati, & innumeris quibus antea ſca-
tebant mendis repurgati.

BARTHOLOMAEO FACIO
uiro doctiſſimo Interprete.

VIRTVTE DVCE. COMITE FORTVNA.

APVD SEB. GRY-
PHIVM LVGD.
M. D. LII.

91 Sebastian Gryphius's printer mark, on the title page of Arrian, De rebus gestis Alexandri Magni *(Deeds of Alexander the Great, but usually called the* Anabasis*), printed in 1552.*

amulet idea, is that griffins badges were heraldic devices of the Montagu Earls of Salisbury and King Edward III, but whether that coat of arms is the source is debated.[19] These accessories continue to acquire new audiences and meanings, for the badge illustrated here is a recent replica crafted with exquisite care for use by historical re-enactors.

Trade Guilds and Trademarks

The heraldic griffin was readily repurposed as a trademark, and one of many instances would be the late sixteenth-century cloth seal that announced a textile as coming from Colchester. The mark indicates the 'brand' of cloth and assured the buyer of its quality but was also part of the taxation system. Colchester clothmakers' choice of the griffin seal seems inspired by Edward III's role in establishing the town's cloth trade by bringing a cohort of skilled workers from the Low Countries. The seal's reverse inscription uses the Dutch word *draet* (thread), suggesting the clothworkers had recently arrived in England.[20] Just as these Anglo-Dutch cloth makers marked their products with the griffin, the creature has been a printer's mark from the early decades of printing books.[21] Printers' marks often integrated mythological creatures, such as griffins and unicorns, drawing from the visual language of heraldry.[22] Seen here on the title page to Sebastian Gryphius' 1552 printing of Arrian's *Deeds of Alexander the Great*, the griffin is poised to take flight from the remarkably book-like pedestal it happily perches upon, advertising the Lyon-based German printer's personal and professional 'brand' (illus. 91). The tradition of griffins as printers' marks has occasionally met with some snark, as in this nineteenth-century assessment: 'As may be imagined, it [the griffin] does not make a pretty device, although under the circumstances its employment is perhaps permissible.'[23] In Gryphius's case, the conceit takes its cue from the printer's name, mirroring the use in heraldry of the griffin by the noble von Greiffenclau family of Mainz, mentioned earlier in connection with a famous drinking horn, and any number of 'allusive arms' referencing the griffin, to wit those of the Silesian Griffen or Neapolitan Griffa

92 Creature commonly known to be a griffin, sculpture by Charles Bell Birch, Temple Bar memorial, London, 1880, bronze.

families. Of course, 'Griffin' in various spellings serves as both a first and last name more widely, turning up as 'Grifin' several times in the Domesday Book of 1086 and a related lineage from the Welsh personal name Gruffudd.[24] In the United States, its use as a first name climbed during the 1990s and has remained fairly popular since then.

Sculptures, commonly known as 'griffins', stand as markers at the entrances to the City of London, the historic commercial core of the broader metropolis. Heraldic-looking in their stylized silhouette, they show another way this formulation connects with the world of business (illus. 92). The first griffin monument was erected in 1880, following the removal of the seventeenth-century Temple Bar gateway. Further griffin statues were added to other City of London entrances in the 1960s. These markers' serpentine, dragon-like character reflects the temporary broadening of what was labelled a griffin, mirrored in a heraldry manual from 1909, which warns that 'in the popular mind any heraldic monster is generically termed a griffin.'[25] The tradition of calling the boundary-marking statues 'griffins' resonates with the special, distinctly mercantile role of the City of London's urban landscape: a guidebook from the turn of the twentieth century notes that, while the sculpture resembles a dragon, the label of griffin might be more appropriate 'to typify the rapacity of its [the City's] citizens'.[26] Given that both mythic beasts share the role of guarding wealth, the fluidity in naming for these City of London statues isn't surprising; our next chapter includes another very dragon-like creature labelled a griffin from around the same time (see illus. 95).

Other places, such as Perugia, have adopted the griffin as an emblem.[27] Griffins feature on large-scale works in the city, notably the Fontana Maggiore completed in 1278.[28] Medieval Perugia's other main fountain, sculpted by Arnolfo di Cambio, also included a griffin.[29] That second fountain was later dismantled, and its griffin was long misinterpreted as an Etruscan work. Griffins appear all around Perugia, even on seals for individuals ranging from financiers to butchers, as commercial tradespeople assumed the emblem of the city as part of their identity.[30]

Heraldic griffins also become identified with specific brands, in another facet of their mercantile connotations. As the public face of a business's identity, the motif hints at loftiness but does so with a vagueness that is particularly useful to marketers. The griffin appears today on many corporate logos such as that of Chrome Industries, a company known for its bike messenger bags, and based in the Pacific Northwest (illus. 93). Out of the many ways in which griffins have been depicted across time, the iteration chosen for the Chrome brand is the one most typical in branding, being grounded in the visual formulas of heraldry – not least in the stark silhouette and pose. The form's blockiness modernizes it, with an edgy appeal evoking the avant-garde of De Stijl or Russian Constructivism, which also resonates in the black, red and white palette. The griffin as corporate branding continues many aspects of its earlier use, tapping into its aspirational

93 Chrome Industries logo.

94 Mascot of William & Mary, a university in Williamsburg, Virginia.

attributes: Chrome's website features it alongside its 'flying lions' clothing line and the work of 'a collective of artists that inspire us'. Other prominent instances of the griffin as a corporate logo even more directly tap into heraldic roots. Vauxhall Motors' visual branding, despite numerous mergers, has kept the griffin derived from the arms of Falkes de Bréauté, whose manor's name over time shifted by the thirteenth century from Fulk's Hall to Vauxhall, the London neighbourhood where the company was founded.

Mascots

Griffins continue to be domesticated in the twenty-first century as American school and college mascots, and many schools, such as Reed College, use heraldic versions as a crest. In a recent analysis of high school mascots across the United States, sixty griffin mascots were counted, and other mythical beasts, including the dragon and the phoenix, were also popular choices.[31] Athletics mascots often date back decades, but not always. The College of William & Mary in Williamsburg, Virginia, picked a griffin mascot in 2010 (illus. 94), following an NCAA (National Collegiate Athletic Association) ruling that their former mascot's portrayal of a Native American was offensive. As the only U.S. college to have arms granted by the College of Arms in London, from 1694, tradition is a key part of the school's 'brand'. Their decision process took years, with a brief, ill-considered flirtation with a frog mascot, and a time with no mascot, before the school settled on the griffin. The mascot selection committee heavily relied on social media, and the goals underlying the ultimate choice become clear in the awards the committee won for alumni relations – a key constituency when refashioning a contested collective identity.[32] University president Taylor Reveley articulated the official rationale for the new mascot at its unveiling ceremony: 'The Griffin . . . unites strength with intelligence, recalls our royal origins and speaks to our deep roots in American history.'[33] The hybrid creature was further parsed in publicity as conjoining, in the eagle, the United States and, in the lion, the English monarchy, which founded the school in 1693 – though one could opine that if it represents the English coming to the New World, we have another quintessentially acquisitive griffin. Ultimately, the college's verbiage implies the same strategically selective approach to heraldry that was used to put an exclusively positive spin on the *Queen's Beasts* griffin.

Jon Stewart, former host of the *Daily Show* and a William & Mary alumnus, took a different approach after his alma mater's announcement, suggesting that '*griffin* . . . is apparently ancient Greek for the rare pantsless tailed eagle'.[34] His commentary on this 'mythological perversion' gets more ribald from there, and that was only the beginning of the sexualization of this school mascot – all the more amusing for the fact that the griffin had likely been chosen in part for its capacity to be inoffensive yet somehow vaguely impressive. Part of what inspires these jokes is the university's playful, cartoon-like mascot, a costumed performer at athletic competitions. However, when a bronze sculpture arrived on campus, more naturalistically rendered than the mascot figure, a minor controversy arose. Unveiled in 2018, this sculpture had been purchased at auction from another school. Columnists for William & Mary's student newspaper criticized the statue's 'anatomically graphic' details, on the grounds that the 'gendering' of the statue gendered the university itself as male.[35] Their concern lays bare the way in which a school mascot, here the griffin, is expected to present a collective identity. In this way, the school mascot's aim at common purpose – not least rousing the fans in a range of competitive sports – is revealed to be distantly connected to the ways in which heraldry evolved to clarify identity in combat and rally troops to a common cause.

Chapter Fourteen
Adventures with Griffins

How was the water, which came from the griffin's mouth, held in the small basin, which had no aperture at all? Or did the water change its direction to escape? But how could the water flow back from the basin's lips? He marvelled at where the water went. Suddenly the griffin stamped away from where it was standing, crossed the river and stood there.

***Velthandros and Chrysandza*, a late Byzantine novel**

Griffins can be spotted roaming many strange and fearsome landscapes in medieval and early modern narratives. Their very presence works like a signpost, indicating remote lands in early epic adventure tales, courtly imagery and saints' lives, and their supposed remains (griffin claws and eggs) could testify to the veracity of these stories. The griffin's part in these processes of cultural remixing is actually not so different from some of the depictions we have already explored, such as those in the *Alexander Romance* cycles, and a closer look at the creature's role will illustrate the ways in which such narratives of exploration and identity continue to be redrawn.

Griffins of Epic and Travellers' Tales

In hagiographical works like the *Life of Saint Imerius*, griffins embody the dangers posed to travellers in remote lands, and likewise in the Middle High German epic *Kudrun* (*c.* 1250) griffins establish the heroic bona fides of the central character. Near *Kudrun*'s beginning, a griffin abducts young Prince Hagen and flies off to offer him as a tasty morsel to griffin nestlings. Baby griffins apparently like to play with their food, for one nestling then soars away with the prince. Hagen escapes, finding his way to a cave inhabited by three princesses, fellow fugitives from the griffins. In due time Hagen manages to slay the griffins, rescuing himself and the princesses, launching his career as a hero.[1] *Kudrun* enjoyed a nineteenth-century revival in several operas and other adaptations. This lithograph from circa 1900 (illus. 95) shows the young hero at the crucial moment, killing his foe, but the pastel glow of the landscape, and Hagen's whimsical, medievalizing garments and armour, further displace any danger to a safely distant dreamscape. As with the City of London griffin monument from about the same time (see illus. 92), the creature is rendered

95 Young Hagen killing the griffin, scene from Kudrun *(c. 1250), lithograph published* c. *1900.*

96 Griffins of Bactria, miniature from Sir John Mandeville, Voyages (Livre des merveilles)*, c. 1410–12 manuscript of 14th-century text.*

with a quite dragon-like appearance, demonstrating the shifting boundaries around what gets the label 'griffin'.

Medieval travel writing, such as the texts ascribed to Sir John Mandeville (probably mid- to late fourteenth century) and Marco Polo (*c.* 1254–*c.* 1324), regularly interweaves the griffin into what we'd now consider a mix of fiction and factual reportage.[2] Depending on expectations, such a blend might seem delightful or exasperating, and in the case of the Mandeville's *Livre des merveilles*, even the existence of the author is disputed (illus. 96). A French manuscript shows griffins fighting centaurs in Bactria: the standard habitat (remote northern or eastern locale) and activity (combat) for the creature. The text avouches that their size and power is eight times that of lions and ten times that of eagles; the illumination emphasizes details like the aquiline talons raised in attack and beaks open to screech, their arcing tongues protrude in a manner reminiscent of the griffin protomes from ancient Greece (see illus. 13). These early travel memoirs catalogued griffins among the marvels of the East, but as we will see, the existence of griffins would soon come under scrutiny.

A Backwards Lady

The focus on griffins' violence lightens up considerably as we look to works coming from late medieval courtly contexts – at last, griffins start to have fun. We see evidence of this shift in an item that initially might seem strictly religious, a

97 Alms purse, c. 1330–40, embroidered silk.

trapezoidal satchel made in Paris, circa 1330–40 (illus. 97). Objects of this sort are referred to as 'alms purses', but they likely served that ongoing human need to carry around odds and ends. Its decoration – rich grey-green silk interthreaded with gold and silver – renders a woman sitting backwards astride a griffin. Her bow aims at a little rabbit under the griffin, and a haloed angel looks down from the upper register. Previously, this imagery has been interpreted according to religious allegory as a scene of chastity defeating lust, with none other than the Angel of the Revelation above; here we'll consider an alternative.[3] Imagery of a woman riding a griffin in reverse is rare, and no instances are convincingly tied to a specific religious significance. For instance, the inventory of Louis, Count of Anjou, from around 1360, mentions an aquamanile with this form, but this does not necessarily link that griffin and backwards rider to an ecclesiastical context, since, as we have seen, aquamanilia were used in courtly settings, too.[4] On the contrary, evidence suggests the design on the purse is worldly rather than religious in its message. While in the nineteenth century this purse was linked to the medieval Comtesse de Bar, no proof supports that connection. In fact, it is more likely to have been the possession of an aristocratic man, based on several medieval depictions of young noblemen holding similar purses.[5] In fourteenth-century Paris, when this object was crafted, there was a flourishing industry that produced alms purses using materials that mimicked luxurious textiles loosely termed 'saracen' in medieval sources.[6] Taken together, these details suggest that overturning the moralizing interpretation of the purse's image might be in order; we might, instead, argue the scene speaks in the sly language of courtly love. The backwards position (as an inversion of norms) of the woman is generally associated with beings such as demons in medieval imagery, and naughty details as in the rabbit – *con* in Old French, a word that was also slang for female genitalia – support this explanation.[7] The griffin was paired with other aspects of this worldly luxury-loving milieu to such an extent that we might wonder whether this purse's scene could even possess an association with a more amorous type of adventure.

Griffins in Love

Griffins gain a speaking role in *Minne* tapestries, the sumptuous hangings from the German courtly love tradition. On a fifteenth-century hanging from Basel, a lean, lusciously plumed griffin strides between a man and woman as graceful banderoles report their conversation – a little like speech bubbles today (illus. 98).[8] Following an ancient trope – disputations on the nature of love – the tapestry's figures join the age-old argument. The fashionable man implores, 'Lady bestow upon me your love,' but his florid chivalric sentiments get him nowhere, for the woman retorts, 'The griffin here tells me of the trick that true love on earth no more exists.'[9] The griffin often connoted love's duplicity in the *Minne* tradition.[10] Alternatively, it might be seen here as giving supernatural force to the woman's pronouncement, as if the griffin has crossed from the world of truth to the world of appearances with this dire warning.[11] The same beast features in verbal skirmishes between lovers in other fifteenth-century tapestries from Basel; in one a griffin and two dragon-like beasts roam among a man and woman, who claim in the banderoles to 'master with my love, wild animals and also man'.[12] Part of courtly love's exotic menagerie, griffins were a component of what made *Minne* tapestries appealing to the emerging class of affluent merchants of that time.[13] This quality bridged social distinctions, a parallel in the adoption of the heraldic griffin within the aspirational realm of contemporary advertising.

98 Fragment of Minneteppich *(Courtly Love Tapestry), c. 1450, silk, linen and wool.*

From Relic to Curiosity: Souvenir Griffin Claws

However, at times, the exotic allure of the griffin assumed a different function. In addition to the painted, sculpted and woven representations already discussed, some objects inside churches were considered to be actual griffin claws, precious evidence of remote adventures.[14] Such an artefact now housed in a museum was once treasured as a griffin claw at an important English pilgrimage site (illus. 99). The silver band around the base bears an inscription that proclaims it 'the claw of a griffin sacred to the blessed Cuthbert of Durham' (GRYPHI UNGUIS DIVO CUTHBERTO DUNELMENSI SACER). The inscribed band was added circa 1600 but likely copies an earlier medieval inscription. The Durham church treasury inventoried two griffin claws as well as three griffin eggs as early as 1383, and while griffin claws are catalogued in numerous other medieval European churches, ostrich eggs venerated as griffin eggs are likely a uniquely English medieval phenomenon, though oddly enough there could be long past Minoan antecedents.[15] By the fourteenth century, some treasuries' 'griffin claws' – along with other eagerly procured curiosities such as ostrich eggs and coconuts – were being used as reliquaries, though the church forbade their use as chalices.[16] A telling corollary is the reliquaries enshrining human remains – the human body part most often given its own reliquary is the arm.[17] Just as these arms emphasize the saint's capacity for good works, the claw spotlights the griffin's frightening imagined ability to harm.

The griffin claw probably left Durham during the Reformation, and it eventually ended up in the British Museum, where the nineteenth-century antiquarian Sir Hercules Read recognized it as the horn of an ibex.[18] The intermediary between Cuthbert's shrine and museum display was likely the endlessly acquisitive Sir Robert Cotton (d. 1631), because a listing of London libraries first published in 1708 follows its mention of Cotton's manuscripts by describing his collection as also including

> other great rarities, taken notice of by very few who have seen that place. There are many old reliques which belonged to the Monasteries here in England before the Dissolution. Among others, the claw of a griffin with a silver hoop, on the great end of it a Saxon inscription; but I take it rather to be the horn of some animal.[19]

99 'Griffin's claw' of St Cuthbert, medieval with c. *1600 silver mount on ibex horn.*

Its sacred meaning fell away as it became valued instead as a precious secular commodity, a marker of Cotton's learning and means as part of his Cabinet of Wonders (*Wunderkammer*), the idiosyncratic personal displays then in vogue. His grandson donated his collection to what would become the British Museum, and today it is catalogued merely as 'animal remains'.[20] A similar transformation of status is witnessed by Lady Montagu, who mentions in a letter from 1716 going to see a German church's 'Relicks', and after being shown one, 'could not forbear asking the reverend Priest that shew'd it, whether the Griffin was a Saint. This Question almost put him beside his Gravity, but he answer'd, they only kept it as a curiosity.'[21]

The Claws of St Imerius and Huon of Bordeaux

The griffin claw was just one of many rare and precious holdings in the treasury of Cuthbert's shrine, an indicator of Durham's pre-eminence as the most visited northern English pilgrimage destination. Sometimes, though, a griffin claw relic could seem to offer tangible evidence of specific miraculous events from a saint's life. The 'griffin claw' displayed in the Swiss town of Saint-Imier was seen as a memento from St Imerius' conquest of a griffin, an act demonstrating his saintliness that also happened to yield a thrillingly exotic object to attract pilgrims. The *Life of Saint Imerius of Immertal*, a text copied circa 1200, describes his encounter with a ferocious griffin en route to the Holy Land. After subduing the creature – testifying to the saint's ability to conquer any adversary, whether earthly or spiritual – Imerius claimed its claw, with his heroism converting the pagans living nearby. The saint's *Life* goes on to affirm that this hard-won claw was the very one exhibited at his pilgrimage site until its disappearance in 1793.[22] A griffin's claw serves as a hero's trophy in other medieval texts. A poem recounting the adventures of a valiant knight, Huon de Bourdeaux, was first written in the thirteenth century but continued to be reprised even two centuries later, making the griffin ever more fearsome, gradually shifting from a more aquiline to leonine depiction.[23] An object displayed as a griffin claw in Paris's Sainte-Chapelle was considered by some viewers to be the very claw taken by the poem's hero, Huon, though also linked to the Crusader Godfrey of Bouillon.[24]

The Castle of Love

If we shift our attention to the eastern Mediterranean, similar features emerge in a Late Byzantine novel, *Velthandros and Chrysandza*. Early in the story, our hero, Velthandros, comes upon the 'Castle of Love'. Being 'remarkable, glorious, and born to the purple', Velthandros bravely enters and encounters a fountain betiding his fantastical setting. Its most wondrous feature, it turns out, is a griffin. After protesting an inability to describe such a fountain, the narrator delves nonetheless into a prolix account:

> A carved griffin was standing there with extended wings and its back arched to a level with them. Its tail was bent round to its head. In its front paws it held a beautiful round basin carved from a precious stone. Water came from its mouth and flowed into the basin without the smallest drop falling down to the ground. For some time Velthandros stood contemplating the griffin's construction and the strange property of the water. How was the water, which came from the griffin's mouth, held in the small basin, which had no aperture at all? Or did the water change its direction to escape? But how could the water flow back from the basin's lips? He marvelled at where the water went. Suddenly the griffin stamped away from where it was standing, crossed the river and stood there.[25]

With that final surprise the griffin transforms from an enigmatic sculpture into a moving creature and sets the terms of the adventure the protagonist is undertaking. Western medieval romances likely influenced this Byzantine text, where griffins mark the transition to the world of the fantastic, but also reprise the pattern seen in Aelian, Herodotus and the like of writing the griffin not as a creature, but as an artistic invention.

The Legendary Griffins of California

Griffins announce a formidable alien landscape into early modern times. An example that epitomizes this, and resonates in unexpected ways into the present day, is Garci Rodríguez de Montalvo's Castilian text from 1510, *Las Sergas de Esplandián*. The tale includes the knight Esplandián's adventures on a fictional island called California, ruled over by Queen Calafia. Montalvo's California is filled with 'an amazing abundance of gold and precious stones', and griffins 'suited to the ruggedness of the terrain' guard the island's riches – an echo of medieval lapidary texts, and ultimately Herodotus.[26] The island's warrior women feed the griffins a diet of 'captured men and the boys they bore'.[27] This baleful place is defined – for men at least – by the hybrid beasts' violence, for

> every man who ventured onto the island was immediately killed and devoured by the griffins; and even though they became stuffed, they never for that reason stopped seizing them, carrying them aloft as they flew through the air, and, when tired of carrying them, dropping them to their certain deaths.[28]

While their vile temperament and unquenchable enthusiasm for guarding gold are well-established clichés by this time, griffins serving Amazonian-type female fighters is a new twist.

Montalvo invented the names of the island California and Queen Calafia, which in their aural intimation of the word 'caliph' would convey the locale's remote and enticing nature to his audience in sixteenth-century Spain.[29] Esplandián's exploits were so popular that in Cervantes's *Don Quixote* they come up as the prime example of the literary confections that inspired the protagonist's chivalric fantasies (pt I, ch. 6). Not only fictional explorers were inspired by this book: real-world toponyms still betray its influence on Spanish conquistadors in the New World. In 1524 Hernán Cortés wrote a report of a land mass he thought was an island that seemed to reflect key details from Montalvo's account of Queen Calafia's realm. The toponym Cortés gave it, California, has stuck.[30] In this way the U.S. state of California and Mexico's Baja California likely received their name from a fictional place where griffins served as a warrior queen's brutal minions.[31]

This conjunction of history, fantasy and exploration is the point of departure for the resplendent 2017 painting by Walton Ford titled *Grifo de California* (illus. 100). Ford fashioned his griffin from two animals indigenous to the state – the California condor and the mountain lion – conjuring both a sense of the specific place and of wonder. The composite creature is incorporated into other paintings of Ford's same series, such as the one soaring over power lines in the recognizably Californian landscape of *Isla de California*.[32] His exquisite attention to detail invites us to think of the invented setting as 'real' and at the same time

100 Walton Ford, Grifo de California, *2017, watercolour, gouache and ink on paper.*

subverts those expectations with the hybrid beast inhabiting it. Ford teasingly conveys a sense of authority, too, by taking a cue from early modern natural history and mock-labelling this exceptionally rare specimen with a handwritten 'Grifo de California 1533' – the date referring to the time of early Spanish intrusions in Baja California.[33] Another layer of inspiration might come from Aelian, whom Walton Ford has mentioned repeatedly as a source for his work. Aelian's third-century CE text describes griffins with the same palette of black, white, red and blue as in the twenty-first-century painting.[34] Part of what imbues *Grifo de California* with its beguiling combination of wit and majesty is how it pushes against our boundaries regarding the fictive in our understanding of the world, all the while commenting on a lesser-known bit of history.

A New Questioning

Doubts about the existence of griffins intensified following the era of Cortés, as evident in Lady Montagu's teasing of the cleric about his 'griffin claw'. Sir Thomas Browne's popular seventeenth-century work debunking 'Vulgar Errors' initially observes, 'That there are Griffins in Nature, that is a mixt and dubious Animal . . . many affirm, and most, I perceive, deny not.' He himself, however, finds strong reason to deny, and then systematically obliterates, earlier suppositions about the creature's existence.[35] Yet the nineteenth-century naturalist M. Roulin, who established the species taxonomy for the South American mammal the tapir, opined that the tapir may have inspired classical depictions of the griffin, a theory then adopted in an 1858 work devoted to 'Popular Errors Explained'.[36]

By 1725, even a heraldry manual is willing to emphatically state, 'A griffon is an imaginary chimerical animal, never to be found anywhere but in painting, feign'd by the Ancients.'[37] Little more than two centuries earlier, Leonardo da Vinci had encapsulated this way of thinking about fictive animals as chimeras. In his writings, gone is the speculation about exotic realms and peculiar habits typical of medieval bestiaries. In its place we find prosaic advice to artists as to how to imbue composite creatures with convincing naturalism. He suggests a dragon, for instance, could be assembled from a laundry list of disparate animal features including a lion's eyebrows and a porcupine's ears.[38] Leonardo's preliminary drawing of a horseman fighting a griffin renders the latter in the cursory lines of a sketch, but nonetheless articulates the powerful leonine rear legs as the beast rears up, and the swipe of a formidable front paw.[39] A late fifteenth-century engraving by Martin Schongauer shows a stilted oddball creature that is part of the artist's wider fascination with chimeras (illus. 101).[40] His engraving, usually entitled *Griffin*, reminds us again that the term comprises a range of winged animal hybrids and embodies Leonardo's artistic procedure for creating chimeras from composite parts.[41] The long, curving tongue emerging from the aquiline beak reminds us of many prior images of griffins, but these elements are affixed to a body that now seems a humorously idiosyncratic combination of animal attributes.

101 Martin Schongauer, The Griffin, c. *1470–91, engraving.*

102 One of two griffins at the pedestrian entrance of the Mandalay Bay Resort and Casino, Las Vegas, Nevada, 2016.

Other griffins can seem like a loose riff on a now-familiar schema, such as the pair that serve as entry sentinels to the rarely walked but often photographed pedestrian entrance to Las Vegas's Mandalay Bay Resort, built in 1999 (illus. 102). The casino company's president envisioned the resort complex thus: 'These are buildings with a story line . . . like a movie set come alive . . . it's part Java, part Bali . . . and a whole lot Shangri-La.'[42] This branding is clear in the choice of Mandalay for the resort's name – former royal capital of Myanmar, then Burma. Despite a tragic mass shooting, the casino continued to embrace its carefree blend of exotic elements, where even in the Nevada desert, griffin imagery is used to welcome visitors into a realm of fantasy.

Chapter Fifteen

Modern Marvels:

The Griffin Imagery of Carroll and Rowling

They very soon came upon a Gryphon, lying fast asleep in the sun. (If you don't know what a Gryphon is, look at the picture.)
Lewis Carroll, *Alice's Adventures in Wonderland* (1865)

Here again we find the notion that seeing is believing with griffins, whereby the Gryphon character is introduced in *Alice's Adventures in Wonderland*, the children's classic from 1865 written by Charles Dodgson under his pseudonym, Lewis Carroll. Starting there and moving into the present with the work of J. K. Rowling, we will see the continued transformation of the idea and image of griffins in literature and popular culture. Earlier views of a griffin's identity deriving from its visual image, or the griffin as an epitome of valour, are now playfully reworked or even subverted in media as diverse as wizarding world fan fiction and Disney Jell-O adverts.

From Tenniel to Disney

The character Alice begins her famous story posing the excellent question, what is the use of a book without pictures? Illustrations by Sir John Tenniel have been integral to the story's cultural force over 150 years (illus. 103–4). The creature's appearances in the book diverge appreciably from prior griffin imagery: the first imbues the Gryphon with the indolent physicality of a sleeping cat, affirming yet domesticating its leonine traits. Tenniel's other two drawings render the creature with a particularly upright gait, which reinforces Carroll's portrayal of a personality that is animated both by a slight haughtiness and an eagerness to engage with Alice. Earlier literary griffins aren't sufficiently developed as characters to possess attributes such as haughtiness – they mostly occupy themselves with trying to harm the hero or more generally being signposts for a certain kind of foreign savagery – but that particular personality trait might be seen as a clever nod to their older association with luxury. The quixotic Queen of Hearts dispatches the Gryphon, with Alice, off to the Mock Turtle, culminating in the two fabulous creatures dancing the Lobster Quadrille around Alice amid lots of absurd prattling. The illustration of the Gryphon with Alice and the Mock Turtle conveys an easy sociability, subverting

103 John Tenniel, 'The Gryphon', illustration for Lewis Carroll, Alice's Adventures in Wonderland *(1865).*

earlier iterations of the hybrid beast for whom Alice and the Mock Turtle would have been considered a tasty snack – part of the inversion of expectations that creates a 'Wonderland'. In the final paragraphs of *Alice's Adventures* the Gryphon reappears briefly, but it is Alice's elder sister who hears 'the shriek of the Gryphon' as she drifts into a reverie contemplating Alice's odd tale. This returns to earlier traditions of the griffin as a supercharged predatory bird, such as in the medieval *Kudrun*, with the more conventional version of the griffin belonging to the older (and more acculturated into conventional thinking) child.[1]

Carroll's choice of archaic spelling, *gryphon*, is telling. Historically the word has a considerable number of spellings: the variants *gryps*, *grypho* and *griffo* all appear in Latin texts from medieval England.[2] In the Middle English manuscripts of Chaucer's *The Knight's Tale*, *grifphon*, *griffon* and *grefoun* are all used (and you might have noticed in Chapter Eleven that the Middle English version of the *Tractatus de armis* used both *gryffyn* and *gryfon*). Other Middle English texts, however, as part of the fallout from the Norman invasion, follow the medieval French convention, using the letter *y* – which is used in Latin to render the letter upsilon found in words assimilated from Greek – instead of *i*. This usage later reverts, and the result of the

104 John Tenniel, 'The Gryphon, Alice and the Mock Turtle', illustration for Lewis Carroll, Alice's Adventures in Wonderland *(1865).*

shift back to the internal *i* is that the *y* spelling in English comes to seem redolent of the past. Looking at later mentions, in Mandeville's *Travels*, Milton's *Paradise Lost* and the letters of Lady Montagu, for example, a similar heterogeneity of spelling persists, with, respectively, 'griffouns', 'Gryphon' and 'Griffin'.[3] Perhaps because of the influence of Carroll, as well as its wider bygone connotations, recent fantasy authors typically prefer the *y* with *ph* spelling variant, for instance the popular *Mage Wars* series by Mercedes Lackey, beginning with *The Black Gryphon* published in 1994.

105 Lewis Carroll (pseud. Charles Dodgson), 'The Mock Turtle and the Gryphon dance the Lobster Quadrille for Alice', drawing from the manuscript 'Alice's Adventures Under Ground', c. 1862–4.

The Gryphon, already with that spelling, appears in the preliminary version of Lewis Carroll's text, the manuscript from 1862 to 1864 entitled 'Alice's Adventures Under Ground', suggesting the creature was integral from the start to the world of fantasy Alice visits, and Chapter Twelve explored a possible early inspiration (see illus. 80). Carroll drew the pen-and-ink illustrations in his manuscript (illus. 105) presented to young Alice Liddell, the book's inspiration, and the author's Gryphon looks decidedly like a rat improbably granted a finch beak and front claws.[4] Tenniel's Gryphon illustrations for the book's publication in 1865 differ to a marked extent. The Gryphon appeared in most later retellings of *Alice's Adventures in Wonderland*, including the gamut of very different films from 1931, 1933, 1966, 1972, 1985 and 1999. A few *Alice* films omit the Gryphon entirely, namely the first short film from 1903 and the 1951 animated Disney version. For the Disney film, the Gryphon was developed in preliminary drawings, and while it did not make the final film, it was later revived for an *Alice in Wonderland*-themed Jell-O television advert that ran in 1956, likely to accompany the weekly Disney show, in which the Gryphon voice actor delivered lines like, 'So when is the Jell-O party?' with an impressive degree of priggishness, taking his cue from the original story. Although colour mock-up drawings for the original Disney character exist, the advert was broadcast in black and white, as was typical for the time. Disney artists such as David Hall drew inspiration from the compositions of Tenniel's drawings, but the adaptation to animation fundamentally shifted the look of the Gryphon.[5]

'A wilderness of crumbling griffins . . .'

The extent of Carroll's own upending of prior griffin representations becomes clear when we contrast his work written for Alice Liddell with another famous English text published shortly before. In Emily Brontë's *Wuthering Heights* (1847), griffins don't serve as characters, but they do appear as doorway sentinels, helping set the scene of the venerable and blighted farmhouse that lends its name as the novel's title. The first chapter opens with the narrator approaching the dwelling named Wuthering Heights, where above the entrance is etched the date 1500, alongside 'a wilderness of crumbling griffins and shameless little boys'.[6] These griffins' liminality is both literal and figurative. Often marking actual doorways (see illus. 51, 70), the griffin motif functions here as an entry point to Gothic decadence and pathos, which entwines many forms of hybridity, as in Heathcliff's mixed social identities. The inclusion of Wuthering Heights' centuries-old date of construction follows, too, the way the griffin motif's vague, rarefied associations become a ready shorthand for the novel's collapsed gentry – comparable, perhaps, to Walton Ford's choice to inscribe a date from the Age of Exploration on his griffin painting (see illus. 100), or the prevalence of archaizing spellings when griffins appear in fantasy writings. Earlier we saw the griffin's remote habitat accentuated; now their temporal distance becomes a defining quality. Likewise in E. M. Forster's 1908 novel, *A Room with a View*, griffins mark a narrative threshold, setting the stage for how Italy will be a place of transformation for the protagonist: 'It was pleasant to wake up in Florence, to open the eyes upon a bright bare room . . . with a painted ceiling whereon pink griffins and blue amorini [cherubs] sport in a forest of yellow violins and bassoons.'[7]

Even recent fiction, such as the novel *Cloud Cuckoo Land* (2021) by Anthony Doerr, follows this strategy. 'Wild griffins' feature in a vignette from the mysterious ancient Greek text resurfacing throughout its narrative, and griffins get embroidered onto precious garments in a Late Byzantine plot fragment, but Doerr forgoes including griffins in the modern and future lines of the book's almost polyphonic structure.[8]

'Gryffindor, where dwell the brave at heart'

Griffins' venerable heraldic symbolism collides with their tradition in fantasy literature with the arrival in popular culture of a young wizard named Harry Potter. Given the way, for centuries, they worked to usher in the marvellous, it is little surprise that griffins feature in many noteworthy children's books. Space does not permit examining the range of stories here – from *The Chronicles of Narnia* and *The Once and Future King* to, of course, *The Griffin and the Minor Canon*, the nineteenth-century story catapulted back to popularity by Maurice Sendak's 1963 illustrated edition – so we can focus on just one storyworld that has enjoyed an exceptionally wide cultural reach.

The ideal of the griffin is a pervasive undercurrent in J. K. Rowling's books, and though no griffin features in the characters of her original seven-book series, several are sprinkled into descriptions of Hogwarts School of Witchcraft and Wizardry, such as a conveniently 'large stone griffin' that Harry and his friend hide behind in the first book. Rather, the griffin's semantic range infuses the name Gryffindor, one of the four Hogwarts boarding houses and a central feature of the protagonist Harry's identity. The name Gryffindor contains a strong homophonic hint of '*griffon d'or*' (golden griffin), common in French heraldry, but with Rowling's more archaizing spelling. The spectrum of earlier associations, from classical griffins' connection with gold to the way in which heraldic griffins signal bravery and nobility, are conflated through Gryffindor.

Rowling has made clear the central importance of names in her worldbuilding: 'I'm very interested in the power of names and naming and I can't really get to grips with characters until I've settled on their name.'[9] As a new Hogwarts student, Harry frets over which house he will be placed into by the magical Sorting Hat. As the young wizard awaits its verdict, the talking hat pontificates aloud:

> You might belong in Gryffindor,
> Where dwell the brave at heart,
> Their daring, nerve, and chivalry
> Set Gryffindors apart.[10]

Gryffindor values echo the attributes of griffins seen in heraldic texts, as in the *Tractactus de armis*'s declaration, 'To bere a gryffyn in armys is a tokyn of a grete man and a strong fighter' (see illus. 85). Likewise, the use of a golden griffin on armaments (echoed in Gryffindor's house colours of gold and red) appears both in heraldic and literary texts, as in the fifteenth-century *Alliterative Morte Arthure*'s reference to Sir Gawain's armour and its 'gryffoune of golde'.[11] Harry actively seeks his Gryffindor identity from the beginning, pleading successfully with the Hogwarts Sorting Hat when it considers placing him in a rival house to assign him to Gryffindor instead. This collective identity gains additional importance in the final book, *Harry Potter and the Deathly Hallows*, when the inter-house rivalry that had played out before largely in sports and behaviour points becomes a life-or-death conflict that implicates the entire wizarding world.[12] After a period of setbacks and stasis in the narrative, Harry and his fellow Gryffindor Ron retrieve the house founder's sword, an act only possible for a 'true Gryffindor', which the voice inside Harry's head reminds him is defined, as the Sorting Hat had proclaimed, by 'daring, nerve and chivalry'.[13]

The house name leads to an opportunity for a coded bit of wordplay: Dumbledore, Harry's mentor and reputedly a Gryffindor in his student days, has a griffin-figured knocker on his office entrance, making it a 'griffin door'; the films transformed this into a moving griffin stairwell (illus. 106).[14] This assimilation in *Harry Potter and the Chamber of Secrets* is direct: 'Harry saw a gleaming oak door ahead, with a brass knocker in the shape of a griffin. He knew now where he was being taken. This must be where Dumbledore lived.'[15]

In Rowling's richly imagined story, the founders of the four Hogwarts houses are loosely dated to a time over a thousand years ago – hence the archaizing *y* redolent of the medieval context of its founder, Godric Gryffindor – and their characteristics continue to be reflected in their houses' pupils.[16] The namesake Gryffindor championed those of 'mixed blood' in the wizarding world, thus the name Gryffindor – the only one of the four houses linked to an animal hybrid – also links to the duality of the griffin. Harry himself is labelled a 'half-blood', with a 'pureblood' father and a mother from a 'Muggle' (non-magical) family.

Following the original seven-book series, *Fantastic Beasts and Where to Find Them*, first mentioned in passing as a Hogwarts textbook, was later developed by Rowling into a short volume sold to benefit charity. As a humorous send-up of medieval bestiaries, the book includes an entry on griffins, emphasizing their hybridity,

> The griffin originated in Greece and has the front legs and head of a giant eagle, but the body and hind legs of a lion. Like sphinxes . . . griffins are often employed by wizards to guard treasure. Though griffins are fierce, a handful of skilled wizards have been known to befriend one. Griffins feed on raw meat.[17]

106 Griffin doorway in Dumbledore's office, from the set of the Harry Potter Warner Bros. studio tour, London.

Here griffins are catalogued alongside many other magical creatures in a mock pedantic tone, offhandedly dismissing both medieval renderings and modern scientific scepticism alike:

> a glance through Muggle art and literature of the Middle Ages reveals that many of the creatures they now believe to be imaginary were then known to be real. The dragon, the griffin . . . these and more are represented in Muggle works of that period, though usually with almost comical inexactitude.[18]

Nonetheless, the wizarding world copies Muggle practices of using griffins as design elements in grand buildings such as Hogwarts – as we have seen with their role as entrance sentinel for the headmaster's office. The screenplay for the 2018 spin-off movie, *Fantastic Beasts: The Crimes of Grindelwald*, promised a shift from the griffin-as-image trope to grant them live creature status, with a passing reference to 'a snoozing griffin with a bandaged beak' glimpsed in Newt Scamander's basement.[19] Sadly, though, the creature was omitted from the film.

Gryffindor Fandoms

Throughout this book we have seen the ways griffin imagery conveys individual and collective identity, with meanings often tapping into the fictive creature's long-standing connotations with dauntlessness, whether on the helmet of an ancient *thraex* gladiator, a coat of arms in medieval heraldry or a college mascot. This elasticity as a symbol becomes even more clear when we now consider the prominence of Hogwarts house identity in the realms of online fan fiction/ transformative fiction – where Gryffindor courage surfaces regularly as a trope. The power of the griffin to symbolize admired personality traits such as bravery, and the extent to which readers and viewers of Rowling's work have internalized her inventions like Gryffindor, becomes clear in the role of house identity in the Harry Potter fandoms. We have studied the way the image and meaning of the griffin has been repurposed across time and space, and this example takes us into an area of contemporary culture in which the roles of consumer and producer blur, as members of Rowling's audience craft their own narratives, to then be shared freely online.

On a leading fan fiction site, *An Archive of Our Own* (often known as AO3), the Harry Potter fandom remains one of the largest, a pattern mirrored on other fan fiction sites. The scale of engagement with these sites is reflected in raw numbers: AO3 tracked 54.1 million daily views in April 2020, with nearly 433,000 'fanfics' devoted to Rowling's wizarding world having been posted at time of writing.[20] Of those many reimaginings of life at and after Hogwarts, many of the stories that have been awarded the most 'kudos' from readers put the Gryffindor–Slytherin house rivalry at the crux of their narrative, with their primary AO3 content descriptor tag denoting the relationship between Gryffindor Harry Potter and his Slytherin nemesis, Draco Malfoy. In the sprawling online realms of fan fiction, house identity works as a convenient shorthand for personality, so Gryffindor identity has an even more prominent role in characterization within these fan-authored stories (and popular culture more widely) than in Rowling's original works.

The transmission of griffin-related references has frequently been multidirectional. Likewise, many fan fiction authors are forthright about their primary point of inspiration often being other fan-authored works and can be sharply disparaging towards Rowling herself. The author of some of this franchise's most popular fan fiction claims to have initially learned about the Harry Potter characters through the online fan-written lexicon – her awareness of Gryffindor traits such as courage came from fan websites before ever encountering Rowling's books or the films.[21] As media consumers become producers, Gryffindor collective identity is reified in the narrative logic of fan fiction author and their reader communities, where familiar formulae scaffold the new narratives.[22] Rowling herself was fairly groundbreaking in her approval of fan fiction based on her work, and the fan identification with Hogwarts houses is encouraged on the corporate website, which offers the opportunity to take a Sorting Hat quiz.[23] Authored by Rowling, the key adjective the online quiz description connects with Gryffindor is 'brave'.[24] Elsewhere in popular culture, in the U.S. version of the television show *The Office*, the martial-arts-loving Dwight Schrute proudly proclaims himself a member of 'Team Gryffindor' in the 'Beach Games' episode first aired in 2007. His misguided valour is a key part of Schrute's characterization over the show's nine-season arc, proudly announcing for instance that he performed his own circumcision ('Baby Shower' episode, 2008). That this comedic take on Gryffindor works as a joke testifies to how widely disseminated Rowling's creations have become.

107 Harry riding a hippogriff named Buckbeak, in Harry Potter and the Prisoner of Azkaban *(dir. Alfonso Cuarón, 2004).*

The Arrival of the Hippogriff

The hippogriff offers another permutation of the griffin within Rowling's wizarding world. While more ancillary to the plot than the concept of Gryffindor, this hybrid is fascinatingly related to the griffin, for the hippogriff combines a horse and a griffin. This creature has its moment in the spotlight during the franchise's third book and film, *Harry Potter and the Prisoner of Azkaban*, when a hippogriff named Buckbeak (illus. 107) is unjustly sentenced to death, then rescued by the rewinding of time, and finally provides an escape ride for a wrongly accused wizard. Rowling describes Buckbeak as more griffin than horse, with his capacity for flight paramount, and by having a personality that is overbearing and easily provoked to violence. As the Hogwarts care of magical creatures teacher, Hagrid, instructs his pupils in his broad accent, 'firs' thing yeh gotta know abou' hippogriffs is, they're proud . . . don't ever insult one, 'cause it might be the last thing yeh do.'[25] Since the hippogriff lacks a strong visual tradition, the Mexican director of *Prisoner of Azkaban*, Alfonso Cuarón, had latitude in rendering Buckbeak, and he saw its composite nature as fundamental to its identity, possessing 'a mixture of regal elegance, particularly when he is flying, and the clumsy and greedy creature that he becomes back on land'.[26] This blend was achieved, in a process echoing Leonardo da Vinci's insight mentioned earlier, by carefully interweaving attributes of real animals, so the special effects team that created this composite animal, largely through digital tools such as Framestore CFC, studied horsehair and different feather types.[27] The Azkaban film's hybrid is reworked from the book by the addition of a heroic moment, saving two Hogwarts children from a werewolf.

The hippogriff's late arrival to the menagerie of imagined animals is easily overlooked. In interviews J. K. Rowling implies that the hippogriff was part of medieval culture, but the creature first appears in Ludovico Ariosto's sixteenth-century epic poem *Orlando Furioso*.[28] Ariosto's coupling of the real (horse) and fictive (griffin) echoes how his poem both celebrates and satirizes the chivalric tradition. In line with many earlier depictions of griffins, hippogriffs, too, provide an especially exciting form of aerial transportation – all the more fleet for the added horse element. This tradition is observed by *Harry Potter*'s Buckbeak – after all, what is the use of having a hippogriff in a story if not to facilitate daring escapes? By the same token, in the fantasy role-playing game Dungeons & Dragons, griffins (spelled as griffon) and hippogriffs were included from the initial 1974 *Monsters and Treasure* booklet, with the latter especially prized as transportation in online fan discussions. Most portrayals of the hippogriff emphasize an unmatched agility, as in a Gustave Doré illustration (illus. 108). Here Ruggieri, on his hippogriff, comes to the rescue of the emphatically nude Angelica, a scene from Ariosto's tale popular with other nineteenth-century artists. Jean-Auguste-Dominique Ingres' painting from 1819 for the Palace of Versailles' Throne Room may have inspired Doré's composition.

After Ariosto, the hippogriff became enough of a fixture in the cultural imagination that a seventeenth-century dictionary included a definition, calling it

108 Gustave Doré, 'Ruggiero on his hippogriff saving Angelica from the sea monster', illustration from a French edition of Ludovico Ariosto, Orlando Furioso *(1879).*

'a kind of feigned beast, in part horse, in part Griffin'.[29] In the meantime, the beast's invention not until *Orlando Furioso* appears to be somewhat forgotten. Classical mythology has often been more read in compilations rather than by doing a deep dive and directly engaging with earlier writers such as Ovid or Hesiod. In the pre-Internet age, *Bulfinch's Mythology* and other collections were a primary point of contact and inspiration for popular reworkings, bringing together ancient and medieval mythology in an accessible manner.[30] The habitual inclusion of hippogriffs in such collections drives the erroneous impression that the beast has a much longer lineage than it actually does, as assumed by Rowling. Her university education included classical studies, in addition to her primary focus on modern languages, especially French literature, and both fields inform her many reworkings of cultural reference points – from the implications of the name Gryffindor to the hippogriff Buckbeak. While it is easy to envision Rowling as an undergraduate student at the University of Exeter in the 1980s sometimes finding inexpensive mythology anthologies a convenient reference point, today, when information is ever more frequently sought online, this distancing from the literary sources becomes even more pronounced. The most consulted websites have the predictable strengths and shortcomings of crowdsourced work: early in the writing of this book, the Wikipedia page on the hippogriff claimed it appears 'in Ancient Greek folklore'.[31] Even some semi-scholarly works claim an ancient lineage for hippogriffs, and online writings about Buckbeak ascribe all sorts of interesting but incorrect provenances to the creature.[32]

Of course, part of why Rowling's archetypes of Gryffindor and her cadre of imagined creatures resonate so widely is the adept way she recasts long-standing cultural motifs, such as those surrounding the griffin and hippogriff. Yet the path from Herodotus' ancient griffins, continually fighting Arimaspi, to Gryffindor valour and hippogriffs is by no means direct. The griffin's cocktail of two apex predators made its early reputation for raw ferocity near-inevitable, but over time that pugnacity became sublimated, such that what was once just a wanton appetite for violence came to be seen as bravery, especially through representation of the creature in the heraldic tradition. Importantly, heraldry not only supported the development of a more nuanced semantic range for the griffin, but ramified how those meanings could signal both individual and collective identity as an aspirational image and a rallying point. In this way, we see how the popular culture phenomenon of Gryffindor both affirms and transfigures preceding ways of using the griffin as a cultural motif.

Epilogue: Thinking with Griffins

It was a Greek voyager who came here and called it a griffin because of its terrifying appearance . . .
***Asterix and the Griffin* (2021)**

Our wayfinding of the griffin motif has encountered many distinct, intertwining and sometimes even divergent paths. Perhaps this multiplicity arises from the inherent contradiction in their identity, yoking attributes of land-bound and airborne creatures – and this cognitive dissonance opens the images up to many interpretations as we have now seen. The urge to represent these leonine–aquiline composites is remarkably widespread, for our examples encircle much of the global north, encompassing Europe, Asia and North America, and date across 5,000 years.

Yet griffins are as often as not presented as recognizable but otherworldly, situated at a remove from our current space and time. While it is commonplace for fictive creatures to reputedly inhabit the margins of the known world, griffins are particularly prone to this treatment as well as being placed in a legendary past. The choice of 'gryphon' (or the related variant used in the wizarding house Gryffindor), with its archaizing flourish, over 'griffin', is favoured across pop culture references. By the same token in the artist Walton Ford's painting of 2017 a splendid griffin combining native Californian animals gets inscribed with the date 1533 (see illus. 100). Even the well-established entry of the griffin motif into Greek art from the visual culture of ancient Egypt and West Asia has recently been muddled, but the theory proposing Greeks invented griffins based on Central Asian dinosaur bones overlooks key facts.[1] The dinosaur theory's reach is so extensive that it provides the basis for a recent reimagining of the griffin tradition: *Asterix and the Griffin* (2021). In this latest offering in the long-standing French comic book series, the Roman-era Asterix travels eastward to find the griffin. The mysterious beast turns out to be dinosaur remains frozen in an ice-covered lake, yet 'It was a Greek voyager who came here and called it a griffin because of its terrifying appearance . . .'[2] Pazyryk visual language (see Chapter Six) influences the way the griffin – an ancient edifice that emerges when the ice melts – is drawn, and Asterix's adventures entail a generous scattering of references to shamanism as well.

109 The Last Guardian *(2016), video game.*

The perpetual recycling of certain griffin tropes, rather than depleting the range of meanings, instead enriches our interpretative possibilities. Earlier scholarship about griffins typically focused on their kinship with various deities and other lofty associations, explaining them and tracking their dissemination primarily though the world of texts. For example, even the suggestion of classical griffins being inspired by dinosaur bones – despite seeming to be a visual, morphological argument – rests mostly on textual references and ignores thousands of years of prior visual representations of the hybrid. Yet wider methodological shifts in art history have made it increasingly clear that sometimes the world of images leads the way. Only after the griffin developed into a well-loved visual formula do the Greeks and other classical sources craft stories around their image, making it their own. To see is to know a griffin – in many instances examined here from Aelian asserting in the third century that a griffin looks 'just as artists portray it in pictures and sculpture' to Lewis Carroll's 'If you don't know what a Gryphon is, look at the picture.' Texts often reference the griffin more as an image than a creature; this pattern embraces writers as varied as the classical Greek historian Herodotus writing of griffins on cauldrons and architectural ornament or the English Gothic novelist Emily Brontë's placement of griffins on the house Wuthering Heights to evoke an atmosphere of decayed grandeur. This framing technique, situating griffins in the past, is adopted even in a video game released in 2016, *The Last Guardian*, for the gameplay unfolds through the recollections of an older man (illus. 109). It also shows the cultural reach of the theme of guardian griffins, for this much-anticipated and popular release for PlayStation 4 is anchored in the relationship of a protective griffin-like titular character named Trico and a boy. Created by Japan Studio and GenDesign, its Japanese title translates as *Trico the Great Man-Eating Eagle*, and gameplay includes phrases such as 'great man-eating beast', making its ties to griffin tradition even more apparent.[3]

The heterogeneity of griffin images makes them challenging to categorize easily, but the most persistent attributes of the griffin motif are a startling cluster of themes: safeguarding/violence, transcendence, riches and moral peril. The staying power of griffins' eternal conflict with the Arimaspi as a literary reference might owe something to its barebones structure, making it both highly portable and malleable. Like the cliché of the popularity of cat videos on the Internet, a tightly circumscribed set of actions are intrinsic to their appeal, and that very narrative paucity leaves the creature more open to be reimagined by viewers and makers.[4] The simplicity of the plot recounted by Herodotus – griffins fight Arimaspi for gold, hit repeat – readily distils down to stock attributes assigned to the hybrid creature, such as violence and greed. Their thin backstory also allow griffins to easily blend with other images that possess a more specific significance, as when the griffin represents Nemesis, the goddess of retributive justice, whenever paired with a wheel of fortune for their ancient Roman audience (see illus. 22). The qualities of transcendence and transformation attributed to griffins in art arise mostly from the possibilities hinted at in their supernatural status uniting creatures of land or air. Conveying divinity across the heavens indicates this special role of griffins: at their most inspirational, they can symbolize the power to transcend our earthbound limitations. Basely violent impulses get revamped in heraldry into rarefied virtues like bravery and nobility; this, in turn, shapes how they are used in commercial branding and as athletics mascots. Earlier art historians might have been inclined to emphasize interpretations of the griffin that, for example, highlight their connection to the mythic or religious (for example, Christian moralizing or classical Apollonian associations) or testify to the specific kinds of cultural transmission privileged in scholarly discourse. This more text-based understanding does not adequately explain the durability of the griffin motif into the present. Looking at a wider range of representations here has clarified that the significance of the griffin comes primarily from visual and material culture.

The frequency on objects like coins, small bronzes and furnishings from antiquity to the present of this imagery is remarkable; for instance, a recent search of the British Museum online collections catalogue for objects with 'griffin' as their subject yielded 1,454 items, mostly representing what has too often been dismissed as 'decorative arts'. The discomfort around this corner of visual culture – Le Corbusier's declaration in 1918 that 'There is a hierarchy in the arts: decorative art at the bottom, and the human form at the top. Because we are men,' sums up the miserable line of dominance nicely – gets to, in part, what is so interesting about this motif. It is no wonder the griffin has been relatively understudied considering its frequent appearance in numerous contexts, for it is easily dismissed as a decorative beast. Art history's long tradition of undervaluing anonymous works and those tainted with the label of 'decoration' or 'craft' has in recent decades been reassessed, and this book takes part in that larger shift. In many places, but especially in textiles and sculpture, the griffin's representation can be visually subsumed into a larger pattern (see illus. 68, 74), and belies long-standing distinctions made between subject and ornament in art.[5] Likewise, the difficulty of assigning a precise origin to many of the works we've discussed, whether a large medieval proto-robot or an exquisitely carved cylinder seal, smaller than a thumb, made thousands of years earlier, is telling (see illus. 9, 38). Chasing the paths of the griffin motif across time and place has led us to understand how profoundly it keeps being repurposed – even into the present with meanings often tied to inspiring wonder or a sense of play.

The breadth of the griffin motif's cultural dispersal and the way in which one composite can be so readily reworked is ultimately the most important story that emerges from gathering these far-flung examples. I would say that this ambiguity is not a problem; rather, it's the whole point. The griffin motif was and is, above all else, highly adaptable and highly transportable, readily slipping into the visual culture of many societies, its meanings ever open to renegotiation.

References

These notes offer a kind of breadcrumb trail to satisfy the curious, but are more concise than in a traditional academic monograph due to space constraints. When possible, I've favoured sources in English, though a few works in other languages were too important for a certain area of research to leave out.

Introduction

1 Key works in this vein include Anna Maria Bisi, *Il Grifone: Storia di un motivo iconografico nell'antico oriente mediterraneo* (Rome, 1965); Christiane Delplace, *Le griffon de l'archaïsme à l'époque impériale: étude iconographique et essai d'interprétation symbolique* (Brussels, 1980); Ingeborg Flagge, *Untersuchungen zur Bedeutung des Greifen* (Sankt Augustin, 1975); Sonja Gerke, *Der altägyptische Greif: von der Vielfalt eines 'Fabeltiers'* (Hamburg, 2014); Nassos Papalexandrou, *Bronze Monsters and the Cultures of Wonder: Griffin Cauldrons in the Preclassical Mediterranean* (Austin, TX, 2021).
2 Laskarina Bouras, *The Griffin through the Ages* (Athens, 1983); Joe Nigg, *The Book of Gryphons* (Cambridge, MA, 1982). Their timing coincides with an uptick of interest in mythic creatures signalled by the huge popularity of Brian Froud's *Faeries* (New York, 1978). Similar to Bouras's book, for a Greek bank's customers, in its bespoke nature was an eight-page handprinted work. Bauer Type Foundry, *The Griffin: A Note on a Fabulous Creature's Rise from a Guardian of Gold to a Symbol of Printing* (New York, 1941).
3 This book is, of course, not alone in questioning this bias, from the more theoretical Martin Jay, *Downcast Eyes: The Denigration of Vision in Twentieth-Century French Thought* (Berkeley, CA, 1993) to recent art-historical case studies such as Daniela Bohde, 'Mary Magdalene at the Foot of the Cross: Iconography and the Semantics of Place', *Mitteilungen des Kunsthistorischen Instituts in Florenz*, I (2019), pp. 3–44.
4 Serinity Young's recent book, *Women Who Fly: Goddesses, Witches, Mystics, and other Airborne Females* (Oxford, 2018), offers an intriguing exploration of another aspect of this phenomenon.

1 What Is a Griffin? Early Depictions from Ancient West Asia

1 Warren Goldfarb, 'Wittgenstein on Fixity of Meaning', in *Early Analytic Philosophy: Frege, Russell, Wittgenstein*, ed. William W. Tait (Chicago, IL, 1997), pp. 75–89 (p. 76); Ludwig Wittgenstein, *Blue Book* (dictated 1933–4, published Oxford, 1958), pp. 17 and 33; Ludwig Wittgenstein, *Philosophical Investigations*, trans. G.E.M. Anscombe (New York, 1953), pp. 31–2, sects 66–8.
2 There is an interesting question of what features define a city. Anatolian Çatalhöyük, with its density of buildings, could be considered a city, but the traditional consensus is that the first cities arose near the end of the fourth millennium BCE in Mesopotamia.
3 This position argued in P.R.S. Moorey, 'On Tracking Cultural Transfers in

Prehistory: The Case of Egypt and Lower Mesopotamia in the Fourth Millennium BC', in *Centre and Periphery in the Ancient World*, ed. M. J. Rowlands et al. (Cambridge, 1987), pp. 36–46 (p. 39); Alice Stevenson, 'Egypt and Mesopotamia', in *The Sumerian World*, ed. Harriet E. W. Crawford (London, 2013), pp. 620–36 (p. 627). Some Egyptologists though argue for Egyptian origins of griffins, as in Nicolas Wyatt, 'Grasping the Griffin: Identifying and Characterizing the Griffin in Egyptian and West Semitic Tradition', *Journal of Ancient Egyptian Interconnections*, I/1 (2009), pp. 29–39 (p. 29).

4 Annie Caubet, 'Animals in Syro-Palestinian Art', in *A History of the Animal World in the Ancient Near East*, ed. Billie Jean Collins (2002), pp. 211–34 (p. 229). Maria Leventopolou, 'Gryps', *Lexicon Iconographicum Mythologiae Classicae (LIMC)* (Zürich, 2009), vol. VIII/1 suppl., p. 609.

5 For an interesting example that illustrates the flexible boundaries around what is labelled a 'griffin': Krzysztof M. Ciałowicz, 'Fantastic Creatures and Cobras from Tell el-Farkha', *Studies in Ancient Art and Civilization*, XV (2011), pp. 13–29 (p. 18).

6 M. Rostovtzeff, *Iranians and Greeks in South Russia* (Oxford, 1922), pp. 24 and 193, is an early observer of this pattern, though his broader idea of 'animal style' is called into question in Petya Andreeva's *Fantastic Beasts of the Eurasian Steppes: Toward a Revisionist Approach to Animal-Style Art* (forthcoming in 2024).

7 Dominique Collon, *First Impressions: Cylinder Seals in the Ancient Near East* (London, 1987), pp. 185–6, cat. no. 885.

8 H.L.J. Vanstiphout, trans., *Epics of Sumerian Kings: The Matter of Aratta* (Atlanta, GA, 2003), p. 139, lines 65–6.

9 Joan Aruz and Ronald Wallenfels, eds, *Art of the First Cities: The Third Millennium BC from the Mediterranean to the Indus,* exh. cat., The Metropolitan Museum of Art (New York, 2003), p. 140.

10 Collon, *First Impressions*, p. 186. Images of lion–eagle hybrids with a more leonine body have been labelled either Anzû or Asakku (a lion–dragon), and neo-Assyrian royal inscriptions often invoke the Anzû legend. Amar Annus, *The Standard Babylonian Epic of Anzu* (Helsinki, 2001), p. xxi.

11 Such as those found in the Early Dynastic I period from Ur. Beatrice Teissier, *Ancient Near Eastern Cylinder Seals from the Marcopoli Collection* (Berkeley, CA, 1984), p. 10.

12 Aruz and Wallenfels, eds, *Art of the First Cities*, p. 175.

13 Ibid., p. 215, no. 142.

14 Edith Porada, 'Why Cylinder Seals? Engraved Cylindrical Seal Stones of the Ancient Near East, Fourth to First Millennium BC', *Art Bulletin*, LXXV/4 (1993), pp. 563–82 (pp. 570–71).

15 Beatrice Teissier, *Egyptian Iconography on Syro-Palestinian Cylinder Seals of the Middle Bronze Age* (Fribourg, 1996), p. 90.

16 Edith Porada, *Corpus of Ancient Near Eastern Seals in North American Collections* (New York, 1948), vol. I, p. 70.

17 A. Green, 'Mischwesen', in *Reallexikon der Assyriologie* (Berlin, 1994), vol. VIII, pp. 222–64 (p. 252).

18 Mehmet-Ali Ataç, *The Mythology of Kingship in Neo-Assyrian Art* (Cambridge, 2010), p. 170.

19 Carolyn Nakamura, 'Dedicating Magic: Neo-Assyrian Apotropaic Figurines and the Protection of Assur', *World Archaeology*, XXXVI/1 (2004), pp. 11–25 (pp. 14, 21).
20 Joan Aruz, 'Intercultural Styles, Animal Combats, and the Art of Exchange', in *Die Bedeutung der minoischen und mykenischen Glyptik*, ed. Walter Müller (Mainz, 2010), pp. 73–82 (pp. 77–9).
21 Georgina Herrmann and Stuart Laidlaw, *Ivories from Rooms SW11/12 and T10 Fort Shalmaneser* (London, 2013), vol. I, pp. 165–7. She points out, too, that the nine ivories share many features with a group of three ivories depicting a kneeling youth.
22 Marian H. Feldman, 'The Legacy of Ivory-Working Traditions in the Early First Millennium BC', in *Beyond Babylon*, ed. Joan Aruz et al. (New York, 2008), pp. 445–8 (p. 447); Claudia E. Suter, 'Classifying Iron Age Levantine Ivories: Impracticalities and a New Approach', *Altorientalische Forschungen*, XLII/1 (2015), pp. 31–45 (pp. 38–40).
23 Nanno Marinatos, *Minoan Kingship and the Solar Goddess: A Near Eastern Koine* (Urbana, IL, 2010), pp. 60–61.
24 Ellen Rehm, *Der Schmuck der Achämeniden* (Münster, 1992), pp. 196–8, recaps earlier scholarship, and the attribution to a Hamadan find-spot is now disputed in Oscar White Muscarella, *Archaeology, Artifacts and Antiquities of the Ancient Near East Sites, Cultures, and Proveniences* (Leiden, 2013), pp. 1059–60.
25 Stavros Paspalas, 'The Achaemenid Lion-Griffin on a Macedonian Tomb Painting and on a Sicyonian Mosaic', in *Ancient Greece and Ancient Iran: Cross-Cultural Encounters*, ed. S.M.R. Darbandi and Antigoni Zournatzi (Athens, 2008), pp. 301–25 (p. 303, fig. 2).
26 David Wengrow, *The Origins of Monsters: Image and Cognition in the First Age of Mechanical Reproduction* (Princeton, NJ, 2014), p. 73.

2 Golden Griffins of Ancient Greece: From Image to Word

1 Nassos Papalexandrou, *Bronze Monsters and the Cultures of Wonder: Griffin Cauldrons in the Preclassical Mediterranean* (Austin, TX, 2021), pp. 27–30; U. Gehrig, *Die Greifenprotomen aus dem Heraion von Samos* (Bonn, 2004).
2 Papalexandrou, *Bronze Monsters*, pp. 6 and 143–4.
3 Marian H. Feldman, *Communities of Style: Portable Luxury Arts, Identity, and Collective Memory in the Iron Age Levant* (Chicago, IL, 2014), pp. 158–60; D. W. Rupp, 'The "Royal Tombs" at Salamis (Cyprus): Ideological Messages of Power and Authority', *Journal of Mediterranean Archaeology*, I/1 (1988), pp. 111–39 (p. 116).
4 Papalexandrou, *Bronze Monsters*, pp. 19–24.
5 Helmut Kyrieleis, *Anfänge und Frühzeit des Heiligtums von Olympia* (Berlin, 2006), pp. 95–100.
6 Joshua Paul Dale, 'The Appeal of the Cute Object: Desire, Domestication, and Agency', in *The Aesthetics and Affects of Cuteness*, ed. Joshua Paul Dale et al. (New York, 2016), pp. 35–55 (pp. 48–9).
7 George H. Chase, 'Three Griffins' Heads', *Bulletin of the Museum of Fine Arts*, XLVIII/272 (1950), pp. 33–7 (p. 37).
8 Ann C. Gunter, 'Orientalism and Orientalization in the Iron Age

Mediterranean', in *Critical Approaches to Ancient Near Eastern Art*, ed. Brian A. Brown and Marian H. Feldman (Boston, MA, 2013), pp. 79–108 (p. 88).

9 Papalexandrou, *Bronze Monsters*, p. 4; Thomas Brisart, *Un art citoyen: recherches sur l'orientalisation des artisanats en Grèce proto-archaïque* (Brussels, 2011), p. 58.

10 Ann C. Gunter, *Greek Art and the Orient* (Cambridge, 2009), pp. 105–6.

11 Its inscription, in the first person, proclaims the king of Paphos Akestor's ownership. The inscription's significance is shown in the care updating it, in the fifth century, with a new owner's name, Timokretes; for more on the Kourion bowl, see Feldman, *Communities of Style*, pp. 111–37.

12 Anna Satraki, 'The Iconography of Basileis in Archaic and Classical Cyprus: Manifestations of Royal Power in the Visual Record', *Bulletin of the American Schools of Oriental Research*, CCCLXX/1 (2013), pp. 123–44 (p. 126); Marian H. Feldman, 'Bowl with Egyptianizing Motifs', in *Assyria to Iberia: At the Dawn of the Classical Age*, ed. Joan Aruz et al., exh. cat., The Metropolitan Museum of Art, New York (2014), pp. 159–60.

13 Hristomir Smilenov Hristov, 'The Griffin-Fight in Ancient Art from Cyprus: Iconography and Interpretation', in *POCA (Postgraduate Cypriot Archaeology) 2012*, ed. Hartmut Matthäus et al. (Newcastle upon Tyne, 2015), pp. 240–65 (p. 242).

14 The Fort Shalmaneser Griffin-Fighter Ivory: Cleveland Museum of Art, inv. no. 1968.45.

15 Darrell A. Amyx, *Corinthian Vase-Painting of the Archaic Period* (Berkeley, CA, 1988), vol. II, p. 457.

16 Ann C. Gunter, 'Animal Friezes in "Orientalizing" Greek Art', in *Animals and Their Relation to Gods, Humans and Things in the Ancient World*, ed. Raija Mattila et al. (Wiesbaden, 2019), pp. 235–48 (p. 242).

17 Aeschylus, *Prometheus Bound*, trans. Herbert Weir Smyth (Cambridge, MA, 1926), vol. I, pp. 134–5, lines 803–7.

18 D. J. Conacher, *Aeschylus' Prometheus Bound: A Literary Commentary* (Toronto, 1980), p. 61.

19 M. L. West, *The Hesiodic Catalogue of Women: Its Nature, Structure, and Origins* (Oxford, 1985), p. 136.

20 Herodotus, *Histories*, trans. Tom Holland (New York, 2014), sects. III.116, IV.13, IV.27, IV.79 and IV.152.

21 Pseudo-Longinus, *On the Sublime* 10.4 and John Tzetzes, *Chiliades* 2.18 'Concerning Aristeas' (Story 50). See James Bolton, *Aristeas of Proconnesus* (Oxford, 1962), for more on Aristeas' later reworkings.

22 Fiona Mitchell, *Monsters in Greek Literature: Aberrant Bodies in Ancient Greek Cosmogony, Ethnography, and Biology* (Abingdon, 2021), p. 89.

23 Robert Beekes, *Etymological Dictionary of Greek* (Leiden, 2010), vol. I, p. 289.

24 There are a few earlier instances, such as on a vase from *c.* 525 BCE, where the griffin rears up behind a figure driving a chariot. The figure has been given an unconvincing identification as an Arimaspean (British Museum inv. no. 1923,0419.1); Maria Cecilia D'Ercole, 'Arimaspes et griffons: de la mer noire à l'adriatique via Athènes', *Dossier: Image mises en forme* (Paris, 2009), pp. 203–25 (pp. 209–10); Christiane Delplace, *Le griffon de l'archaïsme à l'époque impériale:*

étude iconographique et essai d'interprétation symbolique (Brussels, 1980), p. 125.
25 J. D. Beazley, *Attic Red-Figure Vase-Painters*, 2nd edn (Oxford, 1963), p. 1462, no. 8; Karl Schefold, *Untersuchungen zu den Kertscher Vasen* (Leipzig, 1934), p. 57, cat. no. 545.
26 John Boardman, *Athenian Red Figure Vases, The Classical Period: A Handbook* (New York, 1989), p. 193.
27 Jessica Hughes, 'Dissecting the Classical Hybrid', in *Body Parts and Bodies Whole*, ed. Marie L. S. Sorensen et al. (Oxford, 2010), pp. 101–10 (p. 103).
28 Adrienne Mayor, *The First Fossil Hunters: Dinosaurs, Mammoths, and Myth in Greek and Roman Times*, 2nd edn (Princeton, NJ, 2011), p. 58.
29 Ibid., pp. 24–5. Mayor refers vaguely to 'strange creatures' and mysterious 'peacock-headed griffins'. Moreover, her theory does not take into account reference materials widely available at her time of writing, for example, the first page of 'The Griffin' entry by Waltraud Bartscht, in *Mythical and Fabulous Creatures: A Source Book and Research Guide*, ed. Malcolm South (New York, 1987), p. 85.
30 Deborah Ruscillo, 'Review of The First Fossil Hunters: Palaeontology in Greek and Roman Times', *American Journal of Archaeology*, CVII/2 (2003), pp. 293–5 is the only review found that referenced the preceding tradition of griffins in the eastern Mediterranean. The reviews overlooking griffins' preceding representations in ancient West Asia and Egypt appeared in journals including *Antiquity*, *Classical Outlook*, *Classical Review*, *European Legacy*, *Isis*, *Journal of American Folklore*, *Journal of Geology* and *Science*.
31 Art Institute of Chicago, inv. no. 1994.38.1–2 (label on view in galleries as of December 2021, and same verbiage on object's website in August 2022); *Monstrum*, 'Why Has the Majestic Griffin Been Forgotten?', season 4, ep. 5, 2022; Marc Aronson and Adrienne Mayor, *The Griffin and the Dinosaur: How Adrienne Mayor Discovered a Fascinating Link between Myth and Science* (Washington, DC, 2014).
32 These connections across the eastern Mediterranean were so extensive and ongoing that thinking in terms such as 'pre-contact' and 'post-contact' confuses the matter. S. Rebecca Martin, *The Art of Contact: Comparative Approaches to Greek and Phoenician Art* (Philadelphia, PA, 2017), p. 34.
33 The sphinx also has wings in works from the Iron Age Levant, suggesting its depiction in Greek art was heavily inspired by West Asian works, rather than directly coming from Egyptian sources. A number of interesting examples are illustrated in Claudia E. Suter, 'Classifying Iron Age Levantine Ivories: Impracticalities and a New Approach', *Altorientalische Forschungen*, XLII/1 (2015), pp. 31–45.
34 Ctesias as quoted in the Byzantine author Photius' *Biblioteca*, sect. 37; Philostratus, *The Life of Apollonius of Tyana*, trans. Christopher P. Jones (Cambridge, MA, 2005), pp. 312–15, sect. 3.48.
35 Rudolf Wittkower, 'Marvels of the East: A Study in the History of Monsters', *Journal of the Warburg and Courtauld Institutes*, V (1945), pp. 159–97 (p. 164).
36 Aelian, *On the Characteristics of Animals*, trans. A. F. Scholfield (Cambridge, 1958), p. 241, sect. IV.27.

37 Mitchell, *Monsters*, pp. 128–32 (esp. p. 129).
38 D. Felton, 'Rejecting and Embracing the Monstrous in Ancient Greece and Rome', in *The Ashgate Research Companion to Monsters and the Monstrous*, ed. A. Simon Mittman and P. J. Dendle (Abingdon, 2012), pp. 103–31 (pp. 124–5).
39 Pliny the Elder, *Natural History*, VII.2; Solinus, *Collection of Remarkable Facts*; Pomponius Mela, *Description of the World*, II.I.

3 Sacred Griffins: Divine Partners and Symbols

1 August Friedrich von Pauly, ed., *Paulys Realencyclopädie der classischen Altertumswissenschaft: Neue Bearbeitung unter Mitwirkung zahlreicher Fachgenossen* (Stuttgart, 1910), vol. VII, cols. 1901–29. The *Lexicon iconographicum mythologiae classica* (LIMC) gives griffins their own entry in its supplement but mainly their inclusion is through deity entries ranging from Artemis to Tyche; Maria Leventopolou, 'Gryps', *LIMC*, vol. VIII/1 (supplement), pp. 609–11.
2 Andreas Vlachopoulos, 'The Wall Paintings from the Xeste 3 Building at Akrotiri: Towards an Interpretation of the Iconographic Programme', in *Horizon: A Colloquium on the Prehistory of the Cyclades*, ed. Neil Brodie et al. (Cambridge, 2008), pp. 491–506 (p. 493).
3 Louise Hitchcock and Marianna Nikolaidou, 'Gender in Greek and Aegean Prehistory', in *A Companion to Gender Prehistory*, ed. Diane Bolger (Somerset, NJ, 2012), pp. 502–25 (p. 513). While Linear A, the Minoan language, remains undeciphered, a seventh-century BCE Assyrian dictionary testifies to saffron's use for menstrual disorders and childbirth. Susan C. Ferrence and Gordon Bendersky, 'Therapy with Saffron and the Goddess at Thera', *Perspectives in Biology and Medicine*, XLVII/2 (2004), pp. 199–226 (p. 207).
4 Marian H. Feldman, *Diplomacy by Design: Luxury Arts and an 'International Style' in the Ancient Near East, 1400–1200 BCE* (Chicago, IL, 2006), p. 80.
5 Elizabeth Shank, 'The Griffin Motif – An Evolutionary Tale', in *Paintbrushes: Wall-Painting and Vase-Painting of the Second Millennium BC in Dialogue*, ed. Andreas G. Vlachopoulos (Athens, 2018), pp. 235–42 (p. 240); her earlier essay is also informative: Elizabeth Shank, 'Throne Room Griffins from Pylos and Knossos', in *Krinoi kai Limenes: Studies in Honor of Joseph and Maria Shaw*, ed. Philip P. Betancourt et al. (Havertown, PA, 2007), pp. 159–66.
6 Maria Anastasiadou, 'Wings, Heads, Tails: Small Puzzles at LM I Zakros', in *Metaphysis: Ritual, Myth and Symbolism in the Aegean Bronze Age*, ed. Eva Alram-Stern et al. (Leuven, 2016), pp. 77–85 (p. 82).
7 Nanno Marinatos, *Minoan Kingship and the Solar Goddess: A Near Eastern Koine* (Urbana, IL, 2010), pp. 52–5. In a Mycenaean thirteenth-century BCE mural fragment from Orchomenos, a warrior (indicated by a boar tusk helmet) cradles a griffin in her arms, and intriguingly this particular warrior is rendered with white skin, a visual convention to 'depict' women. Hitchcock and Nikolaidou, 'Gender', p. 517.
8 Diodorus claims to here be quoting a now-lost source by Hecataeus.

Diodorus Siculus, trans. C. H. Oldfather (Cambridge, MA, 1950), vol. II, pp. 38–9, sect. II.47.2.
9 Pamela A. Webb, *Hellenistic Architectural Sculpture: Figural Motifs in Western Anatolia and the Aegean Islands* (Madison, WI, 1996), p. 30.
10 Richard D. Weigel, 'Gallienus' "Animal Series" Coins and Roman Religion', *Numismatic Chronicle*, CL (1990), pp. 135–43 (pp. 137–8); Erika Manders, *Coining Images of Power: Patterns in the Representation of Roman Emperors on Imperial Coinage, AD 193–284* (Leiden, 2012), p. 289.
11 Claudian, *Panegyric on the Sixth Consulship of Honorius*, trans. Maurice Platnauer (Cambridge, MA, 1922), vol. II, p. 77, lines 30–31.
12 Elinor Bevan, *Representations of Animals in Sanctuaries of Artemis and other Olympian Deities* (Oxford, 1986), vol. II, pp. 475–9; Ruth M. Léger, *Artemis and Her Cult* (Oxford, 2017), pp. 66–7.
13 Strabo, *The Geography of Strabo*, trans. Duane W. Roller (Cambridge, 2014), p. 345, sect. VIII.3.12.
14 Javier Teixidor, *The Pantheon of Palmyra* (Boston, MA, 1979), p. 47; George W. Houston, 'The Altar from Rome with Inscriptions to Sol and Malakbel', *Syria*, LXVII/I (1990), pp. 189–93 (pp. 192–3).
15 Comte du Mesnil de Buisson, 'Le dieu-griffon à Palmyre et chez les Hittites', *L'Ethnographie* (1963), pp. 16–32 (p. 18).
16 Alison Futrell, *Blood in the Arena: The Spectacle of Roman Power* (Austin, TX, 1997), p. 117.
17 Ammianus Marcellinus, trans. J. C. Rolfe (Cambridge, MA, 1935), vol. I, p. 105, sect. XIV.II.25.
18 Emma Stafford, 'Nemesis: From Myth to Reason?', in *Worshipping Virtues: Personification and the Divine in Ancient Greece* (London, 2000), pp. 75–110 (pp. 76–7).
19 British Museum inv. no. 1910,0414.4; Michael Hornum, *Nemesis, the Roman State, and the Games* (New York, 1993), p. 318.
20 Elizabeth Riefstahl, *Ancient Egyptian Glass and Glazes in the Brooklyn Museum* (New York, 1968), p. 113, cat. no. 90. For more on imagery of griffins with a wheel, see Hornum, *Nemesis*, p. 318; Erika Simon, 'Zur Bedeutung des Greifen in der Kunst der Kaiserzeit', *Latomus*, XXI (1962), pp. 749–80 (pp. 770–78); Ingeborg Flagge, *Untersuchungen zur Bedeutung des Greifen* (Sankt Augustin, 1975), pp. 12–14 and 34–43.
21 J. Quaegebeur, 'De l'origine égyptienne du griffon Némésis', in *Visages du destin dans les mythologies: mélanges Jacqueline Duchemin*, ed. Jacqueline Duchemin and François Jouan (Paris, 1983), pp. 41–54.
22 Garrett S. Olmsted, *The Gundestrup Cauldron: Its Archaeological Context, the Style and Iconography of Its Portrayed Motifs, and Their Narration of a Gaulish Version of Táin bó Cúalnge* (Brussels, 1979), pp. 77–8.
23 For instance, the Thracian *c.* 100 BCE Stara Zagora phalerae (sculpted discs), Flemming Kaul, 'The Gundestrup Cauldron: Thracian Art, Celtic Motifs', *Études celtiques*, XXXVII (2011), pp. 81–110 (p. 91).
24 Ibid., p. 100.
25 Claude Maumené, 'The Gundestrup Cauldron: Is This the Key to the Enigma?', *Mediterranean Archaeology and Archaeometry*, XVI/4 (2016), pp. 351–8 (p. 353).

26 Sunil Gupta, 'Fragment of a Coping: A Winged Griffin and Youthful Combatant', in *Tree and Serpent: Early Buddhist Art in India*, ed. John Guy, exh. cat., The Metropolitan Museum of Art, New York (2023), pp. 171–2. Alternatively, the stupa's animals may have testified to the wealth, offering more of a statement of abundance, just as donations to the religious institution were measured in quantity of cattle. This limestone railing was added to the original granite structure, and faced inwards towards worshippers processing towards the stupa's relic.
27 Aarti Kawlra and Surajit Sarkar, 'Hybrid Creature Motifs as Cross-Cultural Transmission along the Silk Roads', in *Textile and Clothing along the Silk Roads*, ed. Feng Zhao and Marie-Louise Nosch (Paris, 2022), pp. 209–28 (p. 211).

4 Drinking with Griffins

1 Christiane Delplace, *Le griffon de l'archaïsme à l'époque impériale: étude iconographique et essai d'interprétation symbolique* (Brussels, 1980), pp. 372–6; Ruth Westgate, 'Party Animals: The Imagery of Status, Power and Masculinity in Greek Mosaics', in *Sociable Man: Essays on Ancient Greek Social Behaviour in Honour of Nick Fisher*, ed. S. D. Lambert (Swansea, 2011), pp. 291–322 (p. 298).
2 Emma Aston, 'Part-Animal Gods', in *The Oxford Handbook of Animals in Classical Thought and Life*, ed. Gordon Lindsay Campbell (Oxford, 2014), pp. 366–83 (p. 374).
3 For example, Nonnos, *Dionysiaca*, XIV.411–29.
4 Anne-Marie Guimier-Sorbets, 'Dionysos dans l'andrôn: L'iconographie des mosaïques de la maison grecque au IVe et au IIIe siècle avant J.-C.', *Mélanges de l'École Française de Rome. Antiquité*, CXVI/2 (2004), pp. 895–932 (pp. 901–2).
5 Ruth Westgate, 'Greek Mosaics in Their Architectural and Social Context', *Bulletin of the Institute of Classical Studies*, XLII/1 (1998), pp. 93–115 (pp. 94–7).
6 Westgate, 'Party Animals', p. 300.
7 Hallie M. Franks, *The World Underfoot: Mosaics and Metaphor in the Greek Symposium* (Oxford, 2018), p. 44.
8 Westgate, 'Party Animals', p. 294.
9 Paul Kosmin, 'Banqueting on the Move', in *Animal-Shaped Vessels from the Ancient World: Feasting with Gods, Heroes, and Kings*, ed. S. Ebbinghaus and A. C. Albinson, exh. cat., Harvard Art Museums, Cambridge, MA (2018), pp. 310–41 (p. 320).
10 David Stronach, 'Notes on the Iconography of the Senmurv', in *Fabulous Creatures and Spirits in Ancient Iranian Culture*, ed. Matteo Compareti (Bologna, 2018), pp. 77–92 (p. 83). For a breakdown of animals on Sasanian rhyta, see Niccolò Manassero, *Rhyta e corni potori dall'Età del ferro all'epoca sasanide: Libagioni pure e misticismo tra la Grecia e il mondo iranico* (Oxford, 2008), p. 77.
11 Carol Neuman de Vegvar, 'Drinking Horns and the Medieval Church', in *Animal-Shaped Vessels from the Ancient World: Feasting with Gods, Heroes, and Kings*, ed. Ebbinghaus and Albinson, p. 291. For a late medieval example, see Albertus Magnus, *On Animals*, XXIII.46.
12 Philippe Cordez, *Trésor, Mémoire, Merveilles. Les objets des églises au Moyen Âge* (Paris, 2016), p. 198; Pierre Alain

Mariaux, '*Curiositas* et curiosités naturelles au Moyen Âge', *Art + Architecture en Suisse*, LVI (2005), pp. 6–11 (p. 6).
13 Daniel Alcouffe et al., *Le Trésor de Saint-Denis*, exh. cat., Musée du Louvre, Paris (1991), pp. 223–5, cat. no. 41.
14 Jörg W. Busch, '775 Jahre Greiffenclau'scher Weinbau', *Heimatjahrbuch des Rheingau-Taunus-Kreises*, 38 (1987), pp. 158–63 (p. 158); Dora Thornton, *A Rothschild Renaissance: Treasures from the Waddesdon Bequest* (London, 2015), p. 257.
15 Vivian Etting, *The Story of the Drinking Horn: Drinking Culture in Scandinavia during the Middle Ages* (Copenhagen, 2013), pp. 68–9 and 138–9.
16 Antoinette Faÿ-Hallé, 'Nevers, un périlleux apogée', in *La faïence européenne au XVIIe siècle*, ed. Antoinette Faÿ-Hallé and Christine Lahaussois (Paris, 2003), pp. 264–9; Barbara Brejon de Lavergnée, 'New Light on Michel Dorigny', *Master Drawings*, XIX/4 (1981), pp. 445–55 and 491–502 (p. 454).
17 For example, the seventeenth-century maiolica from Urbino, with similarly classical imagery and fanciful animal forms, Metropolitan Museum of Art, inv. no. 1975.1.1123. A set of claw-like feet, which once were a stand very similar to our example, survive in Russia. Elena Ivanova, 'Seventeenth-Century Nevers Faience in St Petersburg Collections', *Burlington Magazine*, CXXXV/1083 (1993), pp. 380–85 (p. 384, fig. 16).
18 Jean Rosen, *La faïence de Nevers, 1585–1900* (Dijon, 2009), vol. II, p. 319, figs 548–9.
19 Alfred Gell, *The Art of Anthropology: Essays and Diagrams* (London, 1999), pp. 166–73.

5 The Art of War: Griffins on Weapons and Armour

1 Nicolas Wyatt, 'Grasping the Griffin: Identifying and Characterizing the Griffin in Egyptian and West Semitic Tradition', *Journal of Ancient Egyptian Interconnections*, I/1 (2009), pp. 29–39 (p. 30, n. 15).
2 Henri Frankfort, *Kingship and the Gods: A Study of Ancient Near Eastern Religion as the Integration of Society and Nature* (Chicago, IL, 1978), p. 11 and fig. 15; Edward K. Werner, 'Montu and the "Falcon Ships" of the Eighteenth Dynasty', *Journal of the American Research Center in Egypt*, XXIII (1986), pp. 107–23.
3 Shih-Wei Hsu (徐詩薇), 'The "Griffin" as a Visual and Written Image for the King', *Göttinger Miszellen – Beiträge zur ägyptologischen Diskussion*, CCXXXI (2011), pp. 45–56 (pp. 50–51).
4 Eckart Köhne et al., *Gladiators and Caesars: The Power of Spectacle in Ancient Rome* (Berkeley, CA, 2000), p. 51.
5 Ibid., pp. 41–3. A typical Greek example is the fourth-century BCE Chalcidian-type helmet, Getty Villa Museum inv. no. 93.AC.27.
6 Suetonius, *Lives of the Caesars*, Gaius Caligula 4.liv.1.
7 Michael Carter, 'Artemidorus and the ἀρβήλας Gladiator', *Zeitschrift für Papyrologie und Epigraphik*, CXXXIV (2001), pp. 109–15 (p. 109).
8 Susan Wood offers an especially interesting recent study of the griffins on the cuirassed statues of Hadrian and Hercules, in which a pair of griffins often frame/support a central figure she posits to be Hercules. 'Hadrian, Hercules and Griffins: A Group of Cuirassed Statues

from Latium and Pamphylia', *Journal of Roman Archaeology*, XXIX (2016), pp. 223–38.
9 J. W. Rich, 'Augustus's Parthian Honours, the Temple of Mars Ultor and the Arch in the Forum Romanum', *Papers of the British School at Rome,* LXVI (1998), pp. 71–128 (p. 86).
10 A. J. Droge, 'Finding His Niche: On the "Autoapotheosis" of Augustus', *Memoirs of the American Academy in Rome*, LVI/LVII (2011/12), pp. 85–112 (p. 104).
11 Tonio Hölscher, *Visual Power in Ancient Greece and Rome: Between Art and Social Reality* (Oakland, CA, 2018), p. 331.
12 Laura Nicotra, 'The Figurative Programme of the Architraval Friezes in the Forum of Trajan, Rome', PhD thesis, University of Leicester, 2015, pp. 1–3, her Type 1a, museum inv. no. FT4000.
13 Ibid., pp. 8, 73-9 and 105. She argues this fragment was specifically from the the eastern exedra of the portico of the square of Trajan's Forum. For more on the way such sculptures were part of a larger, general impression of architectural context, see Hölscher, *Visual Power in Ancient Greece and Rome*, pp. 299–333.
14 Nathalie-Cécile Ginoux, 'Images and Visual Codes of Early Celtic Warrior Elites (5th–4th Centuries BC)', in *Art and Communication: Centralization Processes in European Societies in the 1st Millennium BC*, ed. Christopher Pare (Mainz, 2012), pp. 179–90 (p. 187).
15 Denise Bretz-Mahler, 'La civilisation de la Tène I en Champagne: le faciès marnien', PhD thesis, Centre national de la recherche scientifique, Paris, 1971, pp. 142–3.
16 Ginoux, 'Images and Visual Codes', p. 183.
17 Ursula Brosseder, 'Belt Plaques as an Indicator of East–West Relations in the Eurasian Steppe at the Turn of the Millennia', in *Xiongnu Archaeology: Multidisciplinary Perspectives of the First Steppe Empire in Inner Asia*, ed. Ursula Brosseder and Bryan K. Miller (Bonn, 2011), pp. 349–424, see figs 30–31 for distribution maps; examples of Chinese griffin jades include the fourth- to third-century BCE 'contorted griffin', Harvard University Art Museums inv. no. 1943.50.240.
18 Csanád Bálint, *Der Schatz von Nagyszentmiklós: Archäologische Studien zur frühmittelalterlichen Metallgefäßkunst des Orients, Byzanz' und der Steppe* (Budapest, 2010), pp. 369–72.
19 Ibid., p. 361.
20 Birgit Bühler et al., *Der Goldschatz von Sânnicolau Mare/ Nagyszentmiklós* (Mainz, 2018), p. 29.
21 Bálint, *Der Schatz*, p. 351.
22 Walter Pohl, 'The Century of the Griffin', in *The Avars: A Steppe Empire in Central Europe, 567–822* (Ithaca, NY, 2018), pp. 344–402 (p. 347); Falko Daim, 'Byzantine Belt Ornaments of the 7th and 8th Centuries in Avar Contexts', in *Intelligible Beauty: Recent Research on Byzantine Jewellery*, ed. Christopher Entwistle and Noël Adams (London, 2010), pp. 61–71.
23 Csanád Bálint, *The Avars, Byzantium and Italy: A Study in Chorology and Cultural History* (Budapest, 2019), p. 116.
24 Ivan Gaskell, 'A Limestone Mold: Set in Stone', in *Tangible Things: Making History through Objects*, ed. Laurel Thatcher Ulrich et al. (New York, 2015), pp. 55–9 (p. 57); Samuel Szádeczky-Kardoss, 'The Avars', in *The Cambridge History of Early Inner Asia*, ed. Denis

Sinor (Cambridge, 2008), vol. I, pp. 206–28 (p. 228).
25 Falko Daim, 'Objects and Motifs: On Visual Communication in the Avar Empire', in *Von den Hunnen zu den Türken - Reiterkrieger in Europa und Zentralasien*, ed. Harald Meller et al. (Halle (Saale), 2021), pp. 191–214 (pp. 198–9).
26 Anna Contadini, 'Sharing a Taste? Material Culture and Intellectual Curiosity around the Mediterranean, from the Eleventh to the Sixteenth Century', in *The Renaissance and the Ottoman World*, ed. Anna Contadini and Claire Norton (London, 2016), pp. 23–61 (p. 36, n. 47).
27 Karen R. Mathews, *Conflict, Commerce, and an Aesthetic of Appropriation in the Italian Maritime Cities, 1000–1150* (Leiden, 2018), p. 17; Laskarina Bouras, *The Griffin through the Ages*, ed. Alexandra Petrides and Popi Tsakirakis (Athens, 1983), p. 53.
28 Julian Raby, 'The Inscriptions on the Pisa Griffin and the Mari-Cha Lion: From Banal Blessings to Indices of Origins', in *The Pisa Griffin and the Mari-Cha Lion: Metalwork, Art, and Technology in the Medieval Islamicate Mediterranean*, ed. Anna Contadini (Pisa, 2018), pp. 305–60 (p. 323).
29 Anna Contadini et al., 'Beasts that Roared: the Pisa Griffin and the New York Lion', in *Cairo to Kabul: Afghan and Islamic Studies Presented to Ralph Pinder-Wilson*, ed. Warwick Ball and Leonard Harrow (London, 2002), pp. 65–83 (pp. 68–9).
30 Anna Contadini and Richard Camber, 'Acoustic Automata', in *The Pisa Griffin and the Mari-Cha Lion*, ed. Contadini, pp. 63–75.
31 A.S.M. Chirvani, 'Le griffon iranien de Pise: matériaux pour un corpus de l'argenterie et du bronze iraniens III', *Kunst des Orients*, V/2 (1968), pp. 68–86; Marilyn Jenkins, 'New Evidence for the History and Provenance of the So-called Pisa Griffin', *Islamic Archaeological Studies*, I (1978), pp. 79–85 (p. 79).
32 Ittai Weinryb, *The Bronze Object in the Middle Ages* (Cambridge, 2016), p. 140.
33 Anna Contadini, 'Translocation and Transformation: Some Middle Eastern Objects in Europe', in *The Power of Things and the Flow of Cultural Transformations*, ed. Lieselotte E. Saurma-Jeltsch and Anja Eisenbeiss (Berlin, 2010), pp. 42–65 (p. 50).
34 Mathews, *Conflict,* p. 144.
35 Franco Cardini, 'The Iconic Status of Medieval Pisa and Its Urban Form', in *A Companion to Medieval Pisa*, ed. Karen R. Mathews et al. (Leiden, 2022), pp. 497–518 (p. 518).
36 Mathews, *Conflict,* p. 128.
37 Ibid., p. 143, also see Contadini, 'Translocation', pp. 50–51.
38 Major Scott A. Haines, '18 Hours on the Green Ramp', *Air Force Journal of Logistics*, XXVI/1 (2002), pp. 2–11 (p. 11).

6 Griffins on the Move: Depictions in Nomadic Central Asia

1 Joan Aruz and Ronald Wallenfels, eds, *Art of the First Cities: The Third Millennium BC from the Mediterranean to the Indus*, exh. cat., The Metropolitan Museum of Art, New York (2003), pp. 373–4, cat. no. 264.
2 Henri-Paul Francfort, 'Flying in Steppe: Pictures of Bird Hybrids in the Arts of Ancient Central Asia', in *Altai among the Eurasian Antiquities*, ed. A. R. Derevyanko and V. I. Molodin (Moscow, 2016), pp. 185–200 (p. 187).

3 Henri-Paul Francfort, 'La mort chez les Scythes de l'Europe à l'Altaï: la culture de Pazyryk et ses prédécesseurs à la lumière de quelques découvertes récentes', in *Sépultures et sociétés: du néolithique à l'histoire*, ed. Jean Guilaine (Paris, 2009), pp. 153–92 (pp. 157–61).
4 Henri-Paul Francfort, 'L'aigle qui marche et le cerf qui vole: images d'hybrides ornithologiques en Asie centrale ancienne', in *L'homme-animal dans les arts visuels*, ed. Pascale Linant de Bellefonds and A. Rouveret (Paris, 2017), pp. 222–37 (p. 233).
5 Svetlana Pankova, 'Identifications of Iron Age Tattoos from the Altai-Sayan Mountains in Russia', in *Ancient Ink: The Archaeology of Tattooing*, ed. Lars F. Krutak and Aaron Deter-Wolf (Seattle, WA, 2017), pp. 66–98 (p. 68).
6 J. P. Mallory et al., 'The Date of Pazyryk', in *Ancient Interactions: East and West in Eurasia*, ed. Katherine V. Boyle et al. (Cambridge, 2002), pp. 199–211 (p. 199).
7 Pankova, 'Identifications', p. 88.
8 Sergei I. Rudenko, *Frozen Tombs of Siberia: The Pazyryk Burials of Iron Age Horsemen* (Berkeley, CA, 1970), p. 110.
9 Esther Jacobson, *The Deer Goddess of Ancient Siberia: A Study in the Ecology of Belief* (Leiden, 1993) makes clear, too, the larger context of shamanism for this hybrid imagery.
10 Fredrik Fahlander, 'The Skin I Live in: The Materiality of Body Imagery', in *Own and Be Owned: Archaeological Approaches to the Concept of Possession*, ed. Alison Klevnäs and Charlotte Hedenstierna-Jonson (Stockholm, 2015), pp. 49–71 (p. 56).
11 Petya V. Andreeva, 'Fantastic Beasts of the Eurasian Steppes: Toward a Revisionist Approach to Animal-Style Art', PhD thesis, University of Pennsylvania, 2018, pp. 94–5, fig. 2.18.
12 Ibid., p. 96.
13 N. V. Polosmak, 'Tattoos in the Pazyryk World', *Archaeology, Ethnology and Anthropology of Eurasia*, IV/4 (2000), pp. 95–102 (pp. 95–6).
14 Kim Trainor, *Ledi* (Toronto, 2018).
15 Karina Iwe, 'Tattoos from Mummies of the Pazyryk Culture', in *Tattoos and Body Modifications in Antiquity*, ed. Philippe Della Casa and Constanze Witt (Zürich, 2013), pp. 89–95 (p. 93).
16 Pankova, 'Identifications', p. 70.
17 A. Y. Letyagin et al., 'High Field Magnetic Resonance Imaging of a Mummy from Ak-Alakha–3 Mound 1, Ukok Plateau, Gorny Altai: Findings and Interpretations', *Archaeology, Ethnology and Anthropology of Eurasia*, XLII/4 (2014), pp. 83–91 (p. 89).
18 Polosmak, 'Tattoos', p. 95.
19 Pankova, 'Identifications', p. 70.
20 Ibid., p. 88.
21 Polosmak, 'Tattoos', p. 100. Though others suggest many of the tattoos were often covered: Kenneth Lymer, 'Animals and Decorative Arts: Zoomorphic Imagery and Biographical Objects Among the Pazyryk of the Altai', in *Material Culture, Language and Religion of Central and Inner Asia*, ed. Gillian Long and Michael Gervers (Toronto, 2013), pp. 57–70 (p. 64).
22 Pankova, 'Identifications', p. 83.
23 L. L. Barkova and S. V. Pankova, 'Tattooed Mummies from the Large Pazyryk Mounds: New Findings', *Archaeology, Ethnology and Anthropology of Eurasia*, XXII/2 (2005), pp. 48–59 (p. 50).

24 Barkova and Pankova, 'Tattooed Mummies', p. 50; Iwe, 'Tattoos', p. 92.
25 Iwe, 'Tattoos', p. 89.
26 Pankova, 'Identifications', p. 89.
27 Gala Argent, 'Do the Clothes Make the Horse? Relationality, Roles and Statuses in Iron Age Inner Asia', *World Archaeology*, XLII/2 (2010), pp. 157–74 (p. 163).
28 Ibid., pp. 164–5.
29 Gala Argent, 'Inked: Human-Horse Apprenticeship, Tattoos, and Time in the Pazyryk World', *Society and Animals*, XXI/2 (2013), pp. 178–93 (p. 186).
30 Henri-Paul Francfort et al., 'The Gold of the Griffins: Recent Excavation of a Frozen Tomb in Kazakhstan', in *The Golden Deer of Eurasia: Perspectives on the Steppe Nomads of the Ancient World*, ed. Joan Aruz et al. (New Haven, CT, 2006), pp. 114–27 (p. 122).
31 Esther Jacobson-Tepfer, *The Hunter, the Stag, and the Mother of Animals: Image, Monument, and Landscape in Ancient North Asia* (Oxford, 2015), pp. 285–97.
32 D. V. Cheremisin, 'On the Semantics of Animal Style Ornithomorphic Images in Pazyryk Ritual Artifacts', *Archaeology, Ethnology and Anthropology of Eurasia*, XXXVII/1 (2009), pp. 85–94 (p. 88).
33 Petya V. Andreeva, 'Glittering Bodies: The Politics of Mortuary Self-Fashioning in Eurasian Nomadic Cultures (700 BCE–200 BCE)', *Fashion Theory* (28 October 2021), pp. 1–30 (p. 20).
34 Zainullah Samashev et al., 'Die "goldhütenden Greife" des Herodot und die archäologische Kultur der frühen Nomaden im kazachischen Altai', *Eurasia Antiqua: Zeitschrift für Archäologie Eurasiens*, VIII (2002), pp. 237–76 (p. 271); Jochen Fornasier, *Jagddarstellungen des 6.–4. Jhs. v. Chr.: eine ikonographische und ikonologische Analyse* (Münster in Westfalen, 2001), pp. 268–70.
35 Kenneth Lymer, 'Griffins, Myths and Religion – A Review of the Archaeological Evidence from Ancient Greece and the Early Nomads of Central Asia', *Art of the Orient*, VII (2018), pp. 9–25 (p. 12).
36 Author's communication with Kenneth Lymer; and Lymer, 'Griffins', p. 17.
37 Francfort, 'Flying in Steppe', pp. 185–7.
38 Toshio Hayashi, 'Griffin Motif: From the West to East Asia via the Altai', *Parthica: incontri di culture nel mondo antico*, XIV (2012), pp. 49–64 (p. 57).
39 Gertjan Plets, 'Exceptions to Authoritarianism? Variegated Sovereignty and Ethno-Nationalism in a Siberian Resource Frontier', *Post-Soviet Affairs*, XXXV/4 (2019), pp. 308–22 (p. 314).
40 Agnieszka Halemba, '"What Does It Feel Like When Your Religion Moves under Your Feet?" Religion, Earthquakes and National Unity in the Republic of Altai, Russian Federation', *Zeitschrift für Ethnologie*, CXXXIII/2 (2008), pp. 283–99 (p. 284).
41 E. P. Zaĭt͡seva and I. I. Ortonulov, *Altaĭ kep-kiĭim* (Gorno-Altaĭsk, 1990).
42 One example of the trade publications devoted to Pazyryk tattoos: 'The Ancient Tattoos of a Siberian Ice Princess', *INKED*, www.inkedmag.com, 3 October 2014, updated 10 October 2018.
43 Author's communication with D. Mazierski; Colin Dale and Lars F. Krutak, 'Neo-Pazyryk Tattoos: A Modern Revival', in *Ancient Ink*, ed. Krutak and Deter-Wolf, pp. 99–106.

7 Guardian Griffins

1 Stephen Quirke's monumental study of these objects tabulates the depictions of griffins (his categories 8 and 9) as being on five of the nine tusks with specific provenance, and on 28 of the 66 tusks/wands with no provenance, so 44 per cent have some sort of griffin imagery. *Birth Tusks: The Armoury of Health in Context – Egypt 1800 BC* (London, 2016), pp. 316–21.

2 For example, the Metropolitan Museum of Art, inv. no. 30.8.218.

3 James P. Allen, *The Art of Medicine in Ancient Egypt* (New York, 2005), p. 29.

4 William C. Hayes, *The Scepter of Egypt: A Background for the Study of the Egyptian Antiquities in the Metropolitan Museum of Art* (New York, 1978), p. 249.

5 Kasia Szpakowska, 'Demons in the Dark: Nightmares and other Nocturnal Enemies in Ancient Egypt', in *Ancient Egyptian Demonology: Studies on the Boundaries between the Demonic and the Divine in Egyptian Magic*, ed. Panagiotis Kousoulis (Leuven, 2011), pp. 63–76 (p. 75).

6 Branko F. van Oppen de Ruiter, 'Lovely Ugly Bes! Animalistic Aspects in Ancient Egyptian Popular Religion', *Arts*, IX/2: 51 (2020), pp. 1–27 (p. 3); Sonja Gerke, *Der altägyptische Greif: von der Vielfalt eines 'Fabeltiers'* (Hamburg, 2014), p. 142.

7 For example, the Metropolitan Museum of Art inv. nos. 22.1.65 and 22.1.154.

8 Fred Vink, 'Boundaries of Protection: Function and Significance of the Framing (Lines) on Middle Kingdom Apotropaia, in Particular Magic Wands', in *The World of Middle Kingdom Egypt (2000–1550 BC)*, ed. Gianluca Miniaci and Wolfram Grajetzki (London, 2015), vol. II, pp. 257–84 (p. 267, n. 85).

9 Hartwig Altenmüller, 'Der rettende Greif. Zu den Bildern des Greifs auf den sog. Zaubermessem des Mittleren Reiches', in *Kleine Götter – Grosse Götter: Festschrift für Dieter Kessler zum 65. Geburtstag*, ed. M. Flossmann-Schütze (Vattersteten, 2013), pp. 11–28 (pp. 17–20).

10 Joachim F. Quack, 'The Animals of the Desert and the Return of the Goddess', in *Desert Animals in the Eastern Sahara*, ed. Heiko Riemer et al. (Cologne, 2009), pp. 341–61 (p. 350); Gerke, *Der altägyptische Greif*, p. 49.

11 Papyrus Leiden I 384, second century CE; Wilhelm Spiegelberg, *Der ägyptische Mythus vom Sonnenauge: Der Papyrus der Tierfabeln, 'Kufi': nach dem Leidener demotischen Papyrus I. 384* (Strassburg, 1917), pp. 38–9; re-edited in Françoise de Cenival, *Le mythe de l'œil du soleil* (Sommerhausen, 1988), p. 43.

12 Translation from Quack, 'The Animals of the Desert', p. 346.

13 Hartwig Altenmüller, 'Zu den Feindbildern auf den Zauberstäben des Mittleren Reiches und der Zweiten Zwischenzeit', *Études et Travaux*, XXX (2017), pp. 73–94 (pp. 84–7).

14 Lorenz Winkler-Horaček, *Monster in der frühgriechischen Kunst: die Überwindung des Unfassbaren* (Berlin, 2015), p. 214.

15 For example, *Corpus der minoischen und mykenischen Siegel* (*CMS*) cat. no. 1.304; Margaretha Kramer-Hajos argues for these Late Helladic III images being a pointed subversion of palace-era imagery in *Mycenaean Art and the Aegean World: Palace and Province in the Late Bronze Age* (Cambridge, 2016), pp. 149–552.

16 William D. Wixom, 'Two Guardian Griffins. Piazza di Porta Ravennate, Bologna', in *Romanesque Sculpture in American Collections*, ed. Walter Cahn and Linda Seidel (Turnhout, 1999), vol. II, pp. 163–5.
17 Elizabeth Valdez del Alamo, *Palace of the Mind: The Cloister of Silos and Spanish Sculpture of the Twelfth Century* (Turnhout, 2012), pp. 236–7.
18 Thomas E. A. Dale, *Pygmalion's Power: Romanesque Sculpture, the Senses, and Religious Experience* (University Park, PA, 2019), p. 126.
19 Jackie Craven, 'The Griffin in Architecture and Design', *ThoughtCo*, www.thoughtco.com, 27 February 2019; Donald B. Corner and John Rowell, *Architectural Terra Cotta: Design Concepts, Techniques and Applications* (New York, 2022), p. 16.
20 Hütt's suggestion that griffin aquamanilia specifically derive from heraldry does not take into account how widespread griffin imagery was in other settings. Michael Hütt, *Aquamanilien: Gebrauch und Form, 'Quem lavat unda foris'* (Mainz, 1993), pp. 73–4. Recently scholars have raised wide-reaching questions about how to construe objects such as the zoomorphic water vessels, notably Margaret S. Graves, *Arts of Allusion: Object, Ornament, and Architecture in Medieval Islam* (New York, 2018), pp. 61–4.
21 Frits Scholten, *The Robert Lehman Collection, European Sculpture and Metalwork* (New York, 2011), vol. XII, p. 14, cat. no. 5.
22 Ursula Mende, 'Late Gothic Aquamanilia from Nuremberg', in *Lions, Dragons, and other Beasts: Aquamanilia of the Middle Ages, Vessels for Church and Table*, ed. Peter Barnet and Pete Dandridge (New Haven, CT, 2006), pp. 18–33 (p. 30).
23 Louvre, inv. no. OA 3049 and National Museum, Kraców, the Princes Czartoryski Foundation, inv. no. XIII.1233. The griffin sculpture with a very similar beak in the Goslar marketplace has been dated to *c.* 1220–30; Joanna Olchawa, 'Der Greif in Goslar', in *Löwe, Wölfin, Greif: monumentale Tierbronzen im Mittelalter* (Berlin, 2020), pp. 181–200.
24 Louvre, inv. no. OA 6924.

8 In the Halls of Power: Griffins in Byzantine and Sasanian Palaces

1 Jonathan Bardill, 'Visualizing the Great Palace of the Byzantine Emperors at Constantinople', in *Visualisierungen von Herrschaft*, ed. Franz Alto Bauer (Istanbul, 2006), pp. 5–45 (p. 20) nicely encapsulates the rationale for the Heraclius dating here and in his *Brickstamps* two-volume study. The range of dates given in the scholarship extends from Gisela Hellenkemper-Salies's suggestion that the mosaics were a product of the fifth century to Salvador Miranda's suggestion of the ninth century under Emperor Theophilos. A sample of the continuum of datings suggested for the courtyard mosaics includes Martina Müller-Wiener (1977) – places the mosaics in the first half of the sixth century; Jonathan Bardill and John Hayes (2002) – on basis of pottery, no earlier than *c.* 500; Cyril Mango (1960) – Justinian or later; Werner Jobst (2007) – Justinianic era (though the reason given is not archaeological, rather citing that emperor's eminence); José Maria

Blázquez (1989) – seventh century; Per-Jonas Nordhagen (1963) – first reign of Justinian II (685–696); and *c.* 700 by David Talbot Rice (1965).

2 David Parrish, 'The Art-Historical Context of the Great Palace Mosaic at Constantinople', *La Mosaïque Gréco-Romaine IX* (Rome, 2005), vol. II, pp. 1103–17 (p. 1106) construes this portion of the Great Palace mosaics as a venatorial image, likening it to the Worcester Mosaics and Mount Nebo's mosaic in the old *diakonikon*.

3 Athenaeus, *The Learned Banqueters*, trans. S. Douglas Olson (Cambridge, MA, 2006), p. 321, sect. XI.477.

4 Christiane Delplace, *Le griffon de l'archaïsme à l'époque impériale* (Brussels, 1980), pp. 295–7.

5 Eugene Lane, *Corpus Cultus Iovis Sabazii* (Leiden, 1989), vol. III, p. 23.

6 Örgü Dalgiç, 'The Triumph of Dionysos in Constantinople: A Late Fifth-Century Mosaic in Context', *Dumbarton Oaks Papers*, LXIX (2015), pp. 15–48 (p. 36).

7 Nonnos of Panopolis, *Dionysiaca*, trans. W.H.D. Rouse (Cambridge, MA, 1940), vol. III, p. 453, sect. XLVIII.382–3.

8 Anthony Kaldellis, 'The Making of the Hagia Sophia and the Last Pagans of New Rome', *Journal of Late Antiquity*, VI/2 (2013), pp. 347–66 (p. 351).

9 Alan Cameron, 'Paganism in Sixth-Century Byzantium', in *Wandering Poets and other Essays on Late Greek Literature and Philosophy* (Oxford, 2016), pp. 255–86 (p. 264).

10 Ibid., p. 277.

11 David Parrish, 'The Mosaic Program of the "Maison de la Procession Dionysiaque" at El Jem', in *Mosaïque romaine tardive: l'iconographie du temps, les programmes iconographiques des maisons africaines*, ed. Yvette Duval (Paris, 1982), pp. 51–65 (p. 55).

12 Trilling interprets the lizard as an unprecedented allusion to Apollo calculated to appeal to a Christian audience, which sidesteps key features such as the palace mosaics' lack of other explicit Christian iconography, which was the norm for non-church settings at the time. James Trilling, 'The Soul of the Empire: Style and Meaning in the Mosaic Pavement of the Byzantine Imperial Palace in Constantinople', *Dumbarton Oaks Papers*, XLIII (1989), pp. 27–72 (p. 59).

13 Jean-Pierre Sodini, 'Marble Capitals from the Hippodrome', in *Hippodrome/Atmeydanı: A Stage for Istanbul's History*, ed. Brigitte Pitarakis and Ekrem Işın (Istanbul, 2010), pp. 185–92 (pp. 188–90); N. Fıratlı, *La sculpture byzantine figurée au Musée Archéologique d'Istanbul* (Paris, 1990), cat. no. 212.

14 Brigitte Pitarakis and Ekrem Işın, eds, *Hippodrome/Atmeydanı: A Stage for Istanbul's History* (Istanbul, 2010), p. 261.

15 Fredegar, *Chronicle*, sect. IV.65.

16 Ken Dark, 'Roman Architecture in the Great Palace of the Byzantine Emperors at Constantinople during the Sixth to Ninth Centuries', *Byzantion,* LXXVII (2007), pp. 87–105 (p. 97). One problem with making a superficial connection between the mosaics and North African material is that because so much survives from that region, it is tempting to portray the existence of comparanda from there erroneously as evidence of a special connection. Gerald Brett, 'The Brooklyn Textiles and the Great Palace Mosaic', *Coptic Studies in Honor of*

Walter Ewing Crum (Boston, MA, 1950), pp. 433–41 (p. 440). M. Mundell Mango, 'Imperial Art in the Seventh Century', in *New Constantines: The Rhythm of Imperial Renewal in Byzantium, 4th–13th Centuries*, ed. Paul Magdalino (Brookfield, VT, 1994), pp. 109–38 (p. 134).

17 Choricius of Gaza, *Rhetorical Exercises from Late Antiquity: A Translation of Choricius of Gaza's Preliminary Talks and Declamations*, trans. Robert J. Penella (Cambridge, 2009), p. 45, sect. Or. XXI.

18 Catherine Johns, *The Hoxne Late Roman Treasure: Gold Jewellery and Silver Plate* (London, 2010), pp. 36–8.

19 A classic art-historical work on this long-lived symbol, stretching from antiquity to the Mexican flag, is Rudolf Wittkower, 'Eagle and Serpent: A Study in the Migration of Symbols', *Journal of the Warburg Institute*, II/4 (1939), pp. 293–325.

20 Werner Jobst et al., *Istanbul, das grosse byzantinische Palastmosaik* (Istanbul, 1997), p. 56; Trilling, 'The Soul', p. 70.

21 Zoltán Kádár, 'Die älteste Darstellung des Okapis in Europa', in *Festschrift für Claus Nissen*, ed. E. Geck and G. Pressler (Wiesbaden, 1973), pp. 415–22. Alternatively (and erroneously), the horned griffin is viewed as a unicorn, part of a putative larger Chistological programme in Stefan Hiller, 'Divino sensu agnoscere: Zur Deutung des Mosaikbodens im Peristyl des Grossen Palastes zu Konstantinopel', *Kairos; Zeitschrift für Religionswissenschaft und Theologie*, XI (1969), pp. 275–305 (pp. 284 and 302).

22 Hasan Karabulut et al., *Haleplibahçe Mozaikleri Şanlıurfa/Edessa* (Istanbul, 2011), p. 53, fig. 58.

23 Translation by Paul Magdalino, 'The Bath of Leo the Wise and the "Macedonian Renaissance" Revisited: Topography, Iconography, Ceremonial, Ideology', *Dumbarton Oaks Papers*, XLII (1988), pp. 97–118 (p. 118); Leo Choirosphaktes, Vatican mss. Barber. gr. 310.

24 Cyril Mango, 'The Palace of Marina, the Poet Palladas and the Bath of Leo VI', in *Euphrosynon: aphieroma ston Manoli Chatzedake* (Athens, 1991), vol. I, pp. 321–30 (pp. 326–7).

25 Arnaud Zucker, *Physiologos: le bestiaire des bestiaires*, 2nd edn (Grenoble, 2005), p. 264, sect. 51. An earlier theory that the griffin in Leo's bath represents the Prophet Elias isn't persuasive, both because griffins – despite their vast array of associations with divine entities – have no attested connection with Christian prophets, and the poem's survey of Leo's bath mosaics includes no overtly Christian subject-matter. Magdalino, 'The Bath of Leo the Wise, p. 101.

26 Maria Cristina Carile, 'The Imperial Palace Glittering with Light: The Material and Immaterial in the Sacrum Palatium', in *Hierotopy of Fire and Light in the Culture of the Byzantine World*, ed. Alekseĭ Lidov (Moscow, 2013), pp. 105–35 (pp. 115–16).

27 In one Umayyad royal bathing space, the *caldarium* of Quseir Amra, the domed ceiling was frescoed with zodiac imagery copied from a Greek manuscript, and the room suffused with light from four large windows. Garth Fowden, *Quṣayr 'Amra: Art and the Umayyad Elite in Late Antique Syria* (Berkeley, CA, 2004), pp. 42–3.

28 Paul Magdalino, 'The Bath of Leo the Wise', in *Maistor: Classical, Byzantine and*

Renaissance Studies for Robert Browning, ed. Ann Moffatt (Canberra, 1984), pp. 225–40 (p. 239).
29 Anne-Laurence Caudano, 'Astronomy and Astrology', in *A Companion to Byzantine Science*, ed. Stavros Lazaris (Leiden, 2020), pp. 202–30 (p. 210).
30 Sean W. Anthony, *Muhammad and the Empires of Faith: The Making of the Prophet of Islam* (Oakland, CA, 2020), pp. 186–93.
31 Jean Lempire, 'D'Alexandrie à Constantinople. Le commentaire astronomique de Stéphanos', *Byzantion*, LXXXI (2011), pp. 241–66 (pp. 242–8).
32 Anne Tihon, 'Le calcul de la date de Pâques de Stéphanos-Héraclius', in *Philomathestatos: Studies in Greek and Byzantine Texts Presented to Jacques Noret for His Sixty-Fifth Birthday*, ed. B. Janssens et al. (Leuven, 2004), pp. 625–46 (pp. 627–8).
33 St John Simpson, *Afghanistan: A Cultural History* (London, 2012), pp. 76–7.
34 F. Demange, ed., *Les Perses sassanides: fastes d'un empire oublié (224–642)* (Paris, 2006), p. 112; Guitty Azarpay, *Sogdian Painting: The Pictorial Epic in Oriental Art* (Berkeley, CA, 1981), pp. 70–71.
35 Matteo Compareti, 'Assimilation and Adaptation of Foreign Elements in Late Sasanian Rock Reliefs at Taq-i Bustan', in *Sasanidische Spuren in der byzantinischen, kaukasischen und islamischen Kunst und Kultur*, ed. Neslihan Asutay-Effenberger and Falko Daim (Mainz, 2019), pp. 19–36 (pp. 23–4). For a very fine overview of interpretative possibilities for senmurvs, see his 'The So-Called *Senmurv* in Iranian Art: A Reconstruction of an Old Theory', in *Loquentes Linguis: Linguistic and Oriental Studies in Honour of Fabrizio A. Pennacchietti*, ed. Pier Giorgio Borbone et al. (Wiesbaden, 2006), pp. 185–200.
36 Ali Mousavi, 'Two Bronze Statuettes from Tuzandejan, Khurasan', *Bulletin of the Ancient Orient Museum*, XI (1990), pp. 121–34.
37 Maryam Ekhtiar, 'Throne Leg in the Shape of a Griffin', in *Masterpieces from the Department of Islamic Art in the Metropolitan Museum of Art*, ed. Maryam Ekhtiar and Priscilla Parsons Soucek (New York, 2011), p. 28; Roman Ghirshman, *Iran: Parther und Sasaniden* (Munich, 1962), p. 214.
38 Stuart Cary Welch, ed., *The Islamic World* (New York, 1987), p. 15.

9 Griffins Aloft: Griffins as Luminous, Flying and Heavenly Creatures

1 Donald M. Bailey, *Roman Provincial Lamps* (London, 1988), p. 41, cat. no. Q2401.
2 Donald M. Bailey, *A Catalogue of the Lamps in the British Museum* (London, 1975), pp. 41–2.
3 Martin Kemkes, 'Der Wächter an der Tür: ein römischer Bronzegreif aus der "villa rustica" im Beckenhölzle, Stadt Rottweil', in *Im Dienste Roms: Festschrift für Hans Ulrich Nuber*, ed. Gabriele Seitz (Remshalden, 2006), pp. 429–40 (p. 436).
4 Maria Xanthopoulou, *Les lampes en bronze à l'époque paléochrétienne* (Turnhout, 2010), pp. 14–16.
5 Chrysler Museum of Art, inv. no. 71.930. Unfortunately there is no additional information about this lamp available in the Chrysler Museum's records, but the museum conservators have confirmed that its technique and materials are consistent with it being

an early Byzantine lamp, and my examination indicated this as well.

6 The British Museum lamp: inv. no. 1987.8–20.1.

7 Danijela Tešić Radovanović, 'Lamp with a Representation of the Griffin: The Christianisation of Pagan Motifs During Late Antiquity', *Zbornik radova Filozofskog fakulteta*, XLVIII/3 (2018), pp. 219–34 (p. 222).

8 Edward M. Schoolman, 'Image and Function in "Christian" and "Pagan" Late Antique Terracotta Lamps', in *Pagans and Christians in the Late Roman Empire: New Evidence, New Approaches (4th–8th Centuries)*, ed. Marianne Sághy and Edward M. Schoolman (Budapest, 2017), pp. 165–77 (p. 174). Some earlier interpretations of the griffin lamps go further, envisioning that the Wadsworth Athenaeum's griffin lamp, for example, presents a Christianized battle of good versus evil, the shape of the lamp being taken as the boat of the church, the dolphin as 'the Resurrection, the final triumph'. Kurt Weitzmann, ed., *Age of Spirituality: Late Antique and Early Christian Art, Third to Seventh Century* (New York, 1977), p. 624, cat. no. 560.

9 Richard Stoneman, *Alexander the Great: A Life in Legend* (New Haven, CT, 2008), p. 116.

10 Translation from Julie Ann Chappell, 'The Prose "Alexander" of Robert Thornton: The Middle English Text with a Modern English Translation', PhD thesis, University of Washington, 1989, p. 227, folio 45r.

11 For example, a Roman lamp with Apollo's chariot pulled by two griffins, *c.* 200 CE, Getty Museum inv. no. 83.AQ.377.240.

12 Slobodan Ćurčić, 'Some Uses (and Reuses) of Griffins in Late Byzantine Art', in *Byzantine East, Latin West: Art-Historical Studies in Honor of Kurt Weitzmann* (Princeton, NJ, 1995), pp. 597–604, goes back to Greek examples, but the *c.* 1400 BCE Minoan Hagia Triada sarcophagus offers a terrific instance in which a pair of griffins, with their wings unfurled, pull a chariot carrying two women who may be goddesses.

13 Theo Jülich et al., eds, *Die mittelalterlichen Elfenbeinarbeiten des Hessischen Landesmuseums Darmstadt* (Regensburg, 2007), pp. 39–45; Alicia Walker, *The Emperor and the World: Exotic Elements and the Imaging of Middle Byzantine Imperial Power, Ninth to Thirteenth Centuries CE* (Cambridge, 2012), p. 112.

14 Pseudo-Callisthenes, *The Greek Alexander Romance*, trans. Richard Stoneman (London, 1991), p. 123, sect. II. 41.

15 Gerald T. Elmore, *Islamic Sainthood in the Fullness of Time: Ibn al-ʿArabī's Book of the Fabulous Gryphon* (Leiden, 1999), p. 185, esp. n. 134.

16 Thomas Noll, 'The Visual Image of Alexander the Great: Transformations from the Middle Ages to the Early Modern Period', in *Alexander the Great in the Middle Ages: Transcultural Perspectives*, ed. Markus Stock (Toronto, 2016), pp. 244–63 (p. 247).

17 Chiara Settis-Frugoni, *Historia Alexandri elevati per griphos ad aerem: Origine, iconografia e fortuna di un tema* (Rome, 1973), pp. 265–339.

18 Hans Holländer, 'Alexander: Hybris und Curiositas', in *Kontinuität und Transformation der Antike im Mittelalter*,

ed. Willi Erzgräber (Sigmaringen, 1989), pp. 65–79.
19 Victor M. Schmidt, *A Legend and Its Image: The Aerial Flight of Alexander the Great in Medieval Art* (Groningen, 1995), pp. 29–39.
20 Danielle Buschinger, 'German Alexander Romances', in *Companion to Alexander Literature in the Middle Ages*, ed. David Zuwiyya (Leiden, 2011), pp. 291–314 (p. 299).
21 Maud Pérez-Simon, 'The Medieval Alexander: Art and Politics', in *A History of Alexander the Great in World Culture*, ed. Richard Stoneman (Cambridge, 2022), pp. 143–66 (pp. 143–6); Nicolette Sophia Trahoulia, 'The Venice "Alexander Romance", Hellenic Institute Codex Gr. 5: A Study of Alexander the Great as an Imperial Paradigm in Byzantine Art and Literature', PhD thesis, Harvard University, 1997, p. 50.
22 Margaret Carroll, trans., *A Contemporary Greek Source for the Siege of Constantinople, 1453: The Sphrantzes Chronicle* (Amsterdam, 1985), p. 66.
23 Deniz Beyazit, 'Plate of Rukn Al-Dawla Dawud', in *Court and Cosmos: The Great Age of the Seljuqs*, ed. Sheila R. Canby et al. (New York, 2016), pp. 56–7.
24 Eva R. Hoffman, 'Pathways of Portability: Islamic and Christian Interchange from the Tenth to the Twelfth Century', *Art History*, XXIV/1 (2001), pp. 17–50 (p. 39).
25 Eurydice Georganteli, 'Transposed Images: Currencies and Legitimacy in the Late Medieval Eastern Mediterranean', in *Byzantines, Latins, and Turks in the Eastern Mediterranean World after 1150*, ed. Jonathan Harris et al. (Oxford, 2012), pp. 141–79 (p. 144); Scott Redford, 'How Islamic Is It? The Innsbruck Plate and Its Setting', *Muqarnas*, VII/1 (1990), pp. 119–35.
26 See University of Manchester, John Rylands Library, Armenian Mss. 3, made in 1544 in Constantinople, the winged, clawed horse on image 87 in digital version: https://luna.manchester.ac.uk/luna/servlet/s/760jx7.
27 Armen Kazaryan and Lilit Mikayelyan, 'Architectural Decorations of Armenian Churches of the 7th and the 10th–11th Centuries and Their Presumably Sasanian Sources', in *Sasanian Elements in Byzantine, Caucasian and Islamic Art and Culture*, ed. Neslihan Asutay-Effenberger and Falko Daim (Mainz, 2019), pp. 75–92 (p. 82).
28 Zaruhi Hakobyan and Lilit Mikayelyan, 'The Senmurv and Other Mythical Creatures with Sasanian Iconography in the Medieval Art of Armenia and Transcaucasia', in *Fabulous Creatures and Spirits in Ancient Iranian Culture*, ed. Matteo Compareti (Bologna, 2018), pp. 39–76 (pp. 48–9, esp. n. 51).

10 Encircling Griffins: Mapping the Influence of a Motif

1 James Trilling, *The Medallion Style* (New York, 1985) overviews ancient examples of this visual formula.
2 Avinoam Shalem, *Die mittelalterlichen Olifante* (Berlin, 2014), pp. 369–72, cat. no. D2; Miriam Rosser-Owen, 'The Oliphant: A Call for a Shift of Perspective', in *Romanesque and the Mediterranean: Points of Contact Across the Latin, Greek and Islamic Worlds, c. 1000 to c. 1250*, ed. R. M. Bacile and J. McNeill (Leeds, 2015), pp. 15–58 (pp. 18–19).

3 Constantine VII Porphyrogennetos, *The Book of Ceremonies*, trans. Ann Moffatt and Maxeme Tall (Canberra, 2012), vol. II, p. 581, chap. 15 (Reiske 581). The translators suggest the second, 'little' griffin might be a scribal error, vol. II, p. 581, n. 1. My earlier essay on Byzantine textiles offers additional examples, A. L. McClanan, 'Illustrious Monsters: Representations of Griffins on Byzantine Textiles', in *Animals in Text and Textile: Storytelling in the Medieval World,* ed. Evelin Wetter and Kathryn Starkey (Riggisberg, 2019), pp. 133–45.
4 Constantine VII Porphyrogennetos, *The Book of Ceremonies*, vol. II, p. 589, chap. 15 (Reiske 589).
5 George P. Majeska, *Russian Travelers to Constantinople in the Fourteenth and Fifteenth Centuries* (Washington, DC, 1984), p. 142.
6 One page of Greek text contains five references to various 'chlamys', with peacocks, horsemen and eagles decorating the palace. Constantine VII Porphyrogennetos, *The Book of Ceremonies*, vol. II, p. 581, chap. 15 (Reiske 581).
7 Anna Muthesius, 'Byzantine Silks in the Latin West: Economic and Artistic Exchange or Political Ploy?', in *Studies in Byzantine, Islamic, and Near Eastern Silk Weaving* (London, 2008), pp. 116–31 (p. 121).
8 Pierre Müller, *Löwen und Mischwesen in der archaischen griechischen Kunst: eine Untersuchung über ihre Bedeutung* (Zürich, 1978), pp. 79–80.
9 Regula Schorta, *Monochrome Seidengewebe des hohen Mittelalters: Untersuchungen zu Webtechnik und Musterung* (Berlin, 2001), pp. 171–2.
10 Leslie Brubaker and John F. Haldon, *Byzantium in the Iconoclast Era (c. 680–850): The Sources, an Annotated Survey* (Aldershot, 2001), p. 104.
11 Judith H. Hofenk de Graaff et al., *The Colourful Past: Origins, Chemistry and Identification of Natural Dyestuffs* (Riggisberg, 2004), p. 272; Muthesius, *Byzantine Silk Weaving*, cat. no. M48. Legal codes from the early Byzantine period restrict the use of murex. Gerhard Steigerwald, 'Das kaiserliche Purpurprivileg in spätrömischer und frühbyzantinischer Zeit', *Jahrbuch für Antike und Christentum*, XXXIII (1990), pp. 209–39 (pp. 235–9).
12 Liudprand of Cremona, *Legatio*, sect. 55.
13 Gordon Campbell, ed., 'Lampas', in *The Grove Encyclopedia of Decorative Arts,* online version (Oxford, 2006).
14 Julia L. Galliker, 'Middle Byzantine Silk in Context: Integrating the Textual and Material Evidence', PhD thesis, University of Birmingham, 2015, pp. 169–70 and 176; Judith Olszowy-Schlanger, *Karaite Marriage Documents from the Cairo Geniza: Legal Tradition and Community Life in Mediaeval Egypt and Palestine* (Leiden, 1998), cat. nos TS 24.45 and TS NS J86.
15 Arielle Winnik, 'Toward a Grammar of Textiles: A Reconsideration of Medieval Silk Aesthetics and the Impact of Modern Collecting', *Textile Museum Journal*, XLIV (2017), pp. 6–29 (p. 25).
16 Lynn Jones and Henry Maguire, 'A Description of the Jousts of Manuel I Komnenos', *Byzantine and Modern Greek Studies*, XXVI (2002), pp. 104–48 (p. 108).
17 Ibid., p. 108.
18 Alicia Walker, '"The Art That Does Not Think": Byzantine "Decorative Arts" – History and Limits of a Concept', in *From Minor to Major: The Minor Arts*

in *Medieval Art History*, ed. Colum Hourihane (University Park, PA, 2012), pp. 169–93 (p. 183).

19 Eugène Chartraire, *Inventaire du trésor de l'église primatiale et métropolitaine de Sens* (Sens, 1897), p. 373.

20 *The Book of the Eparch*, sect. V.1–5.

21 E. Jane Burns, *Sea of Silk: A Textile Geography of Women's Work in Medieval French Literature* (Philadelphia, PA, 2014), pp. 5–7.

22 For Syrian attribution: Brigitta Schmedding, *Mittelalterliche Textilien in Kirchen und Klöstern der Schweiz* (Bern, 1978), pp. 250–52; for Byzantine attribution: Muthesius, *Byzantine Silk Weaving*, cat. no. M85.

23 Gerhard Wolf, 'Vesting Walls, Displaying Structure, Crossing Cultures: Transmedial and Transmaterial Dynamics of Ornament', in *Histories of Ornament: From Global to Local*, ed. Gülru Necipoğlu and Alina Payne (Princeton, NJ, 2016), pp. 96–105 (p. 105).

24 Robert A. Maxwell, *The Art of Medieval Urbanism: Parthenay in Romanesque Aquitaine* (University Park, PA, 2007), p. 114.

25 Linda Seidel, *Songs of Glory: The Romanesque Façades of Aquitaine* (Chicago, IL, 1981), p. 60.

26 Maxwell, *The Art*, pp. 151–2 and 164.

27 Foucher de Chartres, *A History of the Expedition to Jerusalem, 1095–1127*, trans. Harold S. Fink (Knoxville, TN, 1969), p. 286, sect. III.49.8.

28 Amanda R. Luyster, *English Bodies, Imported Silks: The Crusades, the Chertsey Tiles, and the Cosmopolitan Culture of Display*, forthcoming. Griffins appear of course in many medieval and early modern painted interiors, often taking their visual cue from medallion silks, such as on the Le Puy ceiling.

11 Griffins in the Realms of Death and Transcendence

1 Marian H. Feldman, *Diplomacy by Design: Luxury Arts and an 'International Style' in the Ancient Near East, 1400–1200 BCE* (Chicago, IL, 2006), p. 79.

2 Vibeke Berens, 'Creating the Non-Existent: A Materialistic Approach to the Development of Composite Animals from the Predynastic Period until the Middle Kingdom', master's thesis, Leiden University, 2015, p. 36.

3 Vera Vasilijević, 'Die zꜣgt von Cheti (Beni Hasan Nr. 17)', in *Es werde niedergelegt als Schriftstück: Festschrift für Hartwig Altenmüller zum 65. Geburtstag*, ed. Nicole Kloth et al. (Hamburg, 2003), pp. 433–6.

4 Glenys Davies, 'Before Sarcophagi', in *Life, Death and Representation: Some New Work on Roman Sarcophagi*, ed. Jaś Elsner and Janet Huskinson (New York, 2011), pp. 21–54 (p. 43).

5 Janet Huskinson, *Roman Children's Sarcophagi: Their Decoration and Its Social Significance* (Oxford, 1996), p. 60. Scholars debate whether such imagery is Apollonian or Dionysian. Instead, perhaps the ambiguity suggests it lacked a specific valency either way for its Roman viewers. Barbara Borg, *Roman Tombs and the Art of Commemoration: Contextual Approaches to Funerary Customs in the Second Century CE* (Cambridge, 2019), p. 59. Also see Anne F. Eberle, 'Un sarcophage d'enfant au J. Paul Getty Museum', in *Roman Funerary Monuments in the J. Paul Getty Museum* (Malibu, CA, 1990), vol. I, p. 54.

6 Davies, 'Before Sarcophagi', pp. 50–51.
7 Stine Birk, *Depicting the Dead: Self-Representation and Commemoration on Roman Sarcophagi with Portraits* (Aarhus, 2013), p. 125.
8 Jaś Elsner, 'Ornament, Figure, and *mise en abyme* on Roman Sarcophagi', in *Ornament and Figure in Graeco-Roman Art: Rethinking Visual Ontologies in Classical Antiquity*, ed. Nikolaus Dietrich and Michael Squire (Berlin, 2018), pp. 353–60 (p. 353, n. 2).
9 To illustrate the range, an example from the beginning of the medieval period and distant from the Greek origins of the Metropolitan Museum example would be the seventh-century limestone gravestone found in the Rhineland where griffins' foreparts perch in the stele's three remaining corners. Josef Engemann and Christoph Rüger, eds, *Spätantike und frühes Mittelalter: ausgewählte Denkmäler im Rheinischen Landesmuseum Bonn* (Cologne, 1991), pp. 57–60, inv. no. 35.10.
10 For more comparative examples: Theocharēs Pazaras, *Anaglyphes sarkophagoi kai epitaphies plakes tēs mesēs kai hysterēs vyzantinēs periodou stēn Hellada* (Athens, 1988), especially p. 94, n. 174; Helen C. Evans, ed., *Byzantium: Faith and Power (1261–1557)*, exh. cat. The Metropolitan Museum of Art, New York (2004), pp. 112–13, cat. no. 58.
11 Sharon E. J. Gerstel, *Rural Lives and Landscapes in Late Byzantium: Art, Archaeology, and Ethnography* (Cambridge, 2015), p. 142, n. 75.
12 Helen C. Evans and William D. Wixom, ed., *The Glory of Byzantium: Art and Culture of the Middle Byzantine Era, AD 843–1261*, exh. cat. The Metropolitan Museum of Art, New York (1997), p. 263, cat. no. 185, in reference to Dumbarton Oaks inv. no. BZ.1966.17.
13 An eagle trained this way is described in Geoffrey Moorhouse, *Apples in the Snow: A Journey to Samarkand* (London, 1990), p. 40, and an Indus Valley goshawk blinds a gazelle in Richard F. Burton, *Falconry in the Valley of the Indus* (London, 1852), p. 84.
14 Gönül Öney, 'Lion Figures in Anatolian Seljuk Architecture', *Anadolu/Anatolia*, XIII (1969), pp. 43–69 (pp. 53–4, figs 62–7).
15 Matthias Radscheit, 'Springs and Fountains', *Encyclopaedia of the Qurʾān*, online edition (Leiden, 2012).
16 Katharina Meinecke, 'The Encyclopaedic Illustration of a New Empire: Graeco-Roman-Byzantine and Sasanian Models on the Façade of Qasr al-Mshatta', in *Using Images in Late Antiquity*, ed. Stine Birk et al. (Oxford, 2014), pp. 283–300 (p. 288); Katharina Meinecke, 'Die Bauornamentik von Mschatta', in *Qasr al-Mschatta: ein frühislamischer Palast in Jordanien und Berlin*, ed. J. Cramer et al. (Petersberg, 2016), vol. I, pp. 161–87 (pp. 165–8).
17 Sara Kuehn, *The Dragon in Medieval East Christian and Islamic Art* (Leiden, 2011), pp. 155–6.
18 Elizabeth Jeffreys, 'The Sebastokratorissa Irene as Patron', in *Female Founders in Byzantium and Beyond*, ed. Lioba Theis et al. (Vienna, 2014), pp. 177–95 (p. 182).
19 It was so well regarded that 39 manuscript copies of this grammatical text still survive. Nikolaos Zagklas, 'A Byzantine Grammar Treatise Attributed to Theodoros Prodromos', *Graeco-Latina*

Brunensia, XVI/1 (2011), pp. 77–86 (pp. 80–81); Ingela Nilsson, 'Words, Water, and Power: Literary Fountains and Metaphors of Patronage in Eleventh- and Twelfth-Century Byzantium', in *Fountains and Water Culture in Byzantium*, ed. Brooke Shilling and Paul Stephenson (Cambridge, 2016), pp. 265–80 (p. 270).

20 Pierre and Maria-Teresa Canivet, 'La mosaïque d'Adam dans l'église syrienne de Huarte (Ve s.)', *Cahiers Archéologiques*, XXIV (1975), pp. 49–68; Henry Maguire, 'Adam and the Animals: Allegory and the Literal Sense in Early Christian Art', *Dumbarton Oaks Papers*, XLI (1987), pp. 363–73 (p. 368, n. 27).

21 Herbert L. Kessler, *Spiritual Seeing: Picturing God's Invisibility in Medieval Art* (Philadelphia, PA, 2000), p. 26.

22 George of Pisidia, *Hexaemeron*, col. 1505A.

23 Dante Alighieri, *Purgatorio*, trans. Allen Mandelbaum (Berkeley, CA, 1982), p. 258, sect. XXIX.112–14.

24 Peter Armour, *Dante's Griffin and the History of the World: A Study of the Earthly Paradise (Purgatorio, Cantos XXIX–XXXIII)* (Oxford, 1989), pp. 277–8; David Ruzicka, '"Sì ch'a nulla, fendendo, facea male": Dante's Griffin and Florentine Civic Ritual ("Purgatorio" 29.109–11)', *Dante Studies*, CXXX (2012), pp. 1–45.

25 Colin Hardie, 'The Symbol of the Gryphon in *Purgatorio* XXIX. 108 and Following Cantos', *Centenary Essays on Dante* (Oxford, 1965), pp. 103–31 (pp. 106–7).

26 Ronald E. Pepin, trans., *The Vatican Mythographers* (New York, 2008), p. 278, sect. 16.

27 The Third Vatican Mythographer expands on Late Antique authors such as Servius, who mention the griffin as the middle of Apollo's three key attributes along with the arrow and lyre (*ad Ecl.*, 5.26): 'grypam, quae eum etiam terrenum numen ostendit'. The lyre has celestial connotations, and the arrow is aligned with 'infernus.'

28 Dante, *Purgatorio*, p. 278, sect. XXXI.121–6.

29 For an alternative view, see Chistopher Livanos, 'Dante's Monsters: Nature and Evil in the "Commedia"', *Dante Studies with the Annual Report of the Dante Society*, CXXVII (2009), pp. 81–92.

30 A typical early depiction would be the Florentine manuscript from *c.* 1350, Morgan Library, mss. 676, f. 83v.; Joan Isobel Friedman, 'La processione mistica di Dante: Allegoria e iconografia nel canto XXIX del Purgatorio', in *Dante e le forme dell'allegoresi* (Ravenna, 1987), pp. 125–48 (fig. 8); and for more examples: Peter H. Brieger et al., *Illuminated Manuscripts of the Divine Comedy* (Princeton, NJ, 1969), vol. II, pp. 413–18.

31 Albert S. Roe, *Blake's Illustrations to the Divine Comedy* (Princeton, NJ, 1953), pp. 164–71.

32 Eric Pyle, *William Blake's Illustrations for Dante's Divine Comedy: A Study of the Engravings, Pencil Sketches and Watercolors* (Jefferson, NC, 2015), p. 241.

33 Roe, *Blake's Illustrations*, pp. 169–70. For an alternative reading of this griffin, see Rodney M. Baine, 'Blake's Dante in a Different Light', *Dante Studies, with the Annual Report of the Dante Society*, CV (1987), pp. 113–36 (p. 117).

34 Geneviève Lacambre, *Gustave Moreau: Between Epic and Dream* (Paris, 1999), p. 224, cat. no. 114; Pierre-Louis

Mathieu, *Gustave Moreau: monographie et nouveau catalogue de l'œuvre achevé* (Paris, 1998), cat. no. 216, p. 342.
35 Pierre-Louis Mathieu, *Gustave Moreau: The Watercolors* (New York, 1985), p. 12.
36 Gavin Parkinson, *Enchanted Ground: André Breton, Modernism and the Surrealist Appraisal of Fin-de-Siècle Painting* (New York, 2018), pp. 290–91.

12 Moralizing Griffins

1 Arnaud Zucker, trans., *Physiologos: le bestiaire des bestiaires*, 2nd edn (Grenoble, 2005), p. 264, sect. 51.
2 Isidore of Seville, *Etymologies*, XII.ii.17.
3 Willene B. Clark, *A Medieval Book of Beasts: The Second-Family Bestiary* (Woodbridge, 2006), p. 127; her translation is of British Library mss. Add. 11283.
4 Elizabeth Morrison and Larisa Grollemond, eds, *Book of Beasts: The Bestiary in the Medieval World*, exh. cat., J. Paul Getty Museum, Los Angeles (2019), pp. 98–101, cat. no. 6.
5 T. H. White, trans., *The Book of Beasts* (New York, 1954), p. 105.
6 Clark, *A Medieval Book*, p. 127, n. 42; Christa Tuczay, 'Drache und Greif – Symbole der Ambivalenz', *Mediaevistik*, XIX (2006), pp. 169–211 (p. 196). An example of such a medieval text is that attributed to Hugh of Fouilloy, which offers a generic recap of Isidore of Seville's griffin description in the section devoted to birds (*Patrologia Latina* 177: col. 84, sect. 4), and then in his appendix devoted to gemstones griffins reappear, but as the greedy protectors of emeralds within a larger moral narrative (*PL* 177: 116–17, sect. 58): 'Gryphes qui servunt eas significant diabolos qui pretiosam margaritam fidei . . .'. This negative characterization is echoed in the French prose bestiary attributed to Pierre de Beauvais, *Le bestiaire: version longue attribuée à Pierre de Beauvais*, ed. Craig Baker (Paris, 2010), p. 190, sect. XXXIX.
7 Paul Hardwick, *English Medieval Misericords: The Margins of Meaning* (Woodbridge, 2011), pp. 83 and 149.
8 Frederick Adam Wright, trans., *Select Letters of St Jerome* (Cambridge, MA, 1933), p. 403, letter 125.
9 Andrew Cain, *The Letters of Jerome: Asceticism, Biblical Exegesis, and the Construction of Christian Authority in Late Antiquity* (Oxford, 2009), pp. 151–8.
10 Hrabanus Maurus, *De Universo: The Peculiar Properties of Words and Their Mystical Significance*, trans. Priscilla Throop (Charlotte, VT, 2009), vol. II, p. 171, sect. XVII.7.
11 The Latin word *smaragdus* could refer to a range of green stones, but emerald is the most common translation, more in Brigitte Buettner, *The Mineral and the Visual: Precious Stones in Medieval Visual Culture* (University Park, PA, 2022), p. 109.
12 John T. Appleby, ed. and trans., *The Chronicle of Richard of Devizes of the Time of King Richard the First* (London, 1963), p. 17, f. 29v.
13 Edmond Emplaincourt, 'Notes de lectures à propos des mots grifon et grifaigne', *Oliphant*, XVII/3/4 (1993), pp. 134–44. A similar usage for 'griffin' appears in the nineteenth century, applied to mixed-race individuals in Louisiana (specifically to the child of someone labelled 'Black' and someone labelled 'mulatto'), and in India to newly arrived British. William Dwight

Whitney, *The Century Dictionary: An Encyclopedic Lexicon of the English Language* (New York, 1889), p. 2623; Walter Johnson, 'The Slave Trader, the White Slave, and the Politics of Racial Determination in the 1850s', *Journal of American History*, LXXXVII/1 (2000), pp. 13–38 (p. 16, n. 60).

14 Lindsay Diggelmann, 'Of Grifons and Tyrants: Anglo-Norman Views of the Mediterranean World During the Third Crusade', in *Old Worlds, New Worlds: European Cultural Encounters, c. 1000–c. 1750*, ed. Lisa Kaaren Bailey et al. (Turnhout, 2009), pp. 11–30 (pp. 18–19).

15 Morrison and Grollemond, *Book of Beasts*, pp. 240–44.

16 Marc M. Epstein, *The Medieval Haggadah: Art, Narrative, and Religious Imagination* (New Haven, CT, 2011), pp. 45–63.

17 Ibid., p. 56.

18 Elina Gertsman, 'Animal Affinities: Monsters and Marvels in the Ambrosian Tanakh', *Gesta*, LXI/1 (2022), pp. 27–55 (fig. 1); Bracha Yaniv, 'The Cherubim on Torah Ark Valences', *Assaph, Studies in Art History*, IV (1999), pp. 155–70 (p. 163, n. 17).

19 Epstein, *The Medieval Haggadah*, p. 57, n. 24.

20 Ibid., pp. 100–104. Biddick takes this interpretation of the griffin-headed figures further: 'suturing animal and human forms, these Ashkenazi Jews exposed the sutured nature of sovereign bare life, which to produce "humanness" dominates animals as bare life and in so doing creates the conditions of possibility for naming the state of exception against selected groups of humans and reducing them to the bare life of slavery.' Kathleen Biddick, 'Read Yourself! The Griffin Condition on the Day before the Last Day', *Qui Parle*, XXVII/1 (2018), pp. 77–98 (p. 89).

21 Tade Thompson, *Rosewater* (New York, 2018), p. 386.

13 Making Their Mark with Griffins: From Heraldry to Visual Branding

1 J.M.F. May, *The Coinage of Abdera (540–345 BC)* (London, 1966), p. 49; Katerina Chryssanthaki-Nagle, *L'histoire monétaire d'Abdère en Thrace: VI s. avant J.-C. – IIE s. après J.-C.* (Athens, 2007), pp. 95–7.

2 Alicia Walker, 'Islamicising Motifs in Byzantine Lead Seals: Exoticising Style and the Expression of Identity', *Medieval History Journal*, XV/2 (October 2012), pp. 385–413 (pp. 387–8).

3 Oxford University, Bodleian Library, mss. Laud Misc. 733, f. 10r, lines 798–807.

4 Cambridge University Library, mss. Ee.iv.20, f. 161r, line 88.

5 Richard James Moll, ed., *A Heraldic Miscellany: Fifteenth-Century Treatises on Blazon and the Office of Arms in English and Scots* (Liverpool, 2018), p. 104, lines 105–11.

6 Peter le Neve, British Library, Harley mss. 5801, f. 6.

7 Rodney Dennys, *The Heraldic Imagination* (New York, 1976), pp. 175–7.

8 Brian Abel Ragen, 'Semiotics and Heraldry', *Semiotica*, C/1 (1994), pp. 5–34 (p. 6).

9 W. Mark Ormrod, *Edward III* (New Haven, CT, 2011), p. 135, n. 81.

10 Francis Palgrave, ed., *The Ancient Kalendars and Inventories of the Treasury of His Majesty's Exchequer* (London, 1836), vol. III, p. 340, inv. nos 179 and 180.

11 T. F. Tout, '[Review of] Études de Diplomatique Anglaise, 1272–1485 by

Eugène Déprez', *English Historical Review*, XXIII/91 (1908), pp. 556–9 (p. 559).
12 T. F. Tout, *Chapters in the Administrative History of Mediaeval England; The Wardrobe, the Chamber and the Small Seals* (Manchester, 1928), vol. III, p. 52. P.D.A. Harvey misattributes this griffin seal to Edward II, *A Guide to British Medieval Seals* (Toronto, 1996), p. 36.
13 Hugh Stanford London, *The Queen's Beasts* (London, 1953), p. 22.
14 Ibid., pp. 22–4.
15 *The Kunera Database for Late Medieval Badges and Ampullae*, www.kunera.nl, accessed 6 September 2020. Ann Marie Rasmussen points to the complexity of this corner of material culture, and how it's not always possible to differentiate secular and religious badges, *Medieval Badges: Their Wearers and Their Worlds* (Philadelphia, PA, 2021), p. 15.
16 Sarah Blick, 'Bringing Pilgrimage Home: The Production, Iconography, and Domestic Use of Late-Medieval Devotional Objects by Ordinary People', *Religions*, X/6 (2019), pp. 1–26 (pp. 8–9).
17 Ruth Mellinkoff, *Averting Demons* (Los Angeles, CA, 2004), vol. I, pp. 62–3.
18 Michael Mitchiner, *Medieval Pilgrim and Secular Badges* (Sanderstead, 1986), p. 119, cat. nos 299–300.
19 Argues for this connection to Edward III: Brian Spencer, *Pilgrim Souvenirs and Secular Badges* (Woodbridge, 2010), p. 291; argues against this connection to Edward III: Geoff Egan, *The Medieval Household: Daily Living, c. 1150–c. 1450* (Woodbridge, 2010), p. 266.
20 Geoff Egan et al., *Lead Cloth Seals and Related Items in the British Museum* (London, 1994), pp. 29–30, cat. no. 25.
21 Bauer Type Foundry, *The Griffin: A Note on a Fabulous Creature's Rise from a Guardian of Gold to a Symbol of Printing* (New York, 1941). This booklet, itself an exquisite product of fine printing, briefly sketches the griffin's role in early printing, though overstates its case a bit.
22 Luuk Houwen, 'Beastly Devices: Early Printer's Marks and Their Medieval Origins', in *Typographorum Emblemata: The Printer's Mark in the Context of Early Modern Culture*, ed. Bernhard F. Scholz and Anja Wolkenhauer (Berlin, 2018), pp. 49–75 (p. 52).
23 W. Roberts, *Printers' Marks: A Chapter in the History of Typography* (London, 1893), p. 36.
24 'Griffin', *The Oxford Dictionary of Family Names in Britain and Ireland*, ed. Patrick Hanks et al. (Oxford, 2017), p. 1132; 'Griffin', *Dictionary of American Family Names,* ed. Patrick Hanks, online edition (Oxford, 2003).
25 Arthur Charles Fox-Davies, *A Complete Guide to Heraldry* (London, 1909), p. 222.
26 *A Pictorial and Descriptive Guide to London and Its Environs*, 38th edn (London, 1914), p. 192.
27 This long-standing connection continued to be reinforced, such as with the gift of a 'griffin claw' by King Charles VII before 1454. Philippe Cordez, *Trésor, Mémoire, Merveilles. Les objets des églises au Moyen Âge* (Paris, 2016), pp. 204–5.
28 Ittai Weinryb, *The Bronze Object in the Middle Ages* (Cambridge, 2016), pp. 191–8.
29 Anita Federer Moskowitz, *Italian Gothic Sculpture: c. 1250–c. 1400* (New York, 2001), p. 45.

30 Mary A. Johnstone, 'The Griffin: The Coat of Arms of Perugia', *Studi Etruschi*, XXX (1962), pp. 335–52 (p. 340).
31 Ezra J. Zeitler, 'A Taxonomy of Secondary School Athletic Team Names and Mascots in the United States', *Names*, LXVI/4 (2018), pp. 219–32 (p. 228).
32 Tyra M. Vaughn, 'William and Mary Recognized for Mascot Search', *Daily Press* (Williamsburg, VA), www.dailypress.com, 26 July 2010.
33 Brian Whitson, '"Get Me the Griffin": William & Mary Announce New Mascot', *William & Mary News Archive*, www.wm.edu, 6 April 2010.
34 Jon Stewart, 'Virginia's Confederate History Month and Griffin Mascot', *The Daily Show with Jon Stewart* (video clip), Comedy Central, www.cc.com, 8 April 2010.
35 Sarah Fearing, 'Bronze Griffin's "Graphic" Testicles Prompt Student, Alumni Debate at William & Mary', *Williamsburg Yorktown Daily*, www.wydaily.com, 10 November 2018.

14 Adventures with Griffins

1 Winder McConnell, trans., *Kudrun* (Columbia, SC, 1992), pp. 8–13, ch. 2.
2 In the text attributed to Mandeville's notoriously fraught manuscript lineage, its griffin account usually features in chapter 29; in Marco Polo's *Book of Marvels* the creature features in book three, chapter 33. For more consideration of how in the early modern era 'genres were not defined by their allegiance to truth-telling or invention' a good starting point is Chapter Three of Lennard J. Davis, *Factual Fictions: The Origins of the English Novel* (Philadelphia, PA, 1997), p. 67.
3 Charles de Linas, 'Aumônières tirées de la collection de M. Oudet, architecte à Bar-le-Duc', *Revue de l'art chrétien*, IV (1860), pp. 393–401.
4 Léon de Laborde, *Glossaire français du moyen âge: à l'usage de l'archéologue et de l'amateur des arts* (Paris, 1872), p. 18.
5 Julie Laurenge, 'Les aumônières de forme trapézoïdale à partie supérieure arrondie dans la production brodée du XIVe siècle. Une étude de cas: Les deux aumônières dites d'une Comtesse de Bar du Musée de Cluny (inv. n° Cl. 11787 et Cl. 11788)', in *Actes du 1er Colloque des étudiants de master en Sciences historiques et artistiques de Lille,* ed. Dominic Moreau et al. (Lille, 2017), pp. 240–46 (p. 245).
6 Sharon Farmer, 'Biffes, Tiretaines, and Aumonières: The Role of Paris in the International Textile Markets of the Thirteenth and Fourteenth Centuries', in *Medieval Clothing and Textiles,* ed. Robin Netherton and Gale R. Owen-Crocker (Woodbridge, 2006), pp. 73–89.
7 Thomas Golsenne, 'La femme-léopard. Histoire de la mode chez les amazones', *Apparence(s),* VIII (2018), pp. 1–28 (p. 10).
8 Anna Rapp Buri, *Zahm und wild: Basler und Strassburger Bildteppiche des 15. Jahrhunderts*, 2nd edn (Mainz, 1990), pp. 157–8, cat. no. 18; Betty Kurth, *Die deutschen Bildteppiche des Mittelalters* (Vienna, 1926), vol. II, pl. 54.
9 Klaus Niehr, 'Mimesis, Stilisierung, Fiktion in spätmittelalterlicher Porträtmalerei. Das sog. Gothaer Liebespaar', *Marburger Jahrbuch für Kunstwissenschaft*, 25 (1998), pp. 79–104 (p. 84).
10 Michael Camille, *The Medieval Art of Love: Objects and Subjects of Desire* (New York, 1998), p. 106.

11 Rapp Buri, *Zahm und wild*, p. 157.
12 Jane Staab, *Dragon, Griffin and Courtly Love: Mainz Tapestries from the Late Gothic Period* (Mainz, 2000), p. 24.
13 Jutta Zander-Seidel, 'Animals on Minne Tapestries: Symbols of Lordship and Ornament', in *Animals in Text and Textile: Storytelling in the Medieval World*, ed. Evelin Wetter and Kathryn Starkey (Riggisberg, 2019), pp. 210–25 (p. 214).
14 A mention circa 1171 offers the first reference to a 'griffin claw' (*Ungula grifonis*), 'Gifts of Bishop Henry of Blois, Abbot of Glastonbury, to Winchester Cathedral', in *Liturgica Historica: Papers on the Liturgy and Religious Life of the Western Church*, ed. Edmund Bishop [1884/1918] (Oxford, 1962), pp. 392–401 (p. 401).
15 Naomi Speakman, '"Griffin's Claw" of St Cuthbert', in *Treasures of Heaven: Saints, Relics, and Devotion in Medieval Europe*, ed. Martina Bagnoli (New Haven, CT, 2010), pp. 229–30, cat. no. 132; Philippe Cordez, *Trésor, mémoire, merveilles. Les objets des églises au Moyen Âge* (Paris, 2016), p. 207; Paul Rehak, 'The Aegean "Priest" on CMS I.223', *Kadmos*, XXXIII/1 (1994), pp. 76–84 (p. 83, n. 31).
16 Cordez, *Trésor*, p. 200.
17 Cynthia J. Hahn, *Strange Beauty: Issues in the Making and Meaning of Reliquaries, 400-circa 1204* (University Park, PA, 2012), p. 135.
18 Sir Charles Hercules Read, 'Note of a Griffin's Claw', *Proceedings of the Society of Antiquaries of London*, II/9 (1881), pp. 250–51.
19 William Oldys, *A Literary Antiquary, Memoir of William Oldys Together with His Diary, Choice Notes from His Adversaria, and an Account of the London Libraries* (London, 1862), p. 68.
20 'Animal Remains', www.britishmuseum.org, inv. no. OA.24, accessed 15 October 2020.
21 Lady Mary Wortley Montagu, 'Letter from Ratisbon/Regensburg, 30 August 1716', *The Complete Letters* (Oxford, 1965), vol. I, pp. 256–8 (p. 258).
22 Cordez, *Trésor*, p. 200.
23 Caroline Cazanave, 'Le griffon des Huon de Bordeaux et les retombées d'une histoire de patte coupée', in *Du temps que les bestes parloient: mélanges offerts au professeur Roger Bellon*, ed. Valérie Méot-Bourquin and Aurélie Barre (Paris, 2018), pp. 366–78 (pp. 368, 371).
24 Ibid., p. 373.
25 Gavin Betts, trans., 'Velthandros and Chrysandza', *Three Medieval Greek Romances* (New York, 1995), pp. 5–32 (pp. 10–11).
26 Garci Rodríguez de Montalvo, *The Labors of the Very Brave Knight Esplandián* (Binghamton, NY, 1992), p. 474, sect. 164.
27 Ibid., p. 459, sect. 157.
28 Ibid.
29 Ibid., p. 456, n. 1; Rose Marie Beebe and Robert M. Senkewicz, eds, *Lands of Promise and Despair: Chronicles of Early California, 1535–1846* (Santa Clara, CA, 2001), p. 10.
30 W. Michael Mathes, 'The Mythological Geography of California: Origins, Development, Confirmation and Disappearance', *The Americas*, XLV/3 (1989), pp. 315–41 (p. 317).
31 Erwin Gustav Gudde, *California Place Names: The Origin and Etymology of Current Geographical Names*, 4th edn (Berkeley, CA, 1998), p. 60.
32 Elizabeth Morrison and Larisa Grollemond, eds, *Book of Beasts: The Bestiary in the Medieval World* (Los

Angeles, CA, 2019), p. 306; Walton Ford, *Walton Ford: Calafia* (Beverly Hills, CA, 2017), p. 63.
33 Ezrha Jean Black, 'Walton Ford's Natural History for California Dreamers', *Artillery Magazine*, https://artillerymag.com, 20 December 2017. Ford elsewhere imparts fictive histories through inscriptions, such as 2006's *Novaya Zemlya Still Life* bearing the date 1596. Bill Buford, *Walton Ford: Pancha Tantra*, 4th edn (Cologne, 2020), pp. 193–5.
34 Arsalan Mohammad, '"A Miraculous Diversity of Beautiful Forms": How a World of Natural History Inspires Walton Ford', www.sothebys.com, 23 November 2022.
35 Thomas Browne, *Pseudodoxia Epidemica, or, Enquiries Into Very Many Received Tenents and Commonly Presumed Truths* [1646], 6th edn (London, 1672), p. 142, sect. 3, ch. II. The matter of the griffin's existence was hardly settled though, for others took up the task of rebutting Browne on the controversy, as in Alexander Ross, *Arcana microcosmi* . . . (London, 1651), p. 220.
36 François Désiré Roulin, *Mémoire pour servir à l'histoire du tapir* (Paris, 1835), pp. 79–80; John Timbs, *Things Not Generally Known: Popular Errors Explained and Illustrated* (London, 1858), pp. 120–21.
37 James Coats, *A New Dictionary of Heraldry* (London, 1725), p. 169.
38 Leonardo da Vinci, *Selections from the Notebooks of Leonardo da Vinci*, ed. Irma A. Richter (Oxford, 1977), p. 167.
39 Oxford University, Ashmolean Museum inv. no. PII 17/ WA1855.86; Martin Kemp and Juliana Barone, *I disegni di Leonardo da Vinci e della sua cerchia nelle collezioni della Gran Bretagna* (Florence, 2010), pp. 82–4.
40 Claudia Swan, 'Counterfeit Chimeras: Early Modern Theories of the Imagination and the Work of Art', in *Vision and Its Instruments: Art, Science, and Technology in Early Modern Europe*, ed. Alina Payne (University Park, PA, 2015), pp. 216–40 (p. 225); Sophie de Bussierre, *Martin Schongauer: maître de la gravure rhénane, vers 1450–1491* (Paris, 1991), p. 250, cat. no. 99.
41 Max Lehrs, ed., *Martin Schongauer, Nachbildungen seiner Kupferstiche 72 Tafeln in Kupfertiefätzung* (Berlin, 1914), cat. no. 92 (cat. no. 93 in 2005 revd edn).
42 Dave Berns, 'Circus Circus Creating Paradise on South Strip', *Las Vegas Review-Journal (NV)*, 1 January 1997.

15 Modern Marvels: The Griffin Imagery of Carroll and Rowling

1 For an interesting discussion of pastoral in this scene, see Gillian Beer, *Alice in Space: The Sideways Victorian World of Lewis Carroll* (Chicago, IL, 2016), p. 183.
2 Ronald Latham, *Dictionary of Medieval Latin from British Sources*, fasc. 4 (London, 1975), p. 1112.
3 *Oxford English Dictionary*, 2nd edn, www.oed.com. Mandeville's *Travels*, Roxb. XXIX. 132 and Montagu Letter, 30 August 1716, line 258 (both discussed in Chapter Fourteen); Milton, *Paradise Lost*, sect. II.943 (discussed in Chapter Twelve).
4 As seen on the pages hand numbered 78, 82 and 84 in the 'Alice's Adventures Under Ground' manuscript, available at www.bl.uk, Add. mss. 46700.
5 Enlarged versions of Tenniel's drawings were found alongside David Hall storybook stills for the Disney movie,

including renderings of the Gryphon with a bowler hat. Matt Crandall blog, https://vintagedisneyalice.blogspot.com, 15–16 January 2009.

6 Emily Brontë, *Wuthering Heights* (London, 1847), chap. 1.

7 E. M. Forster, *A Room with a View* (London, 1908), chap. 2.

8 Anthony Doerr, *Cloud Cuckoo Land: A Novel* (New York, 2021), pp. 242 and 34.

9 Tina Jordan, 'J. K. Rowling's Friend Robert Galbraith Has Something to Say', *New York Times*, 16 September 2018.

10 J. K. Rowling, *Harry Potter and the Philosopher's Stone* (London, 1997), chap. 7. Rowling has indicated that four houses, defined by character traits, were part of her conception of the story from the beginning, J. K. Rowling, 'The Sorting Hat', *Hogwarts: An Incomplete and Unreliable Guide* (London, 2016), ebook.

11 Valerie Krishna, ed., *The Alliterative Morte Arthure: A Critical Edition* (New York, 1976), p. 145, line 3869.

12 Brett M. Rogers, 'Orestes and the Half-Blood Prince: Ghosts of Aeschylus in the Harry Potter Series', in *Classical Traditions in Modern Fantasy*, ed. Brett M. Rogers and Benjamin Eldon Stevens (Oxford, 2017), pp. 209–32 (p. 224).

13 J. K. Rowling, *Harry Potter and the Deathly Hallows* (London, 2007), chap. 9.

14 J. K. Rowling, *Harry Potter and the Chamber of Secrets* (London, 1998), chap. 12; also in *Harry Potter and the Order of the Phoenix* (London, 2003), chap. 22.

15 Rowling, *Chamber of Secrets*, chap. 11.

16 John Algeo, 'A Fancy for the Fantastic: Reflections on Names in Fantasy Literature', *Names*, XLIX/4 (2001), pp. 248–53.

17 Newt Scamander (pseud. for J. K. Rowling), *Fantastic Beasts and Where to Find Them*, American edn (New York, 2017), p. 35.

18 Ibid., p. xxiv.

19 J. K. Rowling, *Fantastic Beasts: The Crimes of Grindelwald, the Original Screenplay* (New York, 2018), scene 39.

20 Deniz Çam, 'In A Lonely Lockdown, With Books Slow to Come, Fanfiction Booms', *Forbes*, www.forbes.com, 21 April 2020.

21 'Author Chat: SenLinYu', 30 December 2019, *Wine, Wands and Waffling* podcast, available at www.podchaser.com.

22 Liz Gallo aligns AO3's values with these goals at the heart of feminist human–computer interaction (HCI), 'Archive of Our Own Shows What Happens When Women Make Websites', Medium.com, https://medium.com, 21 August 2019.

23 Darren Waters, 'Rowling Backs Potter Fan Fiction', BBC News, www.bbc.com/news, 27 May 2004.

24 See www.wizardingworld.com, accessed 20 January 2021.

25 J. K. Rowling, *Harry Potter and the Prisoner of Azkaban* (London, 1999), chap. 6.

26 Russell Scott Smith, 'How the Hippogriff Got Its Wings (And Beak)', *New York Post*, https://nypost.com, 5 June 2004.

27 Mary Ann Skweres, 'The Real Magic of "Harry Potter and the Prisoner of Azkaban"', Animation World Network, www.awn.com, 24 June 2004.

28 For example, J. K. Rowling, National Press Club's Author Luncheon, 20 October 1999, https://legacy.npr.org/programs/npc/1999/991020.jkrowling.html.

29 Thomas Blount, *Glossographia; or, A Dictionary, Interpreting the Hard Words of Whatsoever Language Now Used in Our Refined English Tongue* (London, 1674), p. 310.
30 Thomas Honegger, 'Draco litterarius: Some Thoughts on an Imaginary Beast', in *Tiere und Fabelwesen im Mittelalter*, ed. Sabine Obermaier (Berlin, 2009), pp. 131–43 (p. 143).
31 'Hippogriff', www.wikipedia.org, accessed 27 September 2020.
32 Louis Charbonneau-Lassay, *Le bestiaire du Christ* (Bruges, 1940), p. 335.

Epilogue: Thinking with Griffins

1 This theory presented in Adrienne Mayor, 'The Gold-Guarding Griffin: A Paleontological Legend', in *The First Fossil Hunters: Dinosaurs, Mammoths, and Myth in Greek and Roman Times*, 2nd edn (Princeton, NJ, 2011), pp. 15–53. Chapter Two here outlines why it requires reconsideration.
2 Jean-Yves Ferri, *Asterix and the Griffin*, trans. Adriana Hunter (London, 2021), p. 44.
3 The game designer Fumito Ueda and lead animator, Masanobu Tanaka, discuss the naming process in an interview from gen DESIGN, www.gendesign.co.jp, 22 June 2018.
4 E. J. White, *A Unified Theory of Cats on the Internet* (Stanford, CA, 2020), especially pp. 89–106.
5 The ancient Greek concept of *parergon* (ornament, supplemental matter), as reformulated by Enlightenment philosopher Immanuel Kant, had enormous influence, but the wider intellectual currents represented by the twentieth-century deconstructionist Jacques Derrida have seen the distinction between *ergon/parergon* (subject/ornament) questioned and even subverted, for a cogent recent look: Rebecca Zorach, 'Envoi', in *The Frame in Classical Art: A Cultural History*, ed. Verity J. Platt and Michael Squire (Cambridge, 2017), pp. 583–603.

Select Bibliography

Here you find a selection of key books and articles used while exploring the many different ways griffins are portrayed. This list focuses on sources that happen to be in English and that otherwise seem potentially most helpful to a range of *Griffinology* readers.

Algeo, John, 'A Fancy for the Fantastic: Reflections on Names in Fantasy Literature', *Names*, XLIX/4 (2001), pp. 248–53

Andreeva, Petya V., 'Fantastic Beasts of the Eurasian Steppes: Toward a Revisionist Approach to Animal-Style Art', PhD thesis, University of Pennsylvania, 2018, book publication forthcoming

Argent, Gala, 'Do the Clothes Make the Horse? Relationality, Roles and Statuses in Iron Age Inner Asia', *World Archaeology*, XLII/2 (2010), pp. 157–74

Armour, Peter, *Dante's Griffin and the History of the World: A Study of the Earthly Paradise (Purgatorio, Cantos XXIX–XXXIII)* (Oxford, 1989)

Aruz, Joan, 'Intercultural Styles, Animal Combats, and the Art of Exchange', in *Die Bedeutung der minoischen und mykenischen Glyptik*, ed. W. Müller (Mainz, 2010), pp. 73–82

—, and Ronald Wallenfels, eds, *Art of the First Cities: The Third Millennium BC from the Mediterranean to the Indus*, exh. cat., The Metropolitan Museum of Art, New York (2003)

Barkova, L. L., and S. V. Pankova, 'Tattooed Mummies from the Large Pazyryk Mounds: New Findings', *Archaeology, Ethnology and Anthropology of Eurasia*, XXII/2 (2005), pp. 48–59

Bartscht, Waltraud, 'The Griffin', in *Mythical and Fabulous Creatures: A Source Book and Research Guide*, ed. Malcolm South (New York, 1987), pp. 85–101

Bauer Type Foundry, *The Griffin: A Note on a Fabulous Creature's Rise from a Guardian of Gold to a Symbol of Printing* (New York, 1941)

Biddick, Kathleen, 'Read Yourself: The Griffin Condition on the Day before the Last Day', *Qui Parle*, XXVII/1 (2018), pp. 77–98

Bisi, Anna Maria, *Il Grifone; Storia di un Motivo Iconografico nell'antico Oriente Mediterraneo* (Rome, 1965)

Bouras, Laskarina, *The Griffin through the Ages*, ed. A. Petrides and P. Tsakirakis (Athens, 1983)

Clark, Willene B., *A Medieval Book of Beasts: The Second-Family Bestiary* (Woodbridge, 2006)

Collon, Dominique, *First Impressions: Cylinder Seals in the Ancient Near East* (London, 1987)

Contadini, Anna, ed., *The Pisa Griffin and the Mari-Cha Lion: Metalwork, Art, and Technology in the Medieval Islamicate Mediterranean* (Pisa, 2018)

Cordez, Phillippe, *Trésor, Mémoire, Merveilles. Les objets des églises au Moyen Âge* (Paris, 2016), in English translation as *Treasure, Memory, Nature: Church Objects in the Middle Ages*, trans. Chloe Siner Morgan (London, 2020)

Ćurčić, Slobodan, 'Some Uses (and Reuses) of Griffins in Late Byzantine Art', in *Byzantine East, Latin West: Art-Historical Studies in Honor of Kurt Weitzmann* (Princeton, NJ, 1995), pp. 597–604

Daim, Falko, 'Objects and Motifs: On Visual Communication in the Avar Empire', in *Von den Hunnen zu den Türken – Reiterkrieger in Europa und Zentralasien*, ed. H. Meller et al. (Halle (Saale), 2021), pp. 191–214

Delplace, Chistiane, *Le griffon de l'archaïsme à l'époque impériale: étude iconographique et essai d'interprétation symbolique* (Brussels, 1980)

Diggelmann, Lindsay, 'Of Grifons and Tyrants: Anglo-Norman Views of the Mediterranean World During the Third Crusade', in *Old Worlds, New Worlds: European Cultural Encounters, c. 1000–c. 1750*, ed. Lisa Kaaren Bailey et al. (Turnhout, 2009), pp. 11–30

Ebbinghaus, Susanne, and A. Cassandra Albinson, eds, *Animal-Shaped Vessels from the Ancient World: Feasting with Gods, Heroes, and Kings,* exh. cat., Harvard Art Museums, Cambridge, MA (2018)

Elsner, Jaś, 'Ornament, Figure, and *mise en abyme* on Roman Sarcophagi', in *Ornament and Figure in Graeco-Roman Art: Rethinking Visual Ontologies in Classical Antiquity*, ed. N. Dietrich and M. Squire (Berlin, 2018), pp. 357–60

Epstein, Marc M., *The Medieval Haggadah* (New Haven, CT, 2011)

Feldman, Marian H., *Communities of Style: Portable Luxury Arts, Identity, and Collective Memory in the Iron Age Levant* (Chicago, IL, 2014)

—, *Diplomacy by Design: Luxury Arts and an 'International Style' in the Ancient Near East, 1400–1200 BCE* (Chicago, IL, 2006)

Flagge, Ingeborg, *Untersuchungen zur Bedeutung des Greifen* (Sankt Augustin, 1975)

Francfort, Henri-Paul, 'The Gold of the Griffins: Recent Excavation of a Frozen Tomb in Kazakhstan', in *The Golden Deer of Eurasia; Perspectives on the Steppe Nomads of the Ancient World*, ed. J. Aruz et al. (New Haven, CT, 2006), pp. 114–27

Gerke, Sonja, *Der altägyptische Greif: von der Vielfalt eines 'Fabeltiers'* (Hamburg, 2014)

Gertsman, Elina, 'Animal Affinities: Monsters and Marvels in the Ambrosian Tanakh', *Gesta*, LXI/1 (2022), pp. 27–55

Gunter, Ann C., 'Animal Friezes in "Orientalizing" Greek Art', in *Animals and Their Relation to Gods, Humans and Things in the Ancient World*, ed. R. Mattila et al. (Wiesbaden, 2019), pp. 235–48

—, 'Orientalism and Orientalization in the Iron Age Mediterranean', in *Critical Approaches to Ancient Near Eastern Art*, ed. Brian A. Brown and Marian H. Feldman (Boston, MA, 2013), pp. 79–108

Hardwick, Paul, *English Medieval Misericords: The Margins of Meaning* (Woodbridge, 2011)

Hayashi, Toshio, 'Griffin Motif: From the West to East Asia via the Altai', *Parthica: incontri di culture nel mondo antico*, XIV (2012), pp. 49–64

Hitchcock, Louise, and Marianna Nikolaidou, 'Gender in Greek and Aegean Prehistory', in *A Companion to Gender Prehistory*, ed. D. Bolger (Somerset, NJ, 2012), pp. 502–25

Hoffman, Eva R., 'Pathways of Portability: Islamic and Christian Interchange from the Tenth to the Twelfth Century', *Art History*, XXIV/1 (2001), pp. 17–50

Hornum, Michael B., *Nemesis, the Roman State, and the Games* (New York, 1993)

Hristov, Hristomir Smilenov, 'The Griffin-Fight in Ancient Art from Cyprus: Iconography and Interpretation', in *POCA (Postgraduate Cypriot Archaeology) 2012*, ed. H. Matthäus et al. (Newcastle upon Tyne, 2015), pp. 240–65

Hsu (徐詩薇), Shih-Wei, 'The "Griffin" as a Visual and Written Image for the King', *Göttinger Miszellen – Beiträge zur ägyptologischen Diskussion*, CCXXXI (2011), pp. 45–56

Huskinson, Janet, *Roman Children's Sarcophagi: Their Decoration and Its Social Significance* (Oxford, 1996)

Iwe, Karina, 'Tattoos from Mummies of the Pazyryk Culture', in *Tattoos and Body Modifications in Antiquity*, ed. P. Della Casa and C. Witt (Zürich, 2013), pp. 89–95

Kuehn, Sara, *The Dragon in Medieval East Christian and Islamic Art* (Leiden, 2011)

Lacambre, Geneviève, *Gustave Moreau: Between Epic and Dream* (Paris, 1999)

Leventopolou, Maria, 'Gryps', *Lexicon iconographicum mythologiae Classicae (LIMC)*, VIII/1 (Zürich, 2009), p. 609

Lymer, Kenneth, 'Griffins, Myths and Religion – A Review of the Archaeological Evidence from Ancient Greece and the Early Nomads of Central Asia', *Art of the Orient*, VII (2018), pp. 9–25

McClanan, A. L., 'Architectural Fragment with Griffin', in *Bringing the Holy Land Home: The Crusades, Chertsey Abbey, and the Reconstruction of a Medieval Masterpiece*, ed. Amanda Luyster (Turnhout, 2023), pp. 305–7

—, 'Illustrious Monsters: Representations of Griffins on Byzantine Textiles', in *Animals in Text and Textile: Storytelling in the Medieval World*, ed. Evelin Wetter and Kathryn Starkey (Riggisberg, 2019), pp. 133–45

Magdalino, Paul, 'The Bath of Leo the Wise and the "Macedonian Renaissance" Revisited: Topography, Iconography, Ceremonial, Ideology', *Dumbarton Oaks Papers*, XLII (1988), pp. 97–118

Marinatos, Nanno, *Minoan Kingship and the Solar Goddess: A Near Eastern Koine* (Urbana, IL, 2010)

Mathes, W. Michael, 'The Mythological Geography of California: Origins, Development, Confirmation and Disappearance', *The Americas*, XLV/3 (1989), pp. 315–41

Mathews, Karen R., *Conflict, Commerce, and an Aesthetic of Appropriation in the Italian Maritime Cities, 1000–1150* (Leiden, 2018)

Maxwell, Robert A., *The Art of Medieval Urbanism: Parthenay in Romanesque Aquitaine* (University Park, PA, 2007)

Mitchell, Fiona, *Monsters in Greek Literature: Aberrant Bodies in Ancient Greek Cosmogony, Ethnography, and Biology* (Abingdon, 2021)

Morrison, Elizabeth, and Larisa Grollemond, eds, *Book of Beasts: The Bestiary in the Medieval World*, exh. cat., J. Paul Getty Museum, Los Angeles (2019)

Nakamura, Carolyn, 'Dedicating Magic: Neo-Assyrian Apotropaic Figurines and the Protection of Assur', *World Archaeology*, XXXVI/1 (2004), pp. 11–25

Nicotra, Laura, 'The Figurative Programme of the Architraval Friezes in the Forum of Trajan, Rome', PhD thesis, University of Leicester, 2015

Nigg, Joe, *The Book of Gryphons* (Cambridge, MA, 1982)

Pankova, S. V., 'Identifications of Iron Age Tattoos from the Altai-Sayan Mountains in Russia', in *Ancient Ink: The Archaeology of Tattooing*, ed. L. F. Krutak and A. Deter-Wolf (Seattle, WA, 2017), pp. 66–98
Papalexandrou, Nassos, *Bronze Monsters and the Cultures of Wonder: Griffin Cauldrons in the Preclassical Mediterranean* (Austin, TX, 2021)
Paspalas, Stavros, 'The Achaemenid Lion-Griffin on a Macedonian Tomb Painting and on a Sicyonian Mosaic', in *Ancient Greece and Ancient Iran: Cross-Cultural Encounters*, ed. S.M.R. Darbandi and A. Zournatzi (Athens, 2008), pp. 301–25
Pauly, August Friedrich von, ed., *Paulys Realencyclopädie der classischen Altertumswissenschaft: Neue Bearbeitung unter Mitwirkung zahlreicher Fachgenossen* (Stuttgart, 1910), vol. VII, cols 1901–29
Polosmak, N. V., 'Tattoos in the Pazyryk World', *Archaeology, Ethnology and Anthropology of Eurasia*, IV/4 (2000), pp. 95–102
Quack, Joachim Friedrich, 'The Animals of the Desert and the Return of the Goddess', in *Desert Animals in the Eastern Sahara*, ed. H. Riemer et al. (Cologne, 2009), pp. 41–61
Quirke, Stephen, *Birth Tusks: The Armoury of Health in Context – Egypt 1800 BC* (London, 2016)
Schmidt, Victor M., *A Legend and Its Image: The Aerial Flight of Alexander the Great in Medieval Art* (Groningen, 1995)
Settis-Frugoni, Chiara, *Historia Alexandri elevati per griphos ad aerem: Origine, iconografia e fortuna di un tema* (Rome, 1973)
Shank, Elizabeth B., 'The Griffin Motif – An Evolutionary Tale', in *Paintbrushes: Wall-Painting and Vase-Painting of the Second Millennium BC in Dialogue*, ed. A. G. Vlachopoulos (Athens, 2018), pp. 235–42
Tešić Radovanović, Danijela T., 'Lamp with a Representation of the Griffin: The Christianisation of Pagan Motifs During Late Antiquity', *Zbornik radova Filozofskog fakulteta*, XLVIII/3 (2018), pp. 219–34
Trilling, James, 'The Soul of the Empire: Style and Meaning in the Mosaic Pavement of the Byzantine Imperial Palace in Constantinople', *Dumbarton Oaks Papers*, XLIII (1989), pp. 27–72
Valdez del Alamo, Elizabeth, *Palace of the Mind: The Cloister of Silos and Spanish Sculpture of the Twelfth Century* (Turnhout, 2012)
Walker, Alicia, 'Islamicising Motifs in Byzantine Lead Seals: Exoticising Style and the Expression of Identity', *Medieval History Journal*, XV/2 (2012), pp. 385–413
Wengrow, David, *The Origins of Monsters: Image and Cognition in the First Age of Mechanical Reproduction* (Princeton, NJ, 2014)
Westgate, Ruth, 'Party Animals: The Imagery of Status, Power and Masculinity in Greek Mosaics', in *Sociable Man: Essays on Ancient Greek Social Behaviour in Honour of Nick Fisher*, ed. S. D. Lambert (Swansea, 2011), pp. 291–322
Wood, Susan, 'Hadrian, Hercules and Griffins: A Group of Cuirassed Statues from Latium and Pamphylia', *Journal of Roman Archaeology*, XXIX (2016), pp. 223–38
Wyatt, Nicolas, 'Grasping the Griffin: Identifying and Characterizing the Griffin in Egyptian and West Semitic Tradition', *Journal of Ancient Egyptian Interconnections*, I/1 (2009), pp. 29–39

Acknowledgements

I offer my heartfelt thanks to the scholars whose work has provided the foundation for this study of the free-ranging cultural habitats of the griffin. Likewise, colleagues in a wide range of fields have generously shared their expertise including Roland Betancourt, Karen Carr, Falko Daim, William Diebold, Paul Dryburgh, Marian Feldman, Patrick Geary, Sandy Heslop, Jeff Johnson, Rayna Kalas, Briar Levit, Mark Lewis, Amanda Luyster, Kenneth Lymer, Dave Mazierski, Jordan Miller, Morgan Moroney, Nassos Papalexandrou, Kathryn Starkey, Lee Stewart and Alicia Walker.

My friends, family and students have also provided much-appreciated encouragement and leads on griffins spotted in the wild, particularly Lisa Cannon, Steve Gallagher, my McClanan clan (everyone, but especially Glenn, Martin, Polly and my mother, even though she held to the belief this book was about gremlins), Marcelle Heath, Nate Overmeyer, Chase Spearing, Anna Weltner and Jeremy Berck. Thank you!

The current book has also very much benefited from editorial guidance offered by Matthew Gleeson at the very beginning, and Jon K. Shaw, who with grace and discernment helped see the project through the home stretch. Moreover, the warm support from Reaktion by my publisher, Michael Leaman, as well as his team, especially Alex Ciobanu and Amy Salter, has been deeply appreciated. Rosie Collier proved a tenacious research assistant while I scrambled to get resources during COVID-19 shut-downs. This project couldn't have been brought to completion without the resources provided by Furthermore, a programme of the J. M. Kaplan Fund, Portland State's Faculty Development Grants and the Institute for Advanced Study in Princeton. In addition, The Portland State College of the Arts Dean's Fund for Excellence and the Portland State Judaic Studies programme supplemented the image-related costs not covered by the Furthermore award.

Many museums and other institutions smoothed the way for on-site work and other research queries and, in particular, I want to thank the professionals with whom I worked at the Abegg Stiftung (Riggisberg, Switzerland), the British Museum (especially the Department of Greece and Rome), the Capitoline Museums of Rome, the Chrysler Museum of Art (Norfolk, VA), College of Arms (London, UK), Harvard University Art Museums (Cambridge, MA), the Metropolitan Museum of Art (New York), the Museum of London Archaeological Archive, National Archives (Kew, UK), Opera del Duomo Museum (Pisa, Italy), Treasury of the Cathedral (Sens, France), Treasury of the Basilique de Valère (Sion, Switzerland), the Tyrolean State Museum (Innsbruck, Austria) and the World Center for Birds of Prey Archive (Boise, ID).

Photo Acknowledgements

The author and publishers wish to express their thanks to the sources listed below for illustrative material and/or permission to reproduce it. Some locations of artworks are also given below, in the interest of brevity:

akg-images/Bildarchiv Steffens (Luxor Museum, inv. no. JE 4673): 31; from Ludovico Ariosto, and A.-J. Du Pays, trans., *Roland furieux* (Paris, 1879): 108; Art Institute of Chicago (1994.38.1–2): 13; © Bibliothèques d'Amiens Métropole (MS 399, fol. 241r): 83; © Bibliothèque nationale de France, Paris: 29 (Saint-Denis.1794.4), 96 (MS français 2810, fol. 211v); Bodleian Library, University of Oxford (MS Laud. Misc. 733, fol. 10r): 85; © British Library Board, all rights reserved/Bridgeman Images: 62 (Royal 20 B XX, fol. 76v), 81 (Egerton MS 1121, fol. 114v), 105 (Add MS 46700, fol. 42v); Brooklyn Museum, New York (acc. no. 53.173; CC BY 3.0): 22; courtesy Chrome Industries, Inc.: 93; Chrysler Museum of Art, Norfolk, VA (inv. no. 71.930): 60; The Cleveland Museum of Art, OH (acc. no. 1928.861): 51; College of Arms, London, photos reproduced by permission of the Kings, Heralds and Pursuivants of Arms: 86 (MS 1.2, fol. 13), 87 (MS Vincent 178, p. 139); Cyprus Museum, Nicosia (SAL T.79/202), photo courtesy Department of Antiquities, Cyprus: 12; © The Estate of Edward Bawden: 89; The Fitzwilliam Museum, Cambridge (GR.7.1920), photo © Fitzwilliam Museum, Cambridge: 72; Flickr: 80 (photo Spencer Means, CC BY-SA 2.0); © Walton Ford, courtesy Gagosian (FORD 2017.0001): 100; Getty Images: 28 (National Museum of Turkmenistan, Ashgabat, photo Raimund Franken/ullstein bild), 35 (Kunsthistorisches Museum, Vienna, inv. no. Antikensammlung, VIIb 40, photo De Agostini Picture Library); from József Hampel, *A régibb középkor (IV–X. század) emlékei magyarhonban* (Budapest, 1894): 36; courtesy Marianne Hansen, Billy and Charlie's Pewter Goods, Jeffersonville, PA: 90; Israel Museum, Jerusalem (acc. no. B46.04.0912): 84; iStock.com: 95 (zu_09), 102 (diegograndi); courtesy of J. Paul Getty Museum, Los Angeles, and Koninklijke Bibliotheek, The Hague (MS 72 A 23, fol. 46r): 82; photo Bob Keroack, courtesy William & Mary Athletics: 94; Kunstgewerbemuseum, Staatliche Museen zu Berlin (inv. no. K 6211): 98; photo Matthew Lloyd (Archaeological Museum of Eretria, inv. no. ME 12805): 50; photos A. L. McClanan: 21 (Musei Capitolini, Rome, inv. no. NCE 2412), 27, 34 (Museo dei Fori Imperiali, Rome), 38 (Museo dell'Opera del Duomo, Florence), 56, 57, 61 (Hessisches Landesmuseum, Darmstadt, Kg 54:215a–d), 63, 68, 76, 88 (The National Archives, Kew, E 213/128), 97 (Musée de Cluny, Paris, inv. no. Cl. 11788); photo Glenn McClanan (The Metropolitan Museum of Art, New York, lent by Archaeological Museum (ASI), Amaravati, Guntur District, Andhra Pradesh): 24; Manufacture et musée nationaux, Sèvres (MNC9710), photo © RMN-Grand Palais/ Daniel Arnaudet/Art Resource, NY: 30; The Metropolitan Museum of Art, New York: 8 and 9 (acc. no. 1992.288), 10 (acc. no. 64.37.9), 11 (acc. no. 54.3.2), 14 (acc. no. 74.51.4554),

16 (acc. no. x.21.21), 25 (acc. no. 56.171.64), 40 (acc. no. 1982.5), 53 (acc. no. 1975.1.1413), 59 (acc. no. 1971.143), 71 (acc. no. 33.8.14), 73 (acc. no. 2000.81), 101 (acc. no. 27.54.5); The Morgan Library & Museum, New York, photos courtesy the Morgan Library & Museum: 3 and 4 (Morgan Seal 220), 5 and 6 (Morgan Seal 608), 37 (Thaw Collection, 2012.2:84), 79 (MS M.81, fol. 36v – purchased by J. Pierpont Morgan, 1902); Musée du Louvre, Paris (MNB1167), photos © RMN-Grand Palais/Franck Raux/Art Resource, NY: 1, 2; Museo Archeologico Nazionale di Napoli (acc. no. 5649), photo Giorgio Albano, used with permission of Ministero dei beni e delle attività culturali e del turismo: 32; National Archives at College Park, MD: 39; Nationalmuseet, Copenhagen (c6562–74), photo Roberto Fortuna and Kira Ursem (CC BY-SA 4.0): 23; The New York Public Library: 103, 104; Österreichische Nationalbibliothek, Vienna (Cod. Hist. gr. 53, fol. 291v), photo © ÖNB: 67; Patriarchate Library, Jerusalem (Panaghiou Taphou 52, fol. 50r): 75; courtesy Phillip J. Pirages Fine Books and Manuscripts, McMinnville, OR: 91; © Matthew Plexman 2021: 47; private collection: 78; Shutterstock.com: 19 (Ochkin Alexey), 54 and 55 (alex9330), 92 (Clive Beatty), 106 (chrisdorney); The State Hermitage Museum, St Petersburg: 41 (inv. no. 1684–306), 43 (inv. no. 1684–170, photo © The State Hermitage Museum/Vladimir Terebenin), 45 (inv. no. 1295–150, photo © The State Hermitage Museum/Vladimir Terebenin); courtesy Catherine Swift Alexander: 17 and 18 (after Nanno Marinatos, *Akrotiri, Thera and the East Mediterranean* (Athens, 2015)), 42 (after N. V. Polosmak, 'Tattoos in the Pazyryk World', in *Archaeology, Ethnology & Anthropology of Eurasia*, IV/4 (2000)), 44 (after D. V. Cheremisin, 'On the Semantics of Animal Style Ornithomorphic Images in Pazyryk Ritual Artifacts', in *Archaeology, Ethnology & Anthropology of Eurasia*, XXXVII/1 (2009)), 49 (Archaeological Museum of Olympia (inv. no. B104), drawing after Lorenz Winkler-Horaček, *Monster in der frühgriechischen Kunst: Die Überwindung des Unfassbaren* (Berlin, 2015)); Swiss School of Archaeology in Greece, Eretria: 26; Tate Britain, London: 77; Tiroler Landesmuseum Ferdinandeum, Innsbruck (inv. no. K 1036), photo © TLM/Johannes Plattner: 64; Trésor de la cathédrale de Sens (inv. TC B 8), photo Musées de Sens/E. Berry: 69; © The Trustees of the British Museum: 7 (1851,0902.499), 15 (1958,0721.1), 58 (1897,1231.188), 66 (1923,1205.3), 99 (OA.24); courtesy Constancio and Elizabeth Valdez del Álamo: 52; The Walters Art Museum, Baltimore, MD (acc. no. 71.510): 48; Wikimedia Commons: 21 (photo Rabe!, CC BY-SA 4.0), 33 (Musei Capitolini, Rome (inv. Scu 58), photo Rabax63, CC BY-SA 4.0), 65 (photo Ziegler175, CC BY-SA 4.0), 70 (photo G069, CC BY-SA 4.0), 74 (Museum für Islamische Kunst, Berlin, photo Mike Peel/www.mikepeel.net, CC BY-SA 4.0).

Index

Illustration numbers are indicated by *italics*